Sensibility in the Early Modern Era

Sensibility in the Early Modern Era investigates how the early modern characterisation of sensibility as a natural property of the body could give way to complex considerations about the importance of affect in morality. What underlies this understanding of sensibility is the attempt to fuse Lockean sensationalism with Scottish sentimentalism – being able to have experiences of objects in the world is here seen as being grounded in the same principle that also enables us to feel moral sentiments. Moral and epistemic ways of relating to the world thus blend into one another, as both can be traced to the same capacity that enables us to affectively respond to stimuli that impinge on our perceptual apparatus.

This collection focuses on these connections by offering reflections on the role of sensibility in the early modern attempt to think of the human being as a special kind of sensitive machine and affectively responsive animal. Humans, as they are understood in this context, relate to themselves by sensing themselves and perpetually refining their intellectual and moral capacities in response to the way the world affects them. Responding to the world here refers to the manner in which both natural *and* man-made influences impact on our ability to conceptualise the animate and inanimate world, and our place within that world. This book was originally published as a special issue of the *Intellectual History Review*.

Anik Waldow is Senior Lecturer in the Philosophy Department at the University of Sydney, Australia. She mainly works in early modern philosophy, and has published articles on the moral and cognitive function of Humean sympathy, early modern theories of personal identity, scepticism, and associationist theories of thought and language. She is the author of the book *David Hume and the Problem of Other Minds* (2009) and the co-editor of *Contemporary Perspectives on Early Modern Philosophy*: *Nature and Norms in Thought* (2013).

T0346604

Sensibility in the Early Modern Era

From living machines to affective morality

Edited by
Anik Waldow

Routledge
Taylor & Francis Group

LONDON AND NEW YORK

First published 2016
by Routledge

2 Park Square, Milton Park, Abingdon, Oxfordshire OX14 4RN
711 Third Avenue, New York, NY 10017

Routledge is an imprint of the Taylor & Francis Group, an informa business

First issued in paperback 2017

British Library Cataloguing in Publication Data
A catalogue record for this book is available from the British Library

ISBN 13: 978-1-138-65097-8 (hbk)
ISBN 13: 978-1-138-30975-3 (pbk)

Typeset in Times New Roman
by RefineCatch Limited, Bungay, Suffolk

Publisher's Note
The publisher accepts responsibility for any inconsistencies that may have arisen during the conversion of this book from journal articles to book chapters, namely the possible inclusion of journal terminology.

Disclaimer
Every effort has been made to contact copyright holders for their permission to reprint material in this book. The publishers would be grateful to hear from any copyright holder who is not here acknowledged and will undertake to rectify any errors or omissions in future editions of this book.

Contents

Citation Information

The chapters in this book were originally published in the *Intellectual History Review*, volume 25, issue 3 (September 2015). When citing this material, please use the original page numbering for each article, as follows:

Chapter 6

The Artifice of Human Nature: Rousseau and Herder
Anik Waldow
Intellectual History Review, volume 25, issue 3 (September 2015) pp. 343–356

Chapter 7

Seduced by System: Edmund Burke's Aesthetic Embrace of Adam Smith's Philosophy
Michael L. Frazer
Intellectual History Review, volume 25, issue 3 (September 2015) pp. 357–372

For any permission-related enquiries please visit:
http://www.tandfonline.com/page/help/permissions

Notes on Contributors

Michael L. Frazer is a Lecturer in Social and Political Theory at the University of East Anglia, Norwich, UK. His research focuses on canonical political philosophy and its relevance for contemporary political theory. He is the author of *The Enlightenment of Sympathy: Justice and the Moral Sentiments in the Eighteenth Century and Today* (2010), and has contributed papers to *Political Theory, The Review of Politics,* and *The Journal of Political Philosophy.*

Henry Martyn Lloyd is an Honorary Research Fellow in the School of Historical and Philosophical Inquiry at the University of Queensland, Brisbane, Australia. He is a specialist in the history of French philosophy, and has particular interests in the philosophy of the Enlightenment and twentieth century French philosophy. He is the editor of *The Discourse of Sensibility: The Knowing Body in the Enlightenment* (2013), and has published papers in *Intellectual History Review, Philosophy Today,* and *Parrhesia: A Journal of Critical Philosophy.*

Dalia Nassar is a Lecturer in the Department of Philosophy at the University of Sydney, Australia. She works on German romanticism and idealism, the philosophy of nature, aesthetics and environmental philosophy. She is the author of *The Romantic Absolute: Being and Knowing in German Romantic Philosophy, 1795–1804* (2014), and the editor of *The Relevance of Romanticism: Essays on German Romantic Philosophy* (2014).

Michael J. Olson is based in the Department of Philosophy at Macquarie University, Sydney, Australia. His research interests include Kantian theoretical philosophy, the history of early modern philosophy, and contemporary French philosophy. His work has appeared in journals such as *Intellectual History Review, Angelaki, Kant-Studien,* and *Philosophy Today.*

Jessica Riskin is Professor of History at Stanford University, California, USA. Her research interests include early modern science, politics and culture, and the history of scientific explanation. She is the author of *Science in the Age of Sensibility: The Sentimental Empiricists of the French Enlightenment* (2002), and *The Restless Clock: A History of the Centuries-Long Argument over What Makes Living Things Tick* (2015).

Udo Thiel is Professor of the History of Philosophy, and Director of the Institute of Philosophy, at the University of Graz, Austria. His research focuses on the history of epistemology, metaphysics, the philosophy of the mind, and the aesthetics of the early modern period. His current major project is on theories of self-awareness and personal identity in the eighteenth century. He is the author of *The Early Modern Subject: Self-Consciousness and Personal Identity from Descartes to Hume* (2011).

Anik Waldow is Senior Lecturer in the Philosophy Department at the University of Sydney, Australia. She mainly works in early modern philosophy, and has published articles on the moral and cognitive function of Humean sympathy, early modern theories of personal identity, scepticism, and associationist theories of thought and language. She is the author of the book *David Hume and the Problem of Other Minds* (2009) and the co-editor of *Contemporary Perspectives on Early Modern Philosophy: Nature and Norms in Thought* (2013).

Introduction

Anik Waldow

In the *Encyclopédie* of Diderot sensibility is defined in medical and moral terms. The first definition presents sensibilité as a natural property found in living bodies. Through this property it is possible for "certain parts [to] perceive the impressions of external objects."[1] The second entry defines sensibilité as a tender disposition of the soul through which we are moved to virtue: "Reflection can make a man of probity; but sensibility makes a man virtuous."[2] Through this dual characterisation, the French eighteenth-century understanding of sensibility fuses Lockean sensationism with Scottish sentimentalism: being able to have experiences of objects in the world is grounded in the same principle that also enables us to feel moral sentiments. In this way, moral and epistemic ways of relating to the world blend into one another: both can be traced to the same capacity that enables us to affectively respond to stimuli that impinge on our perceptual apparatus. Furthermore, since sensibility in its medical connotation is defined as "the basis and conserving agent of life" and as "animality par excellence," it would appear that the kind of sentimentalist morality that is grounded in our sensibility is a morality that speaks to our animal nature. This morality engages with our existence as embodied beings and understands the phenomenon of life in terms of our sentience.

This volume will explore the connections between the concept of sensibility and the early modern attempt to think of the human being as a special kind of sensitive machine and affectively responsive animal. Humans, as they are understood in this context, relate to themselves by sensing themselves and perpetually refining their intellectual and moral capacities in response to the way the world affects them. Responding to the world here refers to the way in which both natural *and* man-made influences impact on our ability to conceptualise the animate and inanimate world, and our place within that world.

Each of the seven essays in this collection will approach this theme from a different angle. Udo Thiel traces a specific conception of self-presence from Locke to two French eighteenth-century thinkers: Condillac and Rousseau. By conceiving of this self-presence as an aspect of sensibility, Thiel stresses the importance of the conception of the human subject as a sensible being. Turning from the manner in which the self senses itself to the question of how we think of ourselves as perceiving agents, Michael Olson argues that accounts of visual sensation played a key role in seventeenth- and early eighteenth-century accounts of perceptual cognition. Modelled on Kepler's work with the camera obscura, these accounts were designed to reconcile the competing demands of explicating the behavior of bodies, on the one hand, and the nature and function of the immaterial soul, on the other.

In the second half of the eighteenth century, mechanistic models of perception, and the way they presented matter as passive and dead, came under severe pressure. Part of the problem, as Jessica Riskin shows in her analysis of the relationship between Kant's *Critique of Judgement* and the Romantics, was that the conception of organisms as purposive, striving machines gradually subverted the traditional dichotomy between a passive mechanical universe and purposeful agency, thereby paving the way for the Romantic conception of life as a force that permeates nature. While Riskin's essay examines the connection between Kant and the Romantics from a historical perspective, Dalia Nassar offers a philosophical analysis of the tensions within Kant's concept of the organism. The difference between machines and living creatures, she argues, forced Kant to recognise that the mind is more fundamentally constrained by nature than he had suggested in the *Critique of Pure Reason*. Goethe was inspired by this insight and developed his account of the plasticity of cognition out of it.

Henry Martyn Lloyd's essay on the relationship between Sade and Rousseau extends reflections on the developmental aspect of one's mental capacities into the moral sphere. Crucial to his analysis is the link between sensationist epistemology and sentimentalist morality: on Rousseau's and Sade's account, taking care of one's sensibility involves that one works with the perceptual apparatus of the body. In Sade this work leads to the reorganisation of one's bodily pleasures and pains; in Rousseau it constitutes a crucial step towards a "morality of the heart." Anik Waldow's examination of Rousseau and Herder further pursues the idea that one's sensibility must be actively manipulated in order to turn affectively responsive creatures into accomplished moral judges. This manipulation, she claims, crucially relies on an agent's exposure to learning environments saturated with opinion, history and artefacts. The influences of nature and artifice here flow together in the conception of the body as the locus where we naturally respond to artificially orchestrated stimuli.

The last essay of this collection looks at the dynamics of affective responsiveness in the moral-political context. In his examination of Adam Smith's influence on Edmund Burke, Michael Frazer reveals that a commendable style and the beauty of a systematic presentation of philosophical thought were seen as a double-edged sword. While highly valued in their capacity to provoke aesthetic and moral sentiments that open our hearts to certain ideas, writings such as Smith's were also held to incite the passions, and through this to turn the philosopher/statesman into a "man of system" obsessed with shaping actual societies in accordance with a theoretical ideal.

University of Sydney

Notes

1. Henri Fouquet, "Sensibilité. Sentiment (Médecine)," in Diderot, *Encyclopédie*, xiii. 780.
2. Chevalier Louis de Jaucourt, 'Sensibilité, (Morale)', in Diderot, *Encyclopédie*, xiii. 810.

Bibliography

Diderot, Denis, and d'Alembert, Jean le Rond. *Encyclopédie ou Dictionnaire raisonné des sciences, des arts et des métiers par une société des gens de Lettres, mis en ordre et publié par Diderot et quant à la Partie mathematique par d'Alembert.* 40 vols. 2nd ed. Geneva, 1777–9.

Self and Sensibility: From Locke to Condillac and Rousseau

Udo Thiel

University of Graz, Graz, Austria

1   Introduction: Locke on sensibility and the self

It is well known that Locke's philosophy played an important role in the French Enlightenment. Locke's impact in general has been the subject of several scholarly works, and there are of course also studies on particular issues such as John Yolton's survey of Locke's importance to French materialism.[1] In this paper, I focus on an aspect of Locke and French eighteenth-century thought that has been somewhat neglected: the notion of the human subject as a "sensible Being."[2] In *The Collapse of Mechanism and the Rise of Sensibility* Stephen Gaukroger highlights the significance of the notion of sensibility in mid-eighteenth-century France: sensibility is thought of as "a unified phenomenon having physiological, moral and aesthetic dimensions" and as something that "lies at the basis of our relation to the physical world: it is what natural understanding has to be premised on."[3] Sensibility is considered the foundation of cognition.

This is clearly Locke's idea when he talks about the "sensible Qualities" that are conveyed to the mind from "external Objects." Our relation to the external world "depends wholly on our Senses," Locke says. Sensation is the source of *ideas* that we acquire of qualities in the objects.[4] This is what Locke means when he says in the first sentence of the *Essay* that, like other animals, we are "sensible Beings," i.e., endowed with the faculty of sensation.[5] The world is given to us in an immediate kind of way through sensory perception. Sensation is "immediate" in the sense that no other mental activities, no other ideas are required for the production of sensory ideas. The eye perceives light "only by being directed toward it." The "bright Sun-shine," for example, "forces it self immediately to be perceived, as soon as ever the Mind turns its view that way."[6] It is for this reason that Locke ascribes passivity to sensation, at least "for the most part": what the mind "perceives it cannot avoid perceiving."[7]

There is another sense in which we are "sensible Beings," however. It may seem that for Locke access to the inner world, to our own selves is not immediate, for he says that it requires reflection, an inner sense, which in turn requires a special attention to the operations of our own minds. We do not acquire *ideas* of these operations "till the understanding turns inwards upon itself, reflects on its operations, and makes them the object of its own contemplation."[8] It may seem odd, however, to say, as Locke does here, that we have an immediate relation to the external world but not to our own selves. Are we not present to our own self in an immediate kind of way as well? Locke would say that there is such an immediate self-presence, but that this immediacy does not apply to reflection. Rather such self-presence is an aspect of sensibility – an aspect that is different from the one involved in our relation to the external world. According to Locke, apart from, and prior to, reflection there is a more immediate relating to our own selves, and the capacity to relate to our own selves in this immediate kind of way is a feature of Locke's notion of sensibility. Locke indicates what he means in an early Journal note from 1682 on the question of the immortality of the human soul.

> The usuall physicall proofe (as I may soe call it) of the immortality of the soule is this, Matter cannot thinke ergo the soule is immateriall, noe thing can naturally destroy an immateriall thing ergo the soule is naturally immortall [...] But methinks if I may be permitted to say soe neither of these speake to the point in question and perfectly mistake immortality whereby is not meant a state of bare substantiall existence and duration but *a state of sensibility*. For that way that they use of proveing the soul immortal will as well prove the body soe too. For since noething can naturally destroy a materiall substance more then immateriall, the body will naturally endure as well as the soule for ever [...].

> Since then Experience of what we finde dayly in sleepe and very frequently ins swounings and Apoplexys &c. puts it past doubt that *the soule may subsist in a state of insensibility* without partakeing in the least degree of happynesse misery or any perception whatsoever [...]

> Whatsoever shall establish the existence of the soule will not therefor prove its being in a state of happynesse or misery [i.e., of sensibility], since tis evident that perception is noe more necessary to its being then motion is to the being of body.[9]

So *sensibility* here refers to an immediate awareness or feeling of one's own state, a feeling which is part of being alive. We are sensible or, as we would say, aware or conscious of our own states. Without this kind of sensibility we would not be able to be happy or miserable, and so immortality without sensibility would be pointless as we would not be able to feel the punishments that God inflicts on us. In the *Essay* Locke expresses this idea similarly:

> I do not say there is no Soul in a Man, because he is not sensible of it in his sleep; But I do say, he cannot think at any time waking or sleeping, without being sensible of it. Our being sensible of it is not necessary to any thing, but to our thoughts; and to them it is; and to them it will always be necessary, till we can think without being conscious of it.[10]

In this quotation (and elsewhere) Locke himself links "being sensible of" to "being conscious of," or as we might say, "being aware of." He argues that we may exist without being "sensible" or aware of anything, but we would not be a self or a person if our existence were one of "bare substantiall existence." Thinking, broadly conceived, involves "being sensible of it." As Locke says elsewhere: "When we see, hear, smell, taste, feel, meditate, or will any thing, we know that we do so."[11]

Locke sometimes accounts for this inner-directed sensibility or consciousness in terms of a certain feeling. Thus he draws an analogy between being conscious of thoughts and the feeling of hunger. Just as one cannot separate the hunger from the feeling of hunger, one cannot separate thinking from being conscious or being sensible of thinking. These are not two distinct, separate acts. Consciousness or sensibility is essential to thought: "Hunger consists in that very sensation [of feeling hunger], as thinking consists in being conscious that one thinks."[12]

Locke makes a further claim, however. Not only are we immediately aware of our own activity of thinking, in thinking we also become immediately aware of the existence of our own self as the subject of thought. As we are conscious of thoughts, perceptions and experiences, we become immediately conscious or aware of a self or subject of these thoughts, perceptions and experiences. It seems that, for Locke, being conscious of thoughts and experiences involves a consciousness or an "intuitive knowledge," as he says, of the existence of a self as the subject of those thoughts and experiences. Locke states: "In every Act of Sensation, Reasoning or Thinking, we are conscious to our selves of our own Being."[13]

Further, Locke seems to imply a distinction between this awareness or "intuition" of one's own existence and an explicit consideration of oneself as oneself. Locke says that a self or person is "a thinking intelligent Being, that has reason and reflection, and can *consider it self as it self*, the same thinking thing in different times and places."[14] Clearly, for Locke the thinking being's capacity to "consider it self as it self" involves the capacity explicitly to recognize one's own identity in a discursive kind of way.

Thus Locke implicitly distinguishes between several ways of relating to one's own self: immediately, by being sensible or conscious (1) of one's own thoughts and actions and (2) of the existence of one's own self as the subject of those thoughts and actions; and mediately, for example by (3) reflecting on one's own thoughts and actions and (4) by considering oneself as oneself, recognizing one's own diachronic identity.[15]

Obviously, these ideas are part of Locke's famous account of personal identity.[16] I have explored the latter in detail elsewhere but I give a very brief summary here, as this will be relevant to the discussion of the French material that follows below.[17] First, there is Locke's account of the identity of persons in terms of consciousness uniting thoughts and actions. Here the first kind of relating to one's own self is relevant. Consciousness, Locke says, relates to past and present thoughts and actions and so links the present with the past, thereby constituting personal identity. Second and related to this is his distinction (1) between personal identity and the identity of the thinking substance or soul and (2) between personal identity and the identity of the self as "man" or human being. The self as a person is a self that is sensible of its inner states, including those of happiness and misery. To Locke, I am now the same person I was in the past, not because I am the same living body or because the same substance thinks in me, but because my present conscious experience is connected to my past conscious experiences. Third, there is the affective and forensic or moral aspect of his account. For as long as I am in a state of sensibility, I am concerned for my happiness and so am concerned to be able to ascribe actions to myself that will not result in misery (especially in the afterlife).[18] Here self-consciousness in the sense of "considering oneself as oneself" becomes relevant, and it involves a relating to one's own future.

As one would expect, Lockean ideas dominated the discussions about consciousness and the self in eighteenth-century France. How was Locke's account of the self debated, evaluated and used, however? As it turns out, the fate of Locke's theory in France makes a complex and philosophically important story, to be told more extensively elsewhere.[19] In this paper I attempt to identify and evaluate only one particular strand of Lockean thinking about inner-directed sensibility in French thought. Moreover, as space is limited, I can discuss only a couple of the significant contributions here. I begin with an attempt at what may at first seem to be a very straightforward empiricist account of inner-directed sensibility and the self as it is present in Condillac. I shall then turn to the complex discussion in Rousseau. Locke's presence in Condillac and Rousseau will become obvious. In the conclusion I highlight some significant and philosophically important differences and I end with critical remarks on French sensibilist accounts of the self.

2 Etienne Bonnot de Condillac: "The Sentiment of our Being" and the self as phenomenon and as substance

Condillac's empiricism is usually described as a development of Locke's philosophy, and indeed Condillac explicitly acknowledges his indebtedness to Locke. The early *Essai sur l'origine des conaissances humaines* (1746) operates, in Lockean manner, with sensation and reflection as two independent sources of mental content. In his main later work, the *Traité des sensations* (1754), Condillac, working with the image of a statue that progressively comes to life, abandons the notion of reflection as independent. He attempts to reduce the origin of all thought to sensation. Condillac's discussion of the self, too, is clearly based on Lockean theory. Like Locke, it seems, Condillac assigns a central role to consciousness and memory. Other notions are important as well, however: the notion of a "sentiment of our being" or "sentiment of myself," and the notion of a "connection that preserves the sequence of our perceptions." What is meant by these various notions and how do they relate to the issue of the self? Let us begin with consciousness.

2.1 *Consciousness as sensibility and reminiscence*

The notion of an inner "sentiment" was present in French philosophical thought long before Condillac and even before Locke with his notion of inner sensibility. The French variants for inner sentiment go back at least to the late seventeenth century, to the writings of La Forge and Malebranche who introduced the notion of *sentiment intérieur* as a philosophical concept. Moreover, the problems surrounding the translation of Lockean "consciousness" into French early in the eighteenth century led to the introduction of a variety of terms for relating to one's own self. It is only from the mid-eighteenth century onwards, however, that notions such as that of an inner sentiment were elaborated on and used widely in discussions of the self and personal identity – in thinkers such as Bonnet, Lignac and of course Condillac and Rousseau. The various French terms for inner feeling or inner experience do not always denote the same thing, however.[20]

Condillac defines "consciousness" (*la conscience*) as "the sentiment that produces this knowledge" of the mind's perceptions "and that tells us at least partially what goes on" in the mind.[21] It may seem that consciousness is here understood to be a separate mental act relating to other perceptions. That is not Condillac's considered view, however. For him (as for Locke) consciousness is not a second-order mental operation that has other mental operations as its "objects." Rather, consciousness is an aspect of perception itself and in this sense immediate. Condillac makes explicit the view that was present implicitly in Locke. Indeed, he states that the terms "perception" and "consciousness" denote different aspects of one and the same operation: "Thus perception and consciousness are different names for the same operation. When it is looked upon as the impression made in the mind, we can keep the name 'perception.' When it makes its presence known to the mind, we can call it 'consciousness.'"[22] On this basis Condillac can say that all perceptions have this self-reflexive feature, that all perceptions are conscious in this sense.

Elsewhere in the *Essai* Condillac introduces a distinction between consciousness understood as an immediate relating to the present and as a relating to the past. This latter mode of consciousness is "a new operation," called *réminiscence*.[23] Condillac writes:

> When objects attract our attention, the perceptions they occasion in us become linked with *our sentiment of our being* and to everything that can bear some relation to it. It follows that *consciousness* not only gives us *knowledge of our perceptions*, but furthermore, if those perceptions are repeated, it often makes us aware that we have had them before and makes us recognize them as belonging to us or as affecting *a being that is constantly the same "self,"* despite their variety and succession. Seen in relation to these new effects, *consciousness* is a new operation which is at our service every instant and *is the foundation of experience*. Without it every moment of life would seem the first of our existence, and our knowledge would never advance beyond an initial perception. I shall call it "reminiscence."[24]

Condillac seems to be saying here that without consciousness understood as reminiscence, we could not connect past and present perceptions and could not recognize past perceptions as ours and so could not be convinced that our own self today is the same self it was yesterday. Reminiscence relates both to perceptions and to our own self as the identical subject of those perceptions.

Recalling past perceptions leads to the recognition of our identity through time because recalling past perceptions involves recognizing them "as belonging to us." It is important to note that Condillac does not say that reminiscence constitutes our personal identity; rather, he says that we *recognize* our identity through reminiscence. Thus to Condillac, consciousness as reminiscence fulfils an epistemic and not a constitutive role for personal identity. He seems to assume that personal identity is constituted not by consciousness but by some other principle that is not here identified but thought of as presupposed by consciousness and reminiscence. In this regard, then, Condillac's account differs significantly from Locke's.[25]

2.2 The "Sentiment of our Being" and the recognition of our own identity

How is consciousness understood as reminiscence or recollection linked to the notion of the "sentiment of our being" to which Condillac appeals in the above quotation from the *Essai*? This sentiment or feeling relates to the existence of our own self as the subject of perceptions, and Condillac suggests that it is always linked to all our perceptions. It seems to correspond to Locke's account of the "intuitive" grasp we have of our own existence, cited above. Condillac does not explain this "sentiment" any further here. He suggests, however, that the sentiment of our being is fundamental and presupposed by reminiscence. At the same time Condillac's formulation that reminiscence is "the foundation of experience" seems to suggest, rather, that the ability to recall perceptions must be presupposed by the sense or sentiment of our own self. Without reminiscence we could relate only to individual perceptions, but not to a self understood as a being that persists through time. The ability to recollect the past is required for being sensible of such a self. Indeed, it has been argued that Condillac's account is "circular."[26] He seems to be saying both that the sentiment of our being is presupposed by reminiscence, and that reminiscence is presupposed by the sentiment of our being.

It is not as obvious as it may seem, however, that Condillac is guilty of a circular argument here. The two occurrences of "sentiment of our being" in the last sentence of the previous paragraph do not refer to the same thing. The first refers to a feeling of self that Condillac assumes is directly connected to individual perceptions – and does not presuppose reminiscence but is required *for* reminiscence. The second occurrence of "sentiment of our being," by contrast, refers to consciousness insofar as it is involved in the recognition of our own identity through time and as such presupposes reminiscence.

Moreover, Condillac argues that reminiscence is in one sense a "product" of the connection between perceptions and the sentiment of our being. Only if both past and present perceptions are connected by being linked to the sentiment of our being can we have genuine reminiscence. This is what Condillac expresses in the following passage:

> It is evident that if the connection *between the perceptions* I have now, those that I had yesterday, and *my sentiment of myself* was broken, I could not know that what happened to me yesterday, happened to myself. If this connection was interrupted every night, I would, so to speak, each day begin a new life, and no one would be able to convince me that today's self was the self of the day before. Thus reminiscence is the product of the connection that preserves the sequence of our perceptions.[27]

And insofar as reminiscence recalls perceptions "we have already had," it is in turn required for and can lead to the recognition of our own identity through time. It makes sense, then, that Condillac distinguishes between two conceptions of reminiscence:

> To make a closer analysis of reminiscence, we should give it two names: one insofar as it makes us know our being [as identical through time], the other insofar as it makes us aware of the perceptions that are repeated in it, for those are quite distinct ideas.[28]

Condillac states that he regards "this connection [between perceptions and the sentiment of our being] as a fundamental experience which has a right to be considered sufficient to explain all the others."[29] In terms of this connection itself Condillac does not seem to say explicitly that the sentiment of our being presupposes other perceptions. This view is implied, however, by statements he makes in other contexts. Thus he says that the "connection of ideas, either with signs or among themselves" is a "firm fact of experience" to which "everything that pertains to the human mind" can be reduced.[30] It is the basis for everything to do with the self, i.e., including reminiscence and the sentiment of our own being. In other words, there has to be a connection of perceptions in order for there to be a sentiment of the self, reminiscence and recognition of our own diachronic identity. There could be no sentiment of being without other perceptions, as this sentiment is accounted for in terms of its relation to perceptions. And there could be no remembering of perceptions that could lead us to recognize them as ours and thus make us recognize our diachronic identity, if there were no prior sequence of perceptions. In the last analysis, then, for Condillac both reminiscence and the sentiment of our being are grounded in something fundamental. Prior to any sentiment of self and prior to any act of recalling the past and thus invoking the notion of a continuous self, there is the sequence of connected perceptions.

2.3 Is Condillac a bundle theorist of the mind?

Condillac, then, seems to regard the sequence of connected perceptions as fundamental. Does he reduce the mind to a sequence of connected perceptions, however? Is he, in other words, adopting a bundle theory of the self, according to which the self is essentially nothing over and above those related perceptions that he considers as basic to sensibility, to consciousness, memory and the recognition of personal identity? It certainly has been claimed in the literature that Condillac adopts such a view of the self, abandoning the notion of the self as substance.[31] One passage sometimes cited in support of this reading is from a work entitled *Les monades*, first published anonymously in Berlin in 1748.[32] Here Condillac says that we know our own being only insofar as we feel it and that we feel it only insofar as we have sensations.[33] He says also that our consciousness represents our self only insofar as it is endowed with certain properties and as modified in certain ways.[34]

This does not, however, amount to a rejection of the notion of the self beyond the perceptions. Condillac does not say that these feelings and sensations are all there is to our selves. The consciousness we have of our own self, says Condillac, represents this self only insofar as it is endowed with certain properties and as modified in certain ways. And that is what we *call* our substance.[35] He does not say, however, that these collections of properties or qualities are our essential selves. His point is, again, epistemic. He argues that we do not encounter a substantial self, or a self beyond the collections of properties and perceptions, as an item in inner experience. He believes, however, that there must be something over and above those collections of properties, namely, a subject, capable of thought and experience,[36] and this subject may be a substance. Like Locke, he does not reject the notion of self as substance. All he is saying is that we cannot know its inner nature or, to use Locke's terminology, its real essence.

Still, there are at least a couple of other passages in the *Traité des sensations* that seem to endorse a bundle view of the self. Thus he says about the statue that

> its "I" is only the collection of the sensations which it experiences, and those which memory [*la mémoire*] recalls to it. In a word it is immediate knowledge [*la conscience*] of what it is for itself, and remembrance [*le souvenir*] of what it has been.[37]

And in the very last two sentences of the *Traité des sensations* he states: "The statue is therefore nothing but the sum of all it has acquired. May not this be the same with man?"[38] In the light of what has been said above, however, these passages, too, need not be read as endorsing a bundle view. Condillac is talking here about the self insofar as we can know it through inner experience; he is not saying that the self is nothing over and above the perceptions.

Indeed, Condillac also argues explicitly against the bundle-account of the self and for the notion of a permanent self.[39] In a footnote to *Traité des sensations* I.vi.3 Condillac quotes a famous passage from Pascal that suggests that a person is nothing but the sum-total of its properties or qualities. Condillac says about this suggestion:

> But it is not the assemblage of the qualities which makes the person, for then the same man, young or old, beautiful or ugly, wise or foolish, would be so many different persons. Whatever the qualities for which you love me it is always me you love, for the qualities are only me modified differently [...] In Pascal's meaning God alone can say "I." [40]

Condillac points out, then, that to adopt Pascal's suggestion would give rise to problems with personal identity through time. He clearly indicates that there is a self or "I" beyond the "assemblage of qualities." Against what is implied by Pascal's account he insists that not just God, but human selves, too, can say "I."

In a different context Condillac argues that the inner experience of change itself suggests the notion of a self that persists, a self that is distinct from the phenomenal self of inner sensibility and that remains the same. For Condillac, the notion of self or "I" involves that of relating to one's own sensations, that of combining them into a unitary self or person:

> What we understand by this word "I" seems to be only possible in a being who notices that in the present moment he is no longer what he has been. So long as there is no change, he exists without any reflexion [*retour sur lui-même*] upon himself; but as soon as he changes, he judges that he is the same as he formerly was in another state, and he says "I."[41]

Condillac notes here that without change there would be no consciousness of our own selves as identical at different points of time. Although the point concerns directly only the judgement or recognition of our own diachronic identity, it assumes that change and the experience thereof presuppose the existence of an identical subject that undergoes change. For Condillac the experience of change need not lead us to sceptical conclusions about identity. On the contrary, Condillac argues that

> the succession of my modifications makes me perceive that I endure. It is this variation from moment to moment, this change from pleasure to pain and from pain to pleasure, from one state to its opposite, which was necessary to bring me to the knowledge of myself.[42]

Elsewhere, Condillac explicitly invokes the notion of the self as substance. Thus he states in the *Essai* that "we must admit a point of reunion, a substance that is at the same time a simple and indivisible subject […] and […] consequently distinct from the body – in short, a mind."[43] For Condillac, then, there are at least two aspects under which we can consider the self – (1) phenomenologically, as the collection of perceptions and experiences to which consciousness and *réminiscence* or memory have access, and (2) ontologically, as the underlying but in its nature unknowable substance or soul.[44] In short, there is a distinction in Condillac between the notions of a phenomenal self and a substantial self.

2.4 *The origin of self-consciousness*

Since Condillac argues that both the sentiment of being and reminiscence require a prior sequence of perceptions, it is plain that for him there can be no "original" or "pre-existent" sentiment of being and recognition of one's own diachronic identity. Moreover, Condillac points out not only that the experience of change suggests the notion of a permanent self but also that the recognition of one's own diachronic identity requires the experience of change. In the *Traité des sensations* Condillac states that the statue can say "I" only once it has experienced change.[45] This experience in turn requires memory, for without memory we could not have the experience of change as we would not be able to relate to our own past. In short, self-consciousness depends on memory and the experience of change.

The distinction between the phenomenal self and the substantial self, too, can help to illuminate seemingly contradictory passages concerning the origin of self-consciousness. In the *Traité des sensations* Condillac states: "At the first moment of my existence I knew nothing of what was going on within me. I could not distinguish anything. I had no consciousness of myself."[46] Here Condillac implies that the existence of the self is independent of self-consciousness, that the latter requires experience and is thus a later development. Elsewhere, however, in *Les monades*, he states that the existence of that which I call my self begins at that moment at which I begin to have a consciousness of myself.[47] This suggests that the existence of the self is linked inseparably to the consciousness of self. One cannot have the former without the latter. Yet it is plain that the two passages do not contradict each other. The second passage, from *Les monades*, refers to the "beginning" of the phenomenal, self-conscious self; but for that to come into existence the existence of the self as substance, independently of self-consciousness, is presupposed. Condillac appeals to the latter notion in the first passage quoted from the *Traité des sensations*.

When Condillac speaks in these passages of the "consciousness of myself," it may not seem clear whether he has in mind the mere sentiment of existence, or a notion of self-consciousness that involves a recognition of one's own diachronic identity. As he invokes the notion of the capacity to distinguish between perceptions, however, his idea of consciousness clearly does involve a relating to one's own past perceptions. Further, as a relating to one's own past perceptions involves the recognition of oneself as identical over time, what is said here may relate to both the sentiment of our being and the consciousness of our own diachronic identity.

In Condillac, then, there are three basic forms of sensibility that involve a relating to one's own self, and they are closely interconnected: (1) the sentiment of our own being (linked to individual perceptions); (2) reminiscence or memory (in one sense) as a relating to one's own past perceptions, and (3) a consciousness of self that involves a recognition of one's own diachronic identity. Yet there is at least one other feature of sensibility that is of importance in this context, one that relates to the self as a bodily being.

2.5   *The self and the sense of touch*

The intrinsic nature of the substantial self remains unknown to us, according to Condillac. But how does he account for the nature of the phenomenal self, however? Condillac does not explicitly distinguish between what Locke calls "man" and "person." Locke left open what the real nature of "man" or human being might be, but it was plain that he considered "man" a bodily being. And this seems to be applicable to Condillac's phenomenal self or person, too. Condillac endorses a notion of "man" as a union of soul and body, but he holds that we are aware of our own selves directly only as bodily beings. The phenomenal self consists of a multiplicity of experiences, and these are linked to the body. In *Les monades* Condillac states that "the union of the soul with the body is such that we have a consciousness of ourselves only insofar as we feel the weight of our body."[48] As for Condillac self-consciousness always relates to the body, he would seem to reject the notion that self-consciousness relates in any direct way to the soul.

The body as it is present to us in direct experience is not, however, the body as material substance; rather, it is just part of the multiplicity of subjective experiences. Condillac suggests that we experience our own body and its distinctness from other bodies through the sense of touch. The self discovers the non-self and thereby its distinction from other things through the sense of touch.

> Placing its hands on itself it will discover that it has a body, but only when it has distinguished the different parts of it and recognized in each the same sentient being. It will discover there are other bodies when it touches things in which it does not find itself.[49]

Further, Condillac argues that "the statue learns to know its body and to recognize itself in all its component parts, because as soon as it places its hands upon one of them, the same sentient being replies in some way from one to the other: *this is myself*."[50] Thus, in Condillac's account, we individuate our own selves only as bodily beings, through the sense of touch; and we regard ourselves as diachronically identical beings on the basis of the experience of change and memory of ourselves as bodily beings.

As we saw, however, Condillac reduces the self neither to its sensations nor to its bodily being, for he allows for the notion of a soul as a simple and immaterial substance which underlies all experience and memory. Still, the notion of soul as substance plays no explicit explanatory role in his account of the workings of the mind and indeed in his account of personal identity and self-consciousness.

3 Rousseau on the *sentiment de l'existence* and the self

As in the case of Condillac, the notions of sentiment and sensibility are central in Rousseau's thought. Rousseau was certainly familiar with Locke's work, and he knew and met Condillac and refers to him in his writings.[51] In *Émile ou de l'éducation* (1762) Rousseau states that "to exist, for us, is to sense; our sensibility is incontestably anterior to our intelligence, and we had sentiments before ideas."[52] The notion of the self, too, is central in Rousseau. He discusses a variety of issues relating to the self in various, scattered places of his writings, including literary presentations.[53]

3.1. *Varieties of self-love and sentiments of existence*

Sensibility and selfhood are closely related to one another in Rousseau. There are some sentiments, he believes, that are natural to us, or innate, and these relate to the self. "These sentiments, as far as the individual is concerned, are the love of self [*amour de soi*], the fear of pain, the horror of death, the desire for well-being."[54] Importantly and famously, however, Rousseau distinguishes between two kinds of self-love – between *amour de soi*, as in the passage just quoted, which is a natural feeling and connected with the striving for self-preservation, on the one hand, and *amour-propre*, on the other. The latter is not innate but develops through the association with others. It has to do with the striving for acceptance or recognition; it can become excessive, may have negative effects and turn into a striving for domination. In the *Discours sur l'origine de l'inégalité* (1755) Rousseau explains the distinction thus:

> One must not confuse *amour-propre* with *amour de soi-même*, two very different passions in their nature and their effects. *Amour de soi-même* is a natural sentiment that prompts every animal to watch over its own preservation and that, guided in man by reason and modified by pity, produces humanity and virtue. *Amour-propre* is only a relative, artificial sentiment born in society, a sentiment that prompts each individual to set greater store by himself than by anyone else, that triggers all the evil they do to themselves and others, and that is the real source of honour.[55]

This distinction between two types of self-love is crucial to Rousseau's philosophy as a whole, but although the account in the quoted passage seems clear enough, other passages seem less straightforward and, inevitably, there is an ongoing debate among Rousseau scholars about the precise meaning of the two notions and their relationship to one another.[56] It seems clear, however, that *amour de soi* is the more basic sentiment; Rousseau says in *Émile* that *amour de soi* is "a primitive, innate passion, which is anterior to every other, and of which all others are in a sense only modifications."[57]

Here, my main concern is not with *amour de soi* and its relation to *amour-propre* but with the notion of a sentiment that is even more basic than *amour de soi* and equally important to Rousseau's philosophy: that is, the notion of the sentiment of our own existence. Interpretation of this notion is no easier or more straightforward, however, than that of *amour de soi* and *amour-propre*. As scholars have noted, Rousseau uses this notion in more than one sense, and he provides no systematic discussion of it.[58] Moreover, the terminology is not uniform either. Apart from "sentiment de l'existence" Rousseau uses "conscience de soi-même," "sentiment de notre être," "sentiment interne," "sentiment du moi," "sentiment intérieur," and "sentiment intime."[59] It is not at all clear that these expressions are always used synonymously. Sometimes but not always some of these expressions seem to denote the same as *sentiment de l'existence*.[60] But what is the *sentiment de l'existence*? In one sense the notion would not be basic or fundamental at all. In a letter to Voltaire, for example, Rousseau writes of a "pleasant *sentiment de l'existence*, independent of all other sensation," of an *enjoyment* of life, it seems, that one has in spite of bad experiences.[61] This kind of feeling of existence is not basic as it assumes other sentiments and experiences. Similarly, in *Les rêveries du promeneur solitaire* Rousseau says that the sentiment of existence is "in itself a precious sentiment of contentment and of peace."[62] Elsewhere, Rousseau's *sentiment de l'existence* denotes a sentiment of one's own worth. This sentiment is based "on the judgements of others" and seems to presuppose *amour-propre* and so cannot be basic.[63]

In the context of some of the epistemological considerations in the *Profession de foi du vicaire savoyard* in Book IV of *Émile*, however, a somewhat different and more elementary notion of *sentiment de l'existence* comes into play.[64] This is the notion that we are familiar with from our discussion of Locke and Condillac, a notion that goes back to Malebranche and other broadly Cartesian thinkers in the late seventeenth and early eighteenth centuries. This notion, too, is related to *amour de soi* and *amour-propre*, but in a more fundamental way than *sentiment* understood as enjoyment or contentment. This notion of *sentiment de l'existence* is that of an immediate awareness or consciousness of one's own existence as a subject of perceptions. Clearly, this kind of awareness is presupposed by both kinds of self-love. Both self-preservation and the striving for recognition by others assume that I am aware of my own existence; only if I am aware of my own existence as a subject of perceptions can I become an object of self-love and of recognition. Here, I shall focus on the *sentiment de l'existence* in this basic sense; other aspects of the notion hinted at above cannot be discussed in this context.

3.2 *Sentiment de l'Existence as self-awareness*

Rousseau speaks not only of a sentiment or consciousness of one's own existence, but like Locke and Condillac, also of a "consciousness of our sensations."[65] It is precisely the relationship between these two types of consciousness that raises a fundamental question for Rousseau, relating to the nature of the sentiment of existence:

> I exist, and I have senses by which I am affected. This is the first truth that strikes me and to which I am forced to acquiesce. Do I have a particular sentiment of my existence, or do I sense it only through my sensations? This is my first doubt, which it is for the present impossible for me to resolve; for as I am continually affected by sensations, whether immediately or by memory, how can I know whether the sentiment of the I is something outside these same sensations and whether it can be independent of them?[66]

Rousseau clearly believes that the existence of my own self is immediately and absolutely certain. What is questionable, according to him, is *how* I know this. He presents the reader with two possibilities: (a) there is a sentiment or feeling of existence which is separate from all my other feelings and sensations; (b) the feeling of my existence is felt only through sensations and thus dependent on them. Some commentators have identified (b) with the (allegedly) Humean view that the self does not exist apart from its perceptions.[67] This is not, however, what is stated: (b) makes no claim about the nature of the self and the manner of its existence; it does not suggest that the self is a bundle or collection of perceptions. Rather it makes a statement about the means of knowing the existence of my own self, whatever its nature. It says that the feeling of my own existence depends on other sensations. Only through the consciousness of sensations can I become aware or conscious of the being (my own self) who has those sensations. Further one could ask if (b) is the view that the sentiment of existence is an aspect of the other sensations themselves or derived from them. However that may be, (b) is quite consistent with the view that the self is a unitary thing or substance. Rousseau says that it is difficult to answer the question whether (a) or (b) is true, because we are in fact never without sensations, and we cannot tell whether or not "the sentiment of the I" is something independent of them.

Rousseau does not elaborate further on that issue in the *Profession de foi*. The idea present in the quotation above, however, namely that our own existence is a "first truth," seems to suggest that the sentiment of existence is independent and does not require other sensations. Elsewhere, Rousseau states that the "first" sentiment of a human being is that of its own existence which again indicates the independence of this sentiment.[68] Yet other passages in *Émile* suggest that Rousseau thinks there cannot be a special sentiment of one's own self that is independent of all other sensations. Thus, immediately after the passage quoted above Rousseau says that "my sensations [...] make me sense my existence."[69]

Indeed not unlike Condillac, Rousseau states at one point that at the beginning of our existence we have no inner-directed sensibility, no sentiment of our own existence. "We are born capable of learning but able to do nothing, knowing nothing. The soul, enchained in imperfect and half-formed organs, does not even have the sentiment of its own existence."[70] Also, Rousseau says that the *sentiment de l'existence* depends on the existence of sensations of external things and is thus not independent at all. "To live," he says in *Émile*, "is to act; it is to make use of our organs, our senses, our faculties, of all the parts of our selves which give us the sentiment of our existence."[71] If the sentiment of existence is mediated by other activities in this way, then it cannot be "first" or independent. Possibly, when Rousseau says that one's own existence is the first truth one knows, "first" is not to be taken in a temporal sense, but this is not what his formulations in the relevant passages cited above suggest. In short, the precise relationship between the sentiment of one's own existence and other thoughts and perceptions (and our consciousness of these) remains unclear.[72] While a distinct notion of *sentiment de l'existence* as self-awareness can be identified in the *Profession de foi*, there is no systematic discussion of this idea. Still, Rousseau ascribes to the *sentiment de l'existence* a special function for diachronic self-identity.

3.3 *The sentiment of existence and identity: Rousseau and Buffon*

Rousseau's remarks on personal identity through time appeal to ideas we are familiar with from Locke and Condillac. Like Condillac, Rousseau links the notion of the *sentiment de l'existence* to that of memory. He distinguishes between the *sentiment de l'existence* as a relating to one's own present existence and a consciousness of self which involves linking the present to the past. Here, Buffon seems to be a likely source for Rousseau as well, as there are significant similarities.[73] Buffon's main interest is of course in the workings of physical nature, but in the chapter

"De la nature de l'homme" which opens his *Histoire naturelle de l'homme* (1749) he reflects on how human subjects relate to their own selves. The existence of our own soul is absolutely certain, he argues, for "being and thinking are the same thing in us," this is an intuitive truth, and "independent of our senses, of our imagination, of our memory."[74] Buffon speaks of a "sensation of existence" in both animals and human beings. This "sensation" is a relating to one's own present existence. Only human beings, however, are capable of a "consciousness of existence" that involves a relating to the past; animals do not have that capacity.[75] Thus, "consciousness of existence," for which Buffon also uses the expression *sentiment intérieur*, is composed of the sensation of our present existence and the memory of our past existence. This *sentiment intérieur* is what makes us a proper self.[76] Similarly, Rousseau argues that the *sentiment de l'existence* is a feeling that is always with us and as such relates only to the present. Memory, for Rousseau, extends this sentiment to the whole of our existence. This consciousness of self across time is essential, Rousseau suggests, to the self as a moral being, that is, as a proper human being:

> It is at this second stage that the life of the individual begins. It is then that he gains consciousness of himself. Memory extends the sentiment of identity to all the moments of his existence; he becomes truly one, the same, and consequently already capable of happiness or unhappiness. It is important, therefore, to begin to consider him here as a moral being.[77]

For Rousseau, then (as for Locke), only the self considered in terms of its ability to relate to both its present and past is a moral being or a moral self. The mere sentiment of existence cannot constitute the self as a moral being; memory is required as well. Insofar as memory is understood as "extending" the sentiment of existence beyond the present moment, however, it seems that the latter feeling is prior; there could be no memory without the sentiment of existence.

Now, does memory fulfil a constitutive role for diachronic self-identity? The following passage seems to endorse such a view:

> I sense my soul. I know it by sentiment and by thought without knowing what its essence is, I know that it exists. I cannot reason about ideas I do not have. What I know surely is that the identity of the *I* is prolonged only by memory, and that in order to be actually the same I must remember having been. Now, after my death, I could not recall what I was during my life unless I also recall what I felt, and consequently what I did; and I do not doubt that this memory will one day cause the felicity of the good and the torment of the wicked. Here on earth countless ardent passions absorb the inner sentiment and lead remorse astray.[78]

Like Locke, Rousseau seems to be saying here that, as we do not and cannot know what the real essence of the self is, it can have diachronic identity (for us) only through (consciousness and) memory. Memory, according to this passage, is essential; the self would not have diachronic identity if it did not have memory – "in order *to be* actually the same I must remember having been" (my italics).

This claim seems to be inconsistent, however, with other passages in which Rousseau asserts (without invoking memory) that the self simply exists and continues to exist as the same being. For example, in the earlier quote from the *Profession de foi* Rousseau says: "I exist, and I have senses by which I am affected. This is the first truth that strikes me and to which I am forced to acquiesce."[79] Here, Rousseau seems to be saying that the self is simply given and not constituted by any activity of the self. Once we take a closer look, however, it becomes clear that there is only a seeming inconsistency between the two passages. When Rousseau speaks of the self as simply existing he is speaking metaphysically, referring to the self as a soul or thinking substance; when he invokes memory as constitutive of self-identity he is talking about the self as a "moral being." This is indicated by the comment on immortality in the longer quotation above. Remembering "having been" includes remembering what I have done; and this memory of my deeds "will one day cause the felicity of the good and the torment of the wicked." Thus, again like Locke, Rousseau distinguishes between the self as a mental substance and its identity, on the one hand, and the self and its identity as a moral being requiring memory, on the other.[80] Rousseau is not saying, then, that memory creates the self's identity through time in a metaphysical sense (i.e., as a thinking substance). This is given prior to memory. Rather, memory constitutes the self and its identity in a moral sense, as a being that is capable of happiness and misery.[81]

We noted above that for Locke the self, by being "concerned" for its own happiness, relates to its own future, as well as to its present and past thoughts and actions. In Buffon the relating to the future is also relevant, but he argues for this in a different way. He says that memory is dependent on the power of reflection because our memory of past things supposes not only the renewal of earlier sensations but also comparisons that our souls have made of those sensations. The soul establishes the connections between those things through comparing, that is, through reflecting.[82] It is this power of reflection that enables us, as human beings, not only to be certain of our past life but also to relate to our own future.[83] For Buffon, then, self-conscious existence consists essentially in the activity of linking past, present and an anticipated future.

While Rousseau seems to be focused on the link between past and present, his account of the self, too, invokes a relating to the future, through the notion of the afterlife which is also relevant in Locke's account. Our memory of our past deeds will determine if we will be happy or miserable; therefore, our decisions and actions in this life relate to our future lives. Recall the passage quoted above:

> Now, after my death, I could not recall what I was during my life unless I also recall what I felt, and consequently what I did; and I do not doubt that this memory will one day cause the felicity of the good and the torment of the wicked.[84]

3.4 *Rousseau on the active forces of the self*

Much has been made of Rousseau's emphasis on the active nature of the self. Some scholars have contended for a connection between Rousseau and Kant in this respect.[85] And indeed Rousseau argues that we do not passively perceive the connection between our sensations, but that this perception requires an activity of the self. He states: "I reflect on the objects of my sensations; and finding in myself the faculty of comparing them, I sense myself endowed with an active force which I did not know before I had."[86] Only through my activity can there be a "communication" among my sensations so that I can combine them; and only through our activity of combining is it possible for us "to know that the body we touch and the object we see are the same." Without such activity "either we would never sense anything outside of us, or there would be five sensible substances for us whose identity we would have no means of perceiving."[87] It is the self or "I" or soul that brings about this synthesis and thereby makes possible the knowledge of objects:

> Let this or that name be given to this force of my mind which brings together and compares my sensations; let it be called *attention*, *meditation*, *reflection*, or whatever one wishes. It is still true that it is in me and not in things, that it is I alone who produce it, although I produce it only on the occasion of the impression made on me by objects.[88]

Moreover, at a more fundamental level, Rousseau argues that, in formulating propositions, we connect ideas through the copula "is": "the distinctive faculty of the active or intelligent being is to be able to give sense to the word *is*."[89] This requires a unitary self, understood as an immaterial substance. Buffon, too, in spite of his focus on the physical nature of the self, sees human beings as composed of two substances, one extended, material and mortal, the other not extended, imma-terial and immortal.[90] In Rousseau, the anti-materialist position is, in part at least, arrived at through epistemological considerations. It is plain that for Rousseau the self is not a passive recep-tor of sensations, and it is the active nature of the self that, to him, speaks against materialism:

> A machine does not think; there is neither motion nor figure which produces reflection [...] No material being is active by itself, and I am. One may very well argue with me about this; but I sense it, and this sentiment that speaks to me is stronger than the reason combatting it.[91]

These comments, however, point to the fact that Rousseau's reflections on the active nature of the self may not be as innovative and forward-looking as some have thought. It is obvious that for philosophers such as Locke, too, the mind is active, for example, in the creation of complex ideas, in basic cognitive capacities such as reflecting, comparing and abstracting, and in the formation of propositions that may be true or false. In Locke this does not involve a commitment to an imma-terialist conception of the human mind or soul. It seems doubtful, then, that Rousseau's emphasis on the active nature of the self could be used to establish a special connection between him and Kant.[92] Many anti-materialist philosophers both before and after Rousseau, including Buffon and several German thinkers, such as Kant's teacher Martin Knutzen, made the point that the self or soul is active, for example in connecting ideas in a proposition, and therefore cannot be material (as matter is inert).[93] For the most part, Rousseau reproduces standard anti-materialist arguments here.[94]

Finally, Rousseau does not seem to attempt to combine his various remarks on the self (con-cerning memory and personal identity, the *sentiment de l'existence*, and the active forces) into a coherent account. It remains unclear, for example, how the notion of the active, synthesising self is to be related to the *sentiment de l'existence*. The function ascribed to memory, however, can be made consistent with the notion of the synthesising self: it functions as a unifier of past and present experiences, thus constituting moral personal identity through time.

4 Conclusion

The presence of Locke's ideas about the self and sensibility in French thinkers such as Condillac and Rousseau is obvious from the account above. There are, however, not only similarities but also several philosophically important differences. Condillac and Rousseau (as well as Buffon) work with the notion of an immediate sentiment or consciousness of one's own existence. We saw that in Rousseau this notion has several features and that one of these relates to Locke's idea of the "intuitive knowledge" we have of our own existence, an idea that is present in Con-dillac's notion of the "sentiment of our own being." In Locke and Condillac this kind of self-con-sciousness is derived from the consciousness of other perceptions; there is no "original" self-consciousness independently of other perceptions. Rousseau seems to leave the question open of whether there could be such an independent self-consciousness. It is significant, however, that he considers the nature of the sentiment of existence at all.

Locke, Condillac and Rousseau discuss other ways of relating to one's own self, apart from the mere sentiment or intuition of existence. Most important to all of them is the relating to the past, through memory. According to Locke, the consciousness of the present and the memory of the past are constitutive of our diachronic personal identity. In Condillac, by contrast, we merely recognize our identity through consciousness and memory. Rousseau is closer to Locke here in that he suggests that consciousness and memory are constitutive of the self as a "moral being" (see below). Moreover, Locke distinguishes between the human subject as a person, as a man or human being and as a soul or substance. Certainly, Locke's distinction between the soul, as substance, and the person is present, in different ways, in both Condillac and Rousseau. In Condillac, there is a distinction between the soul and the phenomenal self to which we have access through consciousness and memory; and Rousseau distinguishes between the soul and the self as a moral being. It seems that Rousseau and Condillac highlight different (psychological and moral) aspects of Locke's account of the person. Both Locke and Rousseau also speak of a relating to one's own future. In Locke, this belongs to the "forensic" nature of personhood and to the fact that we are "concerned" for our happiness and misery. In the last analysis, this "concern" relates to the afterlife. We saw that similar ideas are present in Rousseau.

Condillac is sometimes seen as a "bundle" theorist, "radicalising" Locke's account of the mind; even Rousseau is occasionally read as at least playing with this idea. As we saw, however, neither thinker sees the mind essentially as a bundle of perceptions. Both Condillac and Rousseau endorse the notion of the soul as a substance. While Locke leaves open the question about the real essence of the soul, Condillac and Rousseau insist that the soul is a "simple and indivisible," immaterial substance. In Rousseau, the immaterial nature of the soul is even a matter of sentiment. Materialists, he says, are "deaf to the inner voice crying out to them in a tone difficult not to recognize."[95] In this sense at least, Condillac and Rousseau are less "radical" than Locke.

There can be no doubt that the relating to our own body is relevant to both Locke's and Rousseau's accounts. Thus Locke suggests that the body becomes part of the person through consciousness and is in this sense relevant to our personal identity. It seems, however, that the body has a more central and fundamental status in Condillac than it does in Locke and Rousseau. This is evident in Condillac's notion discussed above that the self discovers the non-self and thereby its distinction from other things through the sense of touch.

In short, then, Lockean ideas are taken up, adopted, criticised and modified in a variety of fruitful ways. It would be misleading, however, to speak of a particular, progressive development of thought from Locke to Condillac and Rousseau on this issue. One critical question raised by the French sensibilist accounts of the self may be formulated as an elaboration of Rousseau's question cited above. Rousseau asks if the sentiment of existence is derived from sensations or if it is independent of them. One could ask further, if there is any evidence for the existence of such a "sentiment" at all. Can it be empirically identified? It seems that the sensibilist accounts, for all their emphasis on experience, simply assert the existence of such a sentiment. If we cannot empirically identify a sentiment of existence but still consider the notion of self-consciousness in this basic sense important, then it is obvious that the purely experiential approach has reached its limits.[96]

Notes

1. Yolton, *Locke and French Materialism*.
2. Locke, *Essay* I.i.1.
3. Gaukroger, *Collapse of Mechanism*, 390.
4. Locke, *Essay* II.i.3.
5. Locke, *Essay* I.i.1.
6. Locke, *Essay* IV.ii.1.
7. Locke, *Essay* II.ix.1. It is worth noting that Locke uses sensation to illustrate the immediacy of intuitive knowledge (*Essay* IV.ii.1). For a recent analysis of the latter, see Weinberg, "Locke's Reply to the Sceptic," 394–399.
8. Locke, *Essay* II.i.8.
9. Locke, Journal note of 20 Feb 1682, in Locke, *An Early Draft of Locke's Essay together with Excerpts from His Journals*, 121–123 (my italics).
10. Locke, *Essay* II.i.10.
11. Locke, *Essay* II.xxvii.9.

12. Locke, *Essay* II.i.19.
13. Locke, *Essay* IV.ix.3. For a more detailed discussion of Locke on consciousness and the intuitive knowledge of one's own existence, see Thiel, *Early Modern Subject*, 118–120; and Thiel, "Der Begriff der Intuition bei Locke," 95–112.
14. Locke, *Essay* II.xxvii.9 (my italics).
15. The distinction between (2) and (4) corresponds to Galen Strawson's distinction between self-awareness and "full or express" self-consciousness (Strawson, *Evident Connexion*, 86 and 91).
16. Locke, *Essay* II.xxvii.
17. For a detailed discussion of Locke on personal identity, see Thiel, *Early Modern Subject*, chapters 3–6.
18. "The Sentence shall be justified by the consciousness all Persons shall have, that they *themselves* in what Bodies soever they appear, or what Substances soever that consciousness adheres to, are the *same*, that committed those Actions, and deserve that Punishment for them" (Locke, *Essay* II.xxvii.26).
19. Thiel, *Enlightened Subject*.
20. See Thiel, *Early Modern Subject*, 9–10. Compare also the overview in Spink, "Les avatars," 269–298.
21. Condillac, *Essai* I.ii.1, §4; *Oeuvres philosophiques* I, 11; *Essay on the Origin*, 20. See also *Traité des sensations* IV.vii.4 (*Treatise on the Sensations*, 226; *Oeuvres philosophiques* I, 309). Consciousness is a feeling "of what is passing within us" (*notre conscience, c'est-à-dire, le sentiment de ce qui se passe en nous*). In his *Dictionnaire des synonymes* Condillac defines *conscience* as "sentiment intérieur. Nous connoissons notre ame par conscience" (*Oeuvres philosophiques* III, 143).
22. Condillac, *Essai* I.ii.1, § 13; *Essay on the Origin*, 24 ("Ainsi la perception et la conscience ne sont qu'une même opération sous deux noms. En tant qu'on ne la considère que comme une impression dans l'ame, on peut lui conserver celui de perception; en tant qu'elle avertit l'ame de sa présence, on peut lui donner celui de conscience," *Oeuvres philosophiques* I, 13). Compare also *Essai* I.ii.1 § 16 (*Essay on the Origin*, 26): "This impression, considered as giving the mind notice of its presence, is what I call consciousness […] Somehow consciousness says to the mind: there is a perception" ("Cette impression, considérée comme avertissant l'ame de sa présence, est ce que j'appelle conscience […] La conscience dit en quelque sorte à l'ame, voilà une perception," *Oeuvres philosophiques* I, 14).
23. In the *Essai* Condillac distinguishes between imagination, memory and reminiscence. The imagination "revives the perceptions themselves," memory "recalls only the signs or the circumstances," and reminiscence "reports those we have already had" (*Essai*,I.ii.2, §25; *Essay on the Origin*, 30; *Oeuvres philosophiques* I, 16). In the later *Traité des sensations* Condillac does not seem to make use of this distinction, and he accounts for personal identity in terms of memory (*le souvenir*).
24. Condillac, *Essai* I.ii.1, §15, *Essay on the Origin*, 25–26; my italics. ("Lorsque les objets attirent notre attention, les perceptions qu'ils occasionnent en nous, se lient avec le sentiment de notre être et avec tout ce qui peut y avoir quelque rapport. De-là il arrive que non seulement la conscience nous donne connoissance de nos perceptions, mais encore, si elles se répètent, elle nous avertit souvent que nous les avons déjà eues, et nous les fait connoître comme étant à nous, ou comme affectant, malgré leur variété et leur succession, un être qui est constamment le même *nous*. La conscience, considérée par rapport à ces nouveaux effets, est une nouvelle opération qui nous sert à chaque instant et qui est le fondement de l'expérience. Sans elle chaque moment de la vie nous paroît le premier de notre existence, et notre connoissance ne s'étendroit jamais au-delà d'une première perception: je la nommerai *réminiscence*," *Oeuvres philosophiques* I, 14).
25. The account of personal identity Condillac gives in the *Traité des sensations* (I.vi.1) is consistent with the relevant passages in the *Essai*. Condillac explicitly links the idea we have of our own self to memory (*le souvenir*): "If it [the statue] is able to say 'I' (*moi*) it can say it in all the states of its duration; and at each time its 'I' will embrace all the moments of which it might have preserved recollection" (*Treatise on the Sensations*, 43; "Si elle pouvoit dire *moi*, elle le diroit dans tous les instans de sa durée; et à chaque fois son *moi* embrasseroit tous les momens dont elle conserveroit le souvenir," *Oeuvres philosophiques* I, 238). Sensations which the statue cannot recollect are not part of the idea it has of its personality (*Traité des sensations*, I.vi.3: "Les odeurs, dont la statue ne se souvient pas, n'entrent donc point dans l'idée qu'elle a de sa personne. Aussi étrangères à son *moi*, que les couleurs et les sons, dont elle n'a encore aucune connoissance; elles sont à son égard, comme si elle ne les avoit jamais senties," *Oeuvres philosophiques* I, 239). Again, Condillac comments on *the idea* we have of our own personality and what we regard as ourselves. Unlike Locke, he does not state that personal identity itself is constituted through consciousness and memory.
26. Ryding, "La notion du moi chez Condillac," 126ff.
27. Condillac, *Essai* I.ii.1, § 15; *Essay on the Origin*, 25; my italics. ("Il est évident que si la liaison qui est entre les perceptions que j'éprouve actuellement, celles que j'éprouvai hier, et le sentiment de mon être,

étoit détruite, je ne saurois reconnoître que ce qui m'est arrivé hier, soit arrivé à moi-même. Si, à chaque nuit, cette liaison étoit interrompue, je commencerois, pour ainsi dire, chaque jour une nouvelle vie, et personne ne pourroit me convaincre que le *moi* d'aujourd'hui fût le *moi* de la veille. La réminiscence est donc produite par la liaison que conserve la suite de nos perceptions," *Oeuvres philosophiques* I, 14).

28. Condillac, *Essai* I.ii.1 § 15, *Essay on the Origin*, 25–26. ("Afin de mieux analyser la réminiscence, il faudroit lui donner deux noms: l'un, en tant qu'elle nous fait reconnoître notre être; l'autre en tant qu'elle nous fait reconnoître les perceptions qui s'y répètent: car ce sont-là des idées bien dinstinctes," *Oeuvres philosophiques* I, 14).

29. Condillac, *Essai* I.ii.l, § 15; *Essay on the Origin*, 25 ("Je regarde cette liaison comme une première expérience qui doit suffire pour expliquer toutes les autres," *Oeuvres philosophiques* I, 14).

30. Condillac, *Essai*, Introduction; *Essay on the Origin*, 5; *Oeuvres philosophiques* I, 4.

31. See, for example, Davies, *Conscience as Consciousness*, 81–82. Compare also Aliénor Bertrand, who seems to think that the main difference between Locke and Condillac is that the latter abandons the notion of self as a substance. He sees this as a "radicalisation of Locke's theory" that is linked to Condillac's rejection of the autonomy of reflection in the *Traité des sensations* (Bertrand, "Individualité et personnalité," 483).

32. The work is a prize essay that Condillac submitted to the Berlin Academy. It was rediscovered and republished in 1980 (Condillac, *Les monades*). For commentary on this work, see Kreimendahl, "Condillac und die Monaden," 280–288.

33. "Nous ne connaissons notre être qu'autant que nous le sentons, nous ne le sentons qu'autant que nous avons des sensations" (*Les monades*, 146).

34. "La conscience que nous avons de ce que nous appelons *nous*, le représente d'abord comme revêtu de certaines qualités, et comme modifié d'une certaine manière" (*Les monades*, 145).

35. "Voilà proprement ce que nous nommons notre *substance*" (*Les monades*, 145).

36. As Condillac says: "il y a en nous quelque chose capable de sensation" (*Les monades*, 146). Similarly, when Condillac expresses scepticism about the possibility of knowing the nature of our own self in the *Traité des sensations*, he does not thereby deny the existence of an underlying substantial self whose nature remains unknown to us: "I know this body belongs to me, though how, I cannot understand. I see myself, I touch myself, I am conscious of myself, but I do not know what I am. If I believe myself sound, taste, colour, smell, I am no nearer to the true knowledge of what I myself actually am," *Traité des sensations* IV.8.6; *Treatise on the Sensations*, 235–236. ("Je sais qu'elles [les parties de ce corps] sont à moi, sans pouvoir le comprendre: je me vois, je me touche, en un mot, je me sens, mais je ne sais ce que je suis; et, si j'ai cru être son, saveur, couleur, odeur, actuellement je ne sais plus ce que je dois me croire," *Oeuvres philosophiques* I, 313).

37. *Traité des sensations* I.vi.3; *Treatise on the Sensations*, 44. ("Son *moi* n'est que la collection des sensations qu'elle éprouve, et de celles que la mémoire lui rappelle. En un mot, c'est tout-à-la-fois et la conscience de ce qu'elle est, et le souvenir de ce qu'elle a été," *Oeuvres philosophiques* I, 239).

38. *Traité des sensations* IV.ix.3. *Treatise on the Sensations*, 238. ("Elle n'est donc rien qu'autant qu'elle a acquis. Pourquoi n'en seroit-il pas de même de l'homme?" *Oeuvres philosophiques* I, 314).

39. Thus, my reading is in agreement in this respect with that of Knight and Perkins (rather than with that of Bertrand and Davies). Knight states that Condillac "annexed the collection of sensations to a soul and declared the soul to be a spiritual substance, unified and immortal, doomed by original sin to dependence on the body" (Knight, *Geometric Spirit*, 98). Knight refers to the *Essai*, *Oeuvres philosophiques* I, 7–8, but also to the *Traité des animaux*, in *Oeuvres philosophiques* I, 371. Compare also Perkins who speaks of Condillac's notion of "the true self, the self which exists behind the mere content of the self" (Perkins, *Concept of the Self*, 55). Condillac "always had the metaphysical concept of the soul to fall back on [...] The soul exists as an independent entity, unified and comprehensive, to which all the passing perceptions, emotions and ideas could be attached" (ibid., 56). John C. O'Neal's long chapter on Condillac in *Authority of Experience*, 13–59, does not deal with the issues of substance and personal identity.

40. *Traité des sensations* I.vi.3; *Treatise on the Sensations*, 43. ("Ce n'est pas l'assemblage des qualités qui fait la personne; car le même homme, jeune ou vieux, beau ou laid, sage ou fou, seroit autant de personnes distinctes; et pour quelques qualités qu'on m'aime, c'est toujours moi qu'on aime; car les qualités ne sont que moi modifié différemment [...] Dans le sens de Pascal, Dieu seul pourroit dire, *moi*," *Oeuvres philosophiques* I, 239).

41. *Traité des sensations* I.vi.2; *Treatise on the Sensations*, 43. ("Ce qu'on entend par ce mot [*moi*], ne me paroît convenir qu'à un être qui remarque que, dans le moment présent, il n'est plus ce qu'il a été. Tant

qu'il ne change point, il existe sans aucun retour sur lui-même: mais aussitôt qu'il change, il juge qu'il est le même qui a été auparavant de telle manière, et il dit *moi*," *Oeuvres philosophiques* I, 238). See also the following passage: "By passing [...] through these two states [present smell and remembered smell] the statue feels that it is no longer what it was. The knowledge of this change makes it relate the first smell to a different moment from that in which it is experiencing the second, and this makes it perceive a difference between existing in one state and remembering having existed in another" (*Traité des sensations* I.ii.10; *Treatise on the Sensations*, 7; "En passant [...] par deux manières d' être, la statue sent qu'elle n'est plus ce qu'elle a été: la connaissance de ce changement lui fait rapporter la première à un moment différent de celui où elle éprouve la seconde: et c'est là ce qui lui fait mettre de la différence entre exister d'une manière et se souvenir d'avoir existé d'une autre," *Oeuvres philosophiques* I, 226).

42. *Traité des sensations* IV.viii.1; *Treatise on the Sensations*, 229. ("Par la succession de mes manières d'être, je m'aperçois que je dure. Il falloit donc que ce *moi* variât à chaque instant, au hasard de se changer souvent contre un autre, où il m'est douleureux de me retrouver," *Oeuvres philosophiques* I, 310).

43. *Essai* I.i.1, § 6; *Essay on the Origin*, 13; ("Il faudra donc admettre un point de réunion; une substance qui soit en même temps un sujet simple et indivisible [...] distincte , par conséquent, du corps; une ame, en un mot," *Oeuvres philosophiques* I, 7). See also *Traité des sensations* II.iv: "Since the sensations belong only to the soul, they can be modifications only of that substance." ("Les sensations n'appartenant qu'à l'ame, elles ne peuvent être que des manières d'être de cette substance," *Oeuvres philosophiques* I, 254).

44. Erik Ryding has argued that, in addition to the notions of a phenomenal and a substantial self, there is, third, the notion of a "formal self" in Condillac (Ryding, "La notion du moi chez Condillac," 129). This notion of a *moi formel* is that of a mere unifier of thoughts or perceptions. Acccording to Ryding, the *moi formel* is that which provides a link between our perceptions and guarantees our personal identity. Ryding does not provide sufficient textual evidence, however, for his ascription of such a notion to Condillac. It could perhaps be argued that the "sentiment of our being" fulfils such a role, as it is linked to perceptions and makes reminiscence and self-consciousness possible. This is a "sentiment" in Condillac, however, not a third notion of "self." We have seen also that Condillac postulates a subject that underlies perceptions and that provides the "liaison entre des perceptions" (ibid., 127) required for memory and personal identity. This self beyond the perceptions in Condillac just is the soul, as substance, however. In short, Ryding's rather Kantian-sounding reading of Condillac does not succeed. For a different Kantian reading of Condillac that does not focus on the notion of the self, see M.W. Beal, "Condillac as Precursor of Kant," *Studies on Voltaire and the Eighteenth Century* 102 (1973), 193–229.

45. *Traité des sensations* II.i.3; *Oeuvres philosophiques* I, 251.

46. *Traité des sensations* IV.8.1; *Treatise on the Sensations*, 228. ("Au premier moment de mon existence, je ne savois point ce qui se passoit en moi; je n'y démêlois rien encore; je n'avois aucune conscience de moi-même," *Oeuvres philosophiques* I, 310).

47. "Qu'importe que j'existe, si par moi-même je suis incapable de me sentir? Et proprement l'existence de ce que j'appelle *moi,* où commence-t-elle, si ce n'est au moment où je commence à en avoir conscience?" (*Les monades*, 201–202).

48. "L'union de l'ame avec le corps est telle que nous n'avons conscience de nous-mêmes qu'autant que nous sentons le poids de notre corps," *Les monades*, 145.

49. *Traité des sensations* II.v.2; *Treatise on the Sensations*, 85–86. ("En les portant sur elle-même, elle ne découvrira qu'elle a un corps, que lorsqu'elle en distinguera les différentes parties, et qu'elle se reconnoîtra dans chacune pour le même être sentant; et elle ne découvrira qu'il y a d'autres corps, que parce qu'elle ne se retrouvera pas dans ceux qu'elle touchera," *Oeuvres philosophiques* I, 255).

50. *Traité des sensations* II.v.4; *Treatise on the Sensations*, 89. ("La statue apprend donc à connoître son corps, et à se reconnoître dans toutes les parties qui le composent; parce qu'aussitôt qu'elle porte la main sur une d'elles, le même être sentant se répond en quelque sorte de l'une à l'autre: *c'est moi*," *Oeuvres philosophiques* I, 256).

51. See, for example, the *Discours sur l'origine de l'inégalité*, in *Oeuvres complètes* III, 148, and *Les confessions*, in *Oeuvres complètes* I, 237, 280. Compare Fräßdorf, *Die psychologischen Anschauungen*, 23.

52. *Emile or On Education*, 290; *Oeuvres complètes* IV, 600: "Exister pour nous, c'est sentir; notre sensibilité est incontestablement antérieure à notre intelligence."

53. For references to literary representations of memory and personal identity in Rousseau, see, for example, Perkins, *Concept of Self*, 91,104–106. There are, of course, more detailed discussions of this aspect of Rousseau's writings. Reinhard Brandt, for example, examines the notion of the self in Rousseau's early comedy *Narcisse* (Brandt, "Der Einzelne und die Andern," 263–287). As Brandt shows, *Narcisse* is concerned with the idea that in being oneself one must lose oneself in another. See also Rousseau's adaptation of the Pygmalion-motif, in his "scéne lyrique" entitled *Pygmalion* (*Oeuvres completes* II, 1224–1231). Here, the statue's first perception is to touch itself and say "I" (ibid., 1230). Compare the discussion in Starobinski, *Jean-Jacques Rousseau. Transparency and Obstruction*, chapter 4.

54. *Emile or On Education*, 290. ("Ces sentimens, quant à la individu, sont l'amour de soi, la crainte de la douleur, l'horreur de la mort, le désir du bien-être," *Oeuvres complètes* IV, 600).

55. *Discourse on the Origin of Inequality*, 115. ("Il ne faut pas confondre l'amour-propre et l'amour de soi-même; deux passions très différentes par leur nature et par leurs effets. L'amour de soi-même est un sentiment naturel qui porte tout animal à veiller à sa propre conservation et qui, dirigé dans l'homme par la raison et modifié par la pitié, produit l'humanité et la vertu. L'amour-propre n'est qu'un sentiment relatif, factice et né dans la société, qui porte chaque individu à faire plus de cas de soi que de tout autre, qui inspire aux hommes tous les maux qu'ils se font mutuellement et qui est la véritable source de l'honneur," *Oeuvres complètes* III, 219).

56. I have benefited greatly from the excellent account in Neuhouser, *Rousseau's Theodicy of Self-Love*, especially 13–18, 29–37, 43–45.

57. *Emile or On Education*, 213; ("passion primitive, innée, antérieure à toute autre, et dont toutes les autres ne sont, en un sens, que des modifications," *Oeuvres complètes* IV, 491).

58. See, for example, the discussion in Neuhouser, *Rousseau's Theodicy*, 35f., and in Cooper, *Rousseau, Nature*, 20–30, at 21.

59. For a list of the terms employed by Rousseau for relating to the self, see Davies, *Conscience as Consciousness*, 75.

60. Philip Robinson notes that "conscience" and "sentiment" are "interchangeable in Rousseau when they relate to one's own existence." See Robinson, "*La Conscience*," 1385.

61. Letter to Voltaire of 18 August 1756; "un doux sentiment de l'existence, indépendant de toute autre sensation," *Oeuvres complètes*, IV, 1063. Compare Fräßdorf, *Die psychologischen Anschauungen*, 209. For an account of *sentiment de l'existence* as enjoyment of life, see the discussion in Cooper, *Rousseau, Nature*, 22–25.

62. "Le sentiment de l'existence […] est par lui-même un sentiment précieux de contentement et de paix" (*Oeuvres complètes* I, 1047).

63. *Emile or On Education*, 215; ("sur les jugements d'autrui," *Oeuvres complètes*, IV, 494). See the discussion of this in Neuhouser, *Rousseau's Theodicy*, 83–84, 156.

64. For the *Profession de foi* in general, see the notes in Rousseau, *La Profession de foi*.

65. *Emile or On Education*, 39 ("la conscience de nos sensations," *Oeuvres complètes* IV, 248).

66. *Emile or On Education*, 270. ("J'existe et j'ai des sens par lesquels je suis affecté. Voilà la première vérité qui me frappe, et à laquelle je suis forcé de'acquiescer. Ai-je un sentiment propre de mon existence, ou ne la sens-je que par mes sensations? Voilà mon premier doute, qu'il m'est, quant à présent, impossible de résoudre. Car étant continuellement affecté de sensations, ou immédiatement, ou par la mémoire, comment puis-je savoir si le sentiment du *moi* est quelque chose hors de ces mêmes sensations, et s'il peut être indépendant d'elles?," *Oeuvres complètes* IV, 570–571).

67. Perkins believes that Rousseau's question is "whether in fact a self *exists* apart from its sensations" (Perkins, *Concept of Self*, 86; my emphasis). See also Brandt, "Rousseau und Kant's 'Ich denke,'" 9.

68. See *Discourse on the Origin of Inequality*, 55: "Man's first sentiment was that of his existence." ("Le premier sentiment de l'homme fut celui de son existence," *Oeuvres complètes* III, 164). Rousseau relates this first sentiment to man's "first concern": his own preservation ("son premier soin celui de sa conservation," ibid.).

69. *Emile or On Education*, 270. ("Mes sensations […] me font sentir mon existence," *Oeuvres complètes* IV, 571).

70. *Emile or On Education*, 61 ("Nous naissons capables d'apprendre, mais ne sachant rien, ne connoissant rien. L'ame, enchaînée dans des organes imparfaits et demi-formés, n'a pas même le sentiment de sa propre existence," *Oeuvres complètes* IV, 279–280).

71. *Emile or On Education*, 42 ("Vivre [...] c'est agir; c'est faire usage de nos organes, de nos sens, de nos facultés, de toutes les parties de nous-mêmes, qui nous donnent le sentiment de notre existence," *Oeuvres complètes* IV, 253).

72. Compare the brief account in Fräßdorf, *Die psychologischen Anschauungen*, 209. Manfred Frank's comment on this issue is too one-sided. Frank focuses only on those passages in Rousseau that suggest a distinct feeling of existence. "Dies ursprüngliche Selbstgefühl, das 'j'existe' zum Gehalt hat, ist von den einzelnen Sinneseindrücken verschieden" (Frank, *Selbstgefühl*, 81).

73. For Rousseau and Buffon, see, for example, Jean Starobinski's study, "Rousseau and Buffon," in Starobinski, *Jean-Jacques Rousseau*, 323–333.

74. "Être & penser, sont pour nous la même chose, cette vérité est intime & plus qu'intuitive, elle est indépendante de nos sens, de notre imagination, de notre mémoire, & de toutes nos autres facultés relatives" (Buffon, *Oeuvres philosophiques*, 294).

75. "Les animaux […] ont aussi la conscience de leur existence actuelle, mais ils n'ont pas celle de leur existence passée" (Buffon, *Oeuvres philosophiques*, 331).

76. "La conscience de son existence, ce sentiment intérieur qui constitue le *moi*, est composé chez nous de la sensation de notre existence actuelle, & du souvenir de notre existence passée" (Buffon, *Oeuvres philosophiques*, 332).

77. *Emile or On Education*, 78. ("C'est à ce second degré que commence proprement la vie de l'individu, c'est alors qu'il prend la conscience de lui-même. La mémoire étend le sentiment de l'identité sur tous les momens de son existence; il devient véritablement un, le même, et par conséquent déjà capable de bonheur ou de misère. Il importe donc de commencer à le considérer ici comme un être moral," *Oeuvres complètes* IV, 301). Compare the brief discussions of this point in Davies, *Conscience as Consciousness*, 74; Perkins, *Concept of Self*, 96; Fräßdorf, *Die psychologischen Anschauungen*, 208).

78. *Emile or On Education*, 283. ("Je sens mon ame, je la connais par le sentiment et par la pensée; je sais qu'elle est, sans savoir quelle est son essence; je ne puis raisoner sur des idées que je n'ai pas. Ce que je sais bien, c'est que l'identité du *moi* ne se prolonge que par la mémoire, et que, pour être le même en effet, il faut que je me souvienne d'avoir été. Or je ne saurois me rappeller, après ma mort ce que j'ai été durant ma vie que je ne me rappelle aussi ce que j'ai senti, par consequent ce que j'ai fait, et je ne doute point que ce souvenir ne fasse un jour la félicité des bons et le tourment des méchans. Ici-bas mille passions ardentes absorbent le sentiment interne et donnent le change aux remords," *Oeuvres complètes* IV, 590–591).

79. *Emile or On Education*, 279; *Oeuvres complètes* IV, 570.

80. Reinhard Brandt, too, notes a distinction in Rousseau between the soul or thinking substance and the self. Brandt thinks, however, that this distinction concerns the soul as substance and the self as an active, synthesising force: "Rousseau setzt an die Stelle der Seele und ihrer Vermögen das 'Ich'" (Brandt, "Rousseau und Kant's 'Ich denke,'" 10). We will see below, however, that for Rousseau the soul itself is this synthesising active force. As noted above, the distinction Rousseau invokes is an essentially Lockean distinction betweeen the soul as substance whose essence is unknown to us and the moral self which is constituted by consciousness and memory. In ascribing to Rousseau a different distinction between soul and self, Brandt seems to be guided by the idea of a close link between Rousseau and Kant. It appears, however, that Rousseau's thinking here is closer to Locke's than it is to Kant's.

81. Compare the discusssion in Perkins, *Concept of Self*, 96, 106.

82. "Chez nous la mémoire émane de la puissance de réfléchir, car le souvenir que nous avons des choses passées suppose, non seulement […] le renouvellement de nos sensations antérieures, mais encore les comparaisons que notre ame a faites de ces sensations, c'est à dire, les idées qu'elle en a formées. […] C'est notre ame qui établit ces rapports entre les choses, par la comparaison qu'elle fait des unes avec les autres; c'est elle qui forme la liaison de nos sensations & qui ourdit la trame de nos existences par un fil continu d'idées" (Buffon, *Oeuvres philosophiques*, 333).

83. "C'est par la puissance de réfléchir qu'a notre ame, & par cette seule puissance que nous sommes certains de nos existences passées & que nous voyons nos existences futures" (Buffon, *Oeuvres philosophiques*, 332).

84. *Emile or On Education*, 283. ("Or je ne saurois me rappeller, après ma mort ce que j'ai été durant ma vie que je ne me rappelle aussi ce que j'ai senti, par consequent ce que j'ai fait, et je ne doute point que ce souvenir ne fasse un jour la félicité des bons et le tourment des méchans," *Oeuvres complètes* IV, 590–591).

85. See especially Henrich, "Fichtes ursprüngliche Einsicht," 191; and Brandt, "Rousseau und Kant's 'Ich denke,'" 16. Brandt sees "parallels" between Rousseau's and Kant's notions of the self but he does not claim that Rousseau's remarks on the topic were in any way a decisive influence on Kant.

86. *Emile or On Education*, 270. ("Je réfléchis sur les objets de mes sensations, et trouvant en moi la faculté de les comparer, je me sens doüé d'une force active que je ne savois pas avoir auparavant,"

Oeuvres complètes IV, 571). Comparative ideas (relational ideas), Rousseau says, are not sensations, "although my mind produces them only on the occasion of my sensations" (*Emile or On Education*, 271; "Ces idées comparatives […] ne sont certainement pas des sensations, quoique mon esprit ne les produise qu'à l'occasion de mes sensations," *Oeuvres complètes* IV, 572).

87. *Emile or On Education*, 271. ("Ou nous ne sentirions jamais rien hors de nous, ou il y auroit pour nous cinq substances sensibles, dont nous n'aurions nul moyen d'apercevoir l'identité," *Oeuvres complètes* IV, 573).

88. *Emile or On Education*, 271. ("Qu'on donne tel ou tel nom à cette force de mon esprit qui rapproche et compare mes sensations; qu'on l'appelle attention, méditation, réflexion, ou comme on voudra; toujours est-il vrai qu'elle est en moi et non dans les choses, que c'est moi seul qui la produis, quoique je ne la produise qu'à l'occasion de l'impression que font sur moi les objets," *Oeuvres complètes* IV, 573).

89. *Emile or On Education*, 270. ("La faculté distinctive de l'être actif ou intelligent est de pouvoir donner un sens à ce mot *est*," *Oeuvres complètes* IV, 571).

90. Buffon, *Oeuvres philosophiques*, 293.

91. *Emile or On Education*, 280. ("Une machine ne pense point, il n'y a ni movement ni figure qui produise la réflexion […] Nul être matériel n'est actif par lui-même, et moi je le suis. On a beau me disputer cela, je le sens, et ce sentiment qui me parle est plus fort que la raison qui le combat," *Oeuvres complètes* IV, 585).

92. Scholars who would like to see a connection between Kant and Rousseau on this point typically emphasise the fact that there is a reference to Rousseau on the self in Kant's lectures on anthropology. That reference, however, relates to the notion of the sentiment of existence and identity, not to the active forces that Rousseau discusses elsewhere. See Kant, *Gesammelte Schriften*, vol XXV, 12, for quotations from Rousseau's *Émile* (*Oeuvres complètes* IV, 571 and 590): "Etant continuellement affecté de sensations, ou immédiatement, ou par la mémoire, comment puis-je savoir si le sentiment du *moi* est quelque chose hors de ces mêmes sensations, et s'il peut être indépendant d'elles? Rousseau. L'identité du *moi* ne se prolonge que par la *memoire*." See the discussion in Brandt, "Rousseau und Kant's 'Ich denke,'" 6–7.

93. For Knutzen, see Thiel, *Early Modern Subject*, 329–330.

94. For example, Rousseau repeats the old argument that materialism cannot account for the unity and individuality of the self. See *Emile or On Education*, 279; *Oeuvres complètes* IV, 584.

95. *Emile or On Education*, 280. ("Ils sont sourds […] à la voix intérieure qui leur crie d'un ton difficile à méconoitre," *Oeuvres complètes* IV, 585).

96. Of course, other thinkers of the time developed the foundational role of an immediate relating to one's own self in different ways. See for example the discussion of J.B. Mérian in Thiel, *Early Modern Subject*, 372–376.

Bibliography

Beal, M.W. "Condillac as Precursor of Kant." *Studies on Voltaire and the Eighteenth Century* 102 (1973): 193–229.

Bertrand, Aliénor. "Individualité et personnalité morale chez Condillac." In *L'individu dans la pensée moderne. XVIe-XVIIIe siècles*, edited by G.M. Cazzaniga and Y.Ch. Zarka. vol. 2, 481–495. Pisa: Edizioni ETS, 1995.

Brandt, Reinhard. "Der Einzelne und die Andern: Eine Studie zur Entwicklung Rousseaus." *Archiv für Rechts- und Sozialphilosophie* 52 (1966): 263–287.

Brandt, Reinhard. "Rousseau und Kant's 'Ich denke.'" *Kant-Forschungen* 5 (1994): 1–18.

Buffon, Georges-Louis, Leclerc, Comte de. *Oeuvres philosophiques*, edited by Jean Piveteau. Paris: Presses Universitaires de France, 1954.

Condillac, Étienne Bonnot de. *Dictionnaire des synonymes*. In Condillac, *Oeuvres philosophiques* III.

Condillac, Étienne Bonnot de. *Essai sur l'origine des conaissances humaines*. In Condillac, *Oeuvres philosophiques* I, 1–118. References are to Part, Section, Chapter and Paragraph, and to page-numbers in *Oeuvres philosophiques*.

Condillac, Étienne Bonnot de. *Essay on the Origin of Human Knowledge*. Translated by Hans Aarsleff. Cambridge: Cambridge University Press, 2001.

Condillac, Étienne Bonnot de. *Les monades*, edited by Laurence L. Bongie. Vol. 187 of *Studies on Voltaire and the Eighteenth Century*. Oxford: Voltaire Foundation, 1980.

Condillac, Étienne Bonnot de. *Oeuvres philosophiques*, edited by Georges Le Roy. 3 vols. Paris: Presses Universitaires de France, 1947–1951.

Condillac, Étienne Bonnot de. *Traité des sensations*. In Condillac, *Oeuvres philosophiques* I, 219–335. References are to Part, Chapter and Paragraph and to page-numbers in *Oeuvres philosophiques*.

Condillac, Étienne Bonnot de. *Treatise on the Sensations*. Translated by Geraldine Carr. Los Angeles: University of Southern California, 1930.

Cooper, Laurence D. *Rousseau, Nature and the Problem of the Good Life*. University Park: Pennsylvania State Unversity Press, 1999.

Davies, Catherine Glyn. *Conscience as Consciousness: The Idea of Self-awareness in French Philosophical Writing from Descartes to Diderot. Vol. 272 of Voltaire and the Eighteenth Century*. Oxford: Voltaire Foundation, 1990.

Frank, Manfred. *Selbstgefühl*. Frankfurt: Suhrkamp, 2002.

Fräßdorf, Walter. *Die psychologischen Anschauungen J. J. Rousseaus*. Langensalza: Beyer, 1929.

Gaukroger, Stephen. *The Collapse of Mechanism and the Rise of Sensibility: Science and the Shaping of Modernity, 1680–1760*. Oxford: Clarendon Press, 2010.

Henrich, Dieter. "Fichtes ursprüngliche Einsicht." In *Subjektivität und Metaphysik: Festschrift für Wolfgang Cramer*, edited by D. Henrich & H. Wagner, 188–232. Frankfurt: Klostermann, 1966.

Kant, Immanuel. *Gesammelte Schriften*, edited by Königlich Preussische Akademie der Wissenschaften, and its successors. Berlin: G. Reimer, later de Gruyter, 1900ff. Vol XXV. Edited by R. Brandt and W. Stark. Berlin: de Gruyter, 1997.

Knight, Isabel F. *The Geometric Spirit: The Abbé de Condillac and the French Enlighenment*. New Haven, London: Yale University Press, 1968.

Kreimendahl, Lothar. "Condillac und die Monaden." *Archiv für Geschichte der Philosophie* 64 (1982): 280–288.

Locke, John. *An Early Draft of Locke's Essay together with Excerpts from His Journals*, edited by R.I. Aaron and J. Gibb. Oxford: Clarendon Press, 1936.

Locke, John. *An Essay Concerning Human Understanding*, edited by P.H. Nidditch. Oxford: Clarendon Press, 1975. References are to Book, Chapter and Paragraph.

Neuhouser, Frederick. *Rousseau's Theodicy of Self-Love: Evil, Rationality, and the Drive for Recognition*. Oxford: Oxford University Press, 2008.

O'Neal, John C. *The Authority of Experience: Sensationist Theory in the French Enlightenment*. University Park: Pennsylvania State University Press, 1996.

Perkins, Jean A. *The Concept of the Self in the French Enlightenment*. Geneva: Droz, 1969.

Robinson, Philip. "*La Conscience*: A Perceptual Problem in Rousseau." *Studies on Voltaire and the Eighteenth Century* 90 (1972): 1377–1394.

Rousseau, Jean Jacques. *Discours sur l'origine de l'inégalité*. In *Oeuvres complètes* III.

Rousseau, Jean Jacques. *Discourse on the Origin of Inequality*. Translated by F. Philip. Oxford: Oxford University Press, 1994.

Rousseau, Jean Jacques. *Émile ou de l'éducation*. In *Oeuvres complètes* IV.

Rousseau, Jean Jacques. *Emile or On Education*. Translated by Allan Bloom. Harmondsworth: Penguin, 1979. Reprint 1991.

Rousseau, Jean Jacques. *Les confessions*. In *Oeuvres complètes* I.

Rousseau, Jean Jacques. *La Profession de foi du vicar savoyard de Jean Jacques Rousseau. Edition critique [...] avec une introduction et un commentaire historiques*, edited by Pierre-Maurice Masson. Fribourg: Librairie de l'Université, and Paris: Hachette, 1914.

Rousseau, Jean Jacques. *Oeuvres complètes*, edited by Bernard Gagnebin and Marcel Raymond. 4 vols. Paris: Gallimard, 1959–1969.

Ryding, Erik. "La notion du moi chez Condillac." *Theoria* 21 (1955): 123–130.

Spink, John S. "Les avatars du 'sentiment de l'existence' de Locke a Rousseau." *Dix-huitième siècle* 10 (1978): 269–298.

Starobinski, Jean. *Jean-Jacques Rousseau: Transparency and Obstruction*. Translated by Arthur Goldhammer. Chicago and London: University of Chicago Press, 1988.

Strawson, Galen. *The Evident Connexion: Hume on Personal Identity*. Oxford: Oxford University Press, 2011.

Thiel, Udo. "Der Begriff der Intuition bei Locke." *Aufklärung* 18 (2006): 95–112.

Thiel, Udo. *The Early Modern Subject: Self-consciousness and Personal Identity from Descartes to Hume*. Oxford: Oxford University Press, 2011.

Thiel, Udo. *The Enlightened Subject: Sameness and Self from Condillac to Reinhold*. Oxford: Oxford University Press (in preparation).

Weinberg, Shelley. "Locke's Reply to the Sceptic." *Pacific Philosophical Quarterly* 94 (2013): 389–420.

Yolton, John. *Locke and French Materialism*. Oxford: Clarendon Press, 1991.

The Camera Obscura and the Nature of the Soul: On a Tension between the Mechanics of Sensation and the Metaphysics of the Soul

Michael J. Olson

Loyola University Chicago, Chicago, USA

When considering the period between Kepler's adoption of an instrument otherwise used for the purposes of courtly entertainment and enshrining of it as a kind of sigil for his new mechanistic optics at the beginning of the seventeenth century and Marx and Engels's famous rhetorical appeal to this same instrument as a model for the socio-economic determination of consciousness in *The German Ideology* (1846),[1] the camera obscura provides an fruitful point of entry into an analysis of the development of the relation between early modern metaphysics and natural philosophy or science. In this paper, I consider the way in which mechanical accounts of vision modeled on the camera obscura complicated and contested philosophical analyses of the immateriality of the soul in the seventeenth and early eighteenth centuries. By focusing narrowly on the role of the camera obscura in determining the parameters of the relationship between the new mechanistic conception of vision and the metaphysics of the soul, I hope to shed light on the larger processes by which the tensions between early modern metaphysics and natural science were negotiated. Moreover, an examination of the treatment of the camera obscura during this time indicates the way in which sensation came to occupy a contested, intermediate position between the physical interrogation of the behavior of bodies and the metaphysical investigation of the nature and functions of the soul.

The mechanistic conception of vision that stemmed from Kepler's work with the camera obscura coexisted throughout nearly the entirety of the seventeenth century with a commitment to the immateriality (and so, the incorruptibility and immortality) of the soul. Kepler, Descartes, and Leibniz, for example, all affirm the camera obscura as a fruitful model for the operations of vision without for that matter taking it to undermine metaphysical accounts of the immateriality of the soul. During the second decade of the eighteenth century, however, the complementarity of the physical mechanics of vision and the immaterialist metaphysics of the soul was called into question. In the *Vernünfftige Gedancken von Gott, der Welt, und der Seele des Menschen, auch alle Dinge überhaupt* (1720), the so-called *German Metaphysics*, Christian Wolff identifies mechanical accounts of vision modeled on the camera obscura as a potential threat to a proper understanding of the immateriality of the soul and of the operations of thought more generally. In a central moment in his analysis of the nature of the soul, Wolff attempts to refute the claim that the projective mechanism of the camera obscura models not only vision, but thought in general. His proof of the immateriality of the soul, from Wolff's perspective, depends on an argument showing that the mechanistic representations of the camera obscura are not thoughts.

Broadly, this paper addresses the history of philosophical appeals to the camera obscura and the implications the material models of vision came to have for the metaphysics of the soul over the long seventeenth century. My presentation of this history of reflections on the camera obscura unfolds in two parts. In Section One, I sketch a series of representative moments in seventeenth-century appropriations of the camera obscura as a model of the physical mechanisms of visual sensation. This sketch will illustrate the way in which mechanistic explanations of visual sensation coexisted with immaterialist accounts of the soul and of rational cognition. The camera obscura, on these accounts, explains the operations of the eye and in some instances grants us insight into behavior of the brain and nervous system. This physical explanation must be complemented by an analysis of the activities of an immaterial soul, it was thought, in order to account for rational cognition. In Section Two, I consider the breakdown of the complementary relation of mechanist explanations of visual sensation and metaphysical analyses of the soul in the German academic philosophy in the first decades of the eighteenth century. The rational psychology of Wolff's *German Metaphysics* clearly indicates that the material model of sensation provided by the camera obscura could no longer exist quite so comfortably alongside a metaphysical treatment of the immateriality of the soul. This shift in how the physics of sensation related to the metaphysics of the soul is best explained, I argue, by considering Urban Bucher's attempt to reduce the soul to the physical mechanisms of vision in his 1713 *Zweyer Guten Freunde vertrauter Brief-Wechsel vom Wesen der Seelen*. Regardless of the sketchy character of Bucher's reductionist argument and the relatively minor significance of the *Brief-Wechsel*, once he extended the explanatory power of the camera obscura to the whole of cognition and volition, and so to the nature of the soul in general, the latent challenge to an immaterialist metaphysics of the soul presented by a now pervasive mechanical account of vision could no longer be overlooked.

1. The camera obscura, vision, and the soul in the seventeenth century

Although the phenomenon of the projection of images through small holes in darkened spaces has been remarked upon since at least the time of Aristotle, both the term *camera obscura* and the concerted effort to formalize the mechanisms of this projection for the purposes of expanding optical and astronomical knowledge find their real origin in Johannes Kepler's *Ad Vitellionem Paralipomena* (1604).[2] Kepler explicitly presents this work as a kind of supplement and correction to Erazmus Ciolek Witelo's thirteenth-century studies, which in turn drew heavily on the eleventh-century writings of the Persian Alhazen. In addition to Witelo's *Perspectiva* (c. 1278), Kepler also draws considerable resources from Giambattista della Porta's *Magiae Naturalis* (1558).[3] In particular, della Porta describes the means by which one can project visual images upon an interior wall. He writes:

> You must shut all the chamber windows, and it will do well to shut up all holes besides, lest any light breaking in should spoil all. Only make one hole, that shall be a hand in breadth and length. Above this fit a little leaden or brass table, and glue it, so thick as a paper. Open a round hole in the middle of it, as great as your little finger. Over against this, let there be white walls of paper, or white clothes, so shall you see all that is done without in the sun, and those that walk in the streets, like to antipodes, and what is right will be the left, and all things changed. And the farther they are off from the hole, the greater they will appear. If you bring your paper, or white table nearer, they will show less and clearer, but you must stay a while for the images will not be seen presently.[4]

Though della Porta recommends using the instrument for viewing a solar eclipse, this purpose is subordinated in the text to a use "more pleasant for great men, and scholars, and ingenious persons to behold," namely the dramatic staging of great battles and exotic hunting scenes to impress and entertain those within the chamber.[5]

The camera obscura of course continued to be an object of courtly entertainment and artistic interest for some time.[6] I will leave that trajectory to the side for now, however, in order to pursue the larger natural philosophical implications of the device worked out by Kepler. I would like to highlight two moments of Kepler's appropriation of the philosophical potential of the curiosity he encountered in the Dresden *Kunstkammer*. The first moment of Kepler's philosophical appropriation of his experience with what he called "della Porta's device" is its utility in the articulation and defense of a new account of the role of the retinal image in the operations of vision. In an apostrophic paean to della Porta, Kepler emphasizes the degree to which an encounter with a camera obscura all but guarantees acceptance of a mechanist understanding of vision. He writes:

> To Aristotle, in the book *On Sense*, Empedocles is absurd, because he said that *chromata* are *aporroias*. For [Aristotle] thinks it incongruous that vision should occur when the eye is contacted by an efflux made by colors. But let him into this camera obscura of yours: he will see the wall touched; why can the eye not therefore be touched?[7]

Kepler establishes an analogy between the camera obscura and the eye such that the projected image in the former is now taken to be mirrored in a retinal image in the latter. His explanation of the production of the retinal image on the basis of his geometrical analysis of projections in the camera obscura, as we will see, reoriented subsequent analyses of vision such that the operations of the eye became inseparable from the mechanisms of this device.

The second element of Kepler's natural philosophical use of the camera obscura, we should notice, concerns the limitations he places on the broader metaphysical and epistemological implications of the mechanistic theory of vision he develops. Recognition of the mechanical operations of vision does not in itself commit us, according to Kepler, to any particular account of the metaphysical nature of the soul or its functions in the constitution of perceptual knowledge. Thus, he explains that his experiments with the camera obscura compel him to accept "that vision is carried out exactly through this device,"[8] but he reserves comment regarding the relation between the operations of thought or perception and the mechanics of the eye. He writes:

> How this image or picture is joined together with the visual spirits that reside in the retina and the nerve, and whether it is arraigned within by the spirits into the cavern of the cerebrum to the tribunal of the soul or of the visual faculty; whether the visual faculty, like a magistrate given by the soul, descending from the headquarters of the cerebrum outside to the visual nerve itself and to the retina, as to the lower courts, might go forth to meet this image – this, I say, I leave to the natural philosophers to argue about.[9]

In general, Kepler maintains that it is perfectly coherent to provide a mechanist explanation of vision modeled on the camera obscura, while remaining committed to the immateriality of the soul.[10] The camera obscura, in other words, provides a fruitful model of vision without threatening the prevailing idealist metaphysics of the soul. Despite the difficulties it produces for explaining the interaction of the body and the soul, this separability of the material processes of sensation from their conscious perception by an immaterial soul characterizes much of seventeenth-century philosophical reflection on vision.

Kepler's analysis of vision on the model of the camera obscura and his separation of the mechanics of the eye from the cognitive activities of the soul are repeated with somewhat greater philosophical conviction three decades later in Descartes' *Dioptrics* (1637). In that text, Descartes adds greater anatomical specificity to Kepler's analogy between the camera obscura and the eye:

This [the creation of images in the eyes] has been very ingeniously explained by the following comparison. Suppose a chamber is all shut up apart from a single hole, and a glass lens is placed in front of this whole with a white sheet stretched at a certain distance behind it so that the light coming from objects outside forms images on the sheet. Now it is said that the room represents the eye; the hole the pupil; the lens the crystalline humour, or rather all the parts of the eye which cause some refraction; and the sheet, the internal membrane, which is composed of the optic nerve-endings.[11]

Indeed, the retinal image projected through the crystalline humour resembles the objects it represents, Descartes agrees with Kepler. This resemblance cannot, however, account for our visual perception of the world. Descartes writes:

Now when this picture thus passes to the inside of our head, it still bears some resemblance to the objects from which it proceeds. As I have already amply shown, however, we must not think that it is by means of this resemblance that the picture causes our sensory perception of these objects – as if there were yet other eyes within our brain with which we could perceive it.[12]

If the eye transmitted images to the brain, the brain would require eyes of its own in order to receive those images, and so on *ad infinitum*. The transmission of visual stimuli is instead accomplished through a kind of tactile or haptic translation of the retinal image by the optic nerve, which makes vision possible, much the same as a blind person "sees" with the aid of a cane.

That visual sensations are communicated tactilely through the optic nerve to the brain and eventually, by way of the pineal gland, to the soul buttresses the Keplerian independence of the mechanics of the body and the metaphysics of the soul. Since neither the brain nor the soul really receives an image from the eyes – instead receiving haptic or tactile movements from the nerves – the mechanical model of the camera obscura presents no threat, in Descartes' mind, to the doctrine of the immateriality of the soul. The soul is further insulated from the mechanisms of the body, and of vision in particular, by his conclusion that "We know for certain that it is the soul which has sensory perceptions, and not the body (On sçait desia assés que c'est l'ame qui sent, non le cors)."[13] We surmise this, Descartes explains, inasmuch as perception dissipates or even halts altogether in moments of extreme excitement or deep contemplation despite the continued effects of external objects on the sense organs. The eyes see, in other words, and the mind perceives. The mechanisms of the body, and of vision in particular, are firmly distinguished from the activities of the soul such that the camera obscura can offer clear insight into the former without threatening metaphysical accounts of the latter.

Outside Cartesian substance dualism, we also find writers in the seventeenth century unperturbed by the possibility that the material model provided by the camera obscura might undermine claims concerning the immateriality of the soul. In *An Essay Concerning Human Understanding* (1690), Locke broadens the explanatory power of the camera obscura, relative to its employment by Kepler and Descartes, by claiming that it provides a model not only for vision, but for thought more generally. In Book II, Chapter x, he writes:

For, methinks, the *understanding* is not much unlike a Closet wholly shut from light, with only some little opening left, to let in external visible Resemblances, or *ideas* of things without; would the Pictures coming into such a dark Room but stay there, and lie so orderly as to be found upon occasion, it would very much resemble the Understanding of a Man, in reference to all Objects of sight, and of the ideas of them.[14]

Given that Locke mentions two limitations of the analogy – that the images in the camera obscura are not retained as in memory and that the analogy only sheds light on visual cognitions – its value as a comprehensive model for his conception of thought remains ambiguous. What is clear, however, is that the explanatory power of this physical model of perceptual operations is not confined, as it was for Descartes, to the extra-mental processes of bodily sensation. Nonetheless, Locke is careful to explain that his extension of the analogy does not pretend to explain the existence of thought as emergent from the mechanical interactions of matter alone.

Despite his cautious if inflammatory remarks in Book IV of the *Essay* that God could "if he pleases, superadd to Matter a Faculty of Thinking,"[15] that is, despite the possibility that matter could think, Locke is adamant that matter and motion alone are insufficient to explain the existence or nature of thought. So, even if God saw fit to add the power of thought to a material body, Locke explains, "Yet matter, *incogitative matter* and motion, whatever changes it might produce of figure and bulk, *could never produce thought*: knowledge will still be as far beyond the power of motion and matter to produce, as matter is beyond the power of *nothing*, or *non-entity* to produce."[16] Thus, even when he takes "the *Understanding* [to be] not much unlike" a camera obscura, this still does not present a direct attack, at least to Locke's mind if not Stillingfleet's,[17] to the immaterial nature of the soul.[18]

Locke's expansion of the processes explained by the camera obscura remains, perhaps surprisingly, relatively intact in Leibniz's commentary on Locke's empiricism in the *New Essays on Human Understanding* (1704; published 1765). In Leibniz's remarks on the passage from Locke's *Essay* quoted above wherein the understanding is recognized to be not much unlike the camera obscura, Leibniz affirms Locke's comments, adding another pair of qualifications. He writes:

> For not only do we receive images and traces in the brain, but we form new ones from them when we bring complex ideas to mind: and so the screen that represents our brain must be active and elastic. This analogy would explain reasonably well what goes on in *the brain*. As for *the soul*, which is a simple substance or monad: without being extended it *represents* these various extended masses and has perceptions of them.[19]

Locke is correct, then, provided that the screen upon which the *camera* projects its image is not merely passive, but contributes something through its own activities and characteristics. Moreover, Locke's analysis applies to the brain, but not to the soul, which is, Leibniz maintains, a simple, immaterial substance.[20] For both Locke and Leibniz, then, it is possible to accept the camera obscura as a far-ranging model for both vision and certain elements of cognition without taking such a mechanistic explanation of sensation to present any significant challenge to the metaphysics of the soul.

What is particularly notable about the history of the place of the camera obscura in seventeenth-century analyses of vision and the soul, and what changes considerably in the works I address in the following section, is that natural philosophical appeals to this machine in order to shed light on the mechanisms of vision, and in some cases on the processes of thought more generally, were not taken to present any real threat to the legitimacy of metaphysical analyses of the soul that maintained the soul's transcendence of the very mechanistic principles and material existence central to that natural philosophy.[21] On this issue at least, natural philosophy and metaphysics were taken to be complementary rather than competitive endeavors. This would not always be true, however.

2. Responding to an explicit threat: Wolff's *German Metaphysics*

Although his position in contemporary studies of the history of philosophy is decidedly peripheral, the importance of Christian Wolff in the determination of the course of eighteenth-century German philosophy cannot be denied. His efforts to formalize and disseminate Leibniz's monadology and doctrine of pre-established harmony, coupled with his articulation of the contours the emerging schools of philosophical materialism and idealism and the threat these positions presented to a proper understanding of both theoretical and practical philosophy, set the parameters within which German academic philosophy would operate for more than fifty years. The continuity between Wolffian and Leibnizian thought, as has often been noted, is not nearly as strong as the common use of the phrase "Leibnizian-Wolffian philosophy" to describe the strand of thought prominent in Germany at the time might lead us to think.[22] I will focus on one element of this discontinuity here, not in the interest of deepening our understanding of the relationship between Wolff and Leibniz, but in order to point out a marked divergence from the history of philosophical reflection on the camera obscura I have just sketched. In a moment of initially puzzling departure from what seemed to be a stable and complementary relation between the physics of the camera obscura and the metaphysics of the soul, Wolff presents an argument designed to disprove the claim that the mechanistic projections of this machine themselves amount to thoughts. In what follows, I will lay out Wolff's argument against the conflation of the mechanisms of the camera obscura and the processes of cognition and then turn to a consideration of why Wolff felt such an argument to be necessary in the first place.

In his 1724 *Anmerckungen* to the *German Metaphysics*, Wolff identifies the paragraphs in which he presents the argument against adopting the camera obscura as a model for thought as essential to securing both a true conception of the nature of the soul and a free will as a condition for moral action. Reflecting on a passage I will address in a moment, he writes:

> We see here the fruits of our investigation into how it really occurs that the soul is conscious of itself and what goes before it. In that investigation I show that no body or subtle matter can think, as the materialists advance. Thus I here provide the weapon with which one can challenge the materialists, who abolish the freedom and immortality of the soul, and so nourish a destructive opinion.[23]

Wolff's interest in presenting his metaphysics as essential to combating the deleterious effects of philosophical materialism in these reflections is no doubt colored by his expulsion from Halle for his supposed Spinozism.[24] In fact, the first edition of the *German Metaphysics* makes no explicit mention of materialism, a philosophical school Wolff first explicitly defined in the preface to the second, 1722 edition of that text. Regardless, these comments make it clear that Wolff took an analysis of the camera obscura to be a central component of his conception of the soul as a simple, immaterial substance.

His analysis of the camera obscura turns on a distinction between mechanistic representations (*Vorstellungen*) and thoughts (*Gedancken*). The soul is first and foremost known, according to Wolff, through its capacity to represent the world. What is more, "Because this power [to represent the world] is the ground of everything that occurs in the soul (§754), it is the essence of the soul (§54)."[25] Not all representations are created equal, however. In an early section of the fifth chapter of the *German Metaphysics*, "On the Essence of the Soul and of a Spirit in General," Wolff presents the following argument:

> If however either a machine or a body were present in which, through the action of light and other external contacts, an internal movement were aroused through which a subtle matter were composed in such a way that it represented the external body from which the light originated or which contacted the machine in some other way; there would still be a marked difference between this representation and the thoughts of a soul representing this [external] body. For in the body [or machine] the representation would occur in it; the soul however represents everything to itself as external to itself. And the cause is clear from what we have already said. The soul represents the things about which it thinks as external to itself because it cognizes them as different than itself (§45, 730). It cannot be accomplished through the movement of a machine, however, that the things that are represented in it are held over

against it and their difference from it simultaneously represented. For this reason the material representations in a machine can never become thoughts, no matter how one starts out.[26]

Wolff can only be thinking of the camera obscura here. What differentiates the representations of the camera obscura from those of the soul is the manner in which objects are represented. Both species of representation occur internally to the representing thing; it is only in the soul, however, that objects are internally represented as external. This difference is crucial given Wolff's earlier argument that cognition depends on the differentiation of objects, and primarily on the differentiation of external objects from the soul, which represents them.[27] Insofar as the camera obscura is incapable of distinguishing its representations from itself, its representations are different in kind from the cognitive representations of the soul. Despite some similarity between the representative capacities of the soul and the camera obscura, then, that similarity reveals nothing about the nature of the soul.

What is interesting here is not that Wolff rejects a material or mechanical model for understanding the operations of thought – that is, after all the prevailing philosophical wisdom of the early eighteenth century. What is significant in the present context is that Wolff felt obliged to argue against the claim that the camera obscura might obviate the need for a metaphysical analysis of the immateriality of the soul. As I have indicated, there is a rather broad precedent in the seventeenth century for accepting mechanistic theories of vision modeled on the camera obscura without taking that model to imply anything about the materiality of thought or the soul. Why, then, does Wolff dedicate a central passage in his early rational psychology to refuting a position no one seems to have actually held? How do we explain the emergence of the idea, explicitly articulated in Wolff's *German Metaphysics*, and repeated with some regularity in the Wolffian tradition,[28] that the camera obscura presents a potential challenge to the metaphysics of the soul?

There are certainly a number of factors at work here. First, there is some precedent for arguing against mechanistic explanations of thought in the work Leibniz had published by this time. The *Monadology*, which Wolff was involved in translating and publishing at approximately the same time he published the *German Metaphysics*, of course contains Leibniz's famous mill argument.[29] In the *Monoadology*, Leibniz argues that if perception were explicable on the basis of matter and motion alone, it would be possible to enlarge the material ground of thought while maintaining its proportions such that it would be large enough to walk into and inspect it. Upon such an inspection, he claims, we would "find only parts pushing one another, and never anything by which to explain a perception."[30] Second, Locke's *Essay* had by this time been translated into Latin and published in Leipzig in 1709. The *Essay* received considerable critical response in the German academic fora of the time, including the *Acta Eruditorum*, to which Wolff regularly contributed.[31] Locke's influence on Wolff, particularly in his development of the disciplines of empirical and rational psychology, has been well documented.[32] The hints of materialism in Locke picked out by Stillingfleet and Voltaire[33] might, then, explain Wolff's argument here.

It does not seem to me, however, that Wolff's rather urgent rejection of the camera obscura as a model for the representational power of the soul and the militaristic cast of his reflections on that argument can be explained by appealing to the influence of Leibniz or Locke alone. Leibniz's mill argument, notwithstanding its historical renown, is a decidedly minor moment of the *Monadology*, and its structure does not resemble Wolff's argument in the *German Metaphysics*. Moreover, given Wolff's habit of explicitly referring ideas back to Leibniz, the absence of any such reference in this case further undermines any attempt to take Wolff's position as a development or formalization of Leibniz's position. Locke's suggestion that God might grant material bodies the otherwise inexplicable capacity to think no doubt garnered attention in German academic circles. This claim is entirely distinct from the passage of the *Essay* in which Locke compares the understanding to a camera obscura, and I find no connection between these ideas drawn in the context of the early eighteenth-century German reception of Locke. What is more, Wolff directly addresses and rejects the Lockean claim that God might superadd thought to a material body in a later section of the *German Metaphysics*.[34] The argument of that section proceeds on the basis of Wolff's earlier account of substance and essence, and bears no real conceptual connection to his analysis of the camera obscura. The relevance of Wolff's engagement with Locke appears considerably more formative on this point than does his relationship to Leibniz, but neither of these, it seems to me, explains the breakdown in the previously harmonious relation between the physics of sensation and the metaphysics of the soul.

There is, however, a text, quite well known in German philosophical circles at the time, that clarifies Wolff's interest in distancing the metaphysics of the soul from the mechanics of the camera obscura. That text, the anonymously published *Zweyer guten Freunde vertrauter Brief-Wechsel vom Wesen der Seelen* (1713) gathers three letters between Urban Gottfried Bucher, a well-placed medical doctor, and Johann Baptist Röschel, a theology professor in Wittenberg. In the first and third letters Bucher briefly outlines a mechanistic account of the soul before devoting the majority of his letters to defending the claim that such a psychology has deep roots in both philosophical and Christian traditions.[35] Bucher's first letter opens with the claim, "The actions that are ascribed to the soul are called intellect and will and are in general called inorganic; both however are grounded in sensation."[36] Insofar as sensation admits of a mechanical explanation, then, the operations of thought in general can be explained without appeal to an immaterial soul. Bucher develops this mechanistic explanation of thought as follows:

> The process of understanding occurs in the following way: when the organ of sense, especially that of vision or hearing, is directed toward the object, distinct movements occur in its nerve fibers, which, as is known, all terminate in the sense organ. Such movement in the brain is identical with that of the rays that extend in all directions from the object and fall in various ways on the white sheet in the camera obscura and form a certain idea, which idea is not real on the white sheet, but does exist through the various motions of the optical nerve in the eye. When this nerve is moved in distinct ways, this motion is continued to the brain so that in it the same idea or motion is formed, even if the object is already gone.[37]

We have in this passage an explicit combination of the two elements I have argued were continually held apart in seventeenth-century treatments of the camera obscura. Not only does this device provide us with insight into the operations of vision, in so doing it also lays bare the nature of thought as such, and by extension, the nature of the soul.

Although this text is little known today, it aroused quite a bit of interest in the second decade of the eighteenth century. Not only did it see four printings between 1713 and 1723, it was also the subject of almost immediate critical review in the *Deutsche Acta Eruditorum*,[38] as well as in the writings of Johann Franz Buddeus,[39] his student Johann Jakob Syrbius, and their sometime philosophical opponent Christian Thomasius.[40] Bucher's reduction of the operations of the soul to those of sensation coupled with his mechanistic account of the latter place of the *Brief-Wechsel*, according to Thomasius (and later also to Martin Knutzen[41]), at the heart of a nascent philosophical materialism along with the writings of Hobbes, Gassendi, and William Coward. Against the backdrop of this kind of broad-based response to Bucher's *Brief-Wechsel*, it is not surprising that Wolff would consider a refutation of its use of the camera obscura as a model for the representational powers of the soul to be important.

In addition to having sociological reasons for rejecting Bucher's materialist reduction of the soul to the mechanics of sensation, Wolff has significant philosophical or conceptual reasons for explicitly limiting the explanatory power of the camera obscura. Like the other figures we have considered, Wolff accepts the camera obscura as a model for vision.[42] Given his claim that the essence of the soul lies in its power to represent the world, the visual representations or projections of the camera obscura present a more direct challenge to his account of the immateriality of the soul than it did to those of previous authors. Moreover, Bucher's *Brief-Wechsel* asserts that all mental representations are reducible to the material processes of sensation. Wolff's definition of the soul in terms of representation and Bucher's materialist account of representation together render the implicit tension between seventeenth-century mechanics of vision and its supplementary metaphysics of the soul so explicit that it can no longer be overlooked. In this regard, Wolff does not introduce a new division or opposition into early modern analyses of sensation, cognition, and the soul; his *German Metaphysics* instead makes an already existing implicit tension between natural philosophical and metaphysical analyses of conscious life explicit.

I have sketched an episode in the history of an emerging tension in seventeenth- and early eighteenth-century writings between mechanistic accounts of sensation and accompanying doctrines of the immateriality of the soul. Throughout the seventeenth century, the mechanism of prevailing natural philosophical explanations of visual sensation was in large measure isolated from considerations of the metaphysics of the soul. This separation was effected in some cases by a distinction between sensation and thought and in some cases by a conception of the nature of the soul incompatible with the mechanism of natural philosophy. Once Bucher explicitly challenged the metaphysical accounts of the immateriality of the soul by appealing to the camera obscura as a model not only for vision but for cognition more generally, an implicit tension in early modern analyses of the camera obscura, vision, and the nature of the soul comes into relief. In this context, Wolff's remarks about the limitations of mechanistic explanations with regard to thought mark the breakdown of what was previously a harmonious relation between the mechanics of sensation and the metaphysics of the soul. For Wolff, natural philosophical explanations of the functions of the body's role in sensation are not simply complementary to metaphysical explanations of the soul's power to represent and know; natural philosophy, for him, poses a challenge to metaphysics.[43] Accordingly, the largely implicit boundaries between the domains of natural philosophy and metaphysics in seventeenth-century philosophy come in eighteenth-century German philosophy to be more explicitly defined in order to guard against the encroachment of the physical mechanisms of sensation into the idealist metaphysics of the soul and its cognitions. The texts and authors addressed above by no means exhaust the dense network of seventeenth- and eighteenth-century reflections on the relation between the metaphysics and the emerging natural sciences. Nonetheless, a consideration of the role played by the camera obscura in these texts provides a fruitful vantage from which to consider an important shift in the history of philosophical and scientific conceptions of the relations between sensation, bodies, cognition, and the soul.

Notes

1. Marx and Engels, *Die Deutsche Ideologie* 15:

   Das Bewußtsein kann nie Andres sein als das bewußte Sein, und das Sein der Menschen ist ihr wirklicher Lebensprozeß. Wenn in der ganzen Ideologie die Menschen und ihre Verhältnisse, wie in einer Camera obscura, auf dem Kopf gestellt erscheinen, so geht dies Phänomen ebensosehr aus ihrem historischen Lebensprozeß hervor, wie die Umdrehung der Gegenstände auf der Netzhaut aus ihrem unmittelbar physischen.

2. For a broader account of the history of the camera obscura, see Hammond, *The Camera Obscura*, and Gernsheim and Gernsheim, *The History of Photography*, 17–30.
3. On the relation of Kepler's optics to its medieval influences, see Lindberg, "Continuity and Discontinuity."
4. della Porta, *Natural Magick*, Book 17, Chap. 6; *Magiae Naturalis Libri Viginti* 545:

Cubiculi fenestras omnes claudas oportet, proderitque si spiramenta quoque obturentur, ne lumen aliquod intro irrumpens, omne destruat: unam tantum terebrato, & foramen palmare aperito palmaris longitudinis, & latitudinis, supra tabellam plumbeam, vel æneam accommodabis, & glutinabis, papyri soliditatis, in cuisu medioforamen aperiesbalbos vel papyrum, vel alba lintea appones. Sic a Sole foris illustrate Omnia, & deambulantes per plateas, uti Antipodes spectabis: quæque dextra sinistra, commutataque Omnia videbuntur, & quo lagius a foramine distabunt, tanto maiorem sibi adsciscunt formam. Si papyrum, vel albam tabulam appropinquabis, ea visuntur minora, clarioraque: alinquanisper tamen immorando, non enim ellico simulachra apparebunt: quia simile validum maximam cum sensu nonnunquam efficit sensationem, talemque ineuhit affectionem, ut non solum quum sensus agunt, sensoriis insint, eaque lacessant, sed etiam quum ex operibus discessere, diutius immorentur, quod liquide potest perspici.

5. Ibid.
6. That the roles of the camera obscura as an object of entertainment and of natural philosophical investigation cannot be finally separated is shown in Dupré, "Playing with Images" and "Inside the Kunstkammer."
7. Kepler, *Optics*, 224–225; *Ad Vitellionem Paralipomena* 210 : "Absurdus est Aristoteli libello de sensili Empedocles, quod *chromata* dixerit *aporroias*. Incommodum enim putat, visionem fieri cum oculus effluxia coloribus facto contingitur. At in hanc tuam obscuram cameram intueatur, videbit parietem tangi, quin igitur oculus tangi possit?"
8. Ibid., 225; 210–11: "Et per se procliue est, viso artificio illo tuo capitis tui sexti, statim hac persuasione occupari, visionem peritus hoc artificio persici."
9. Ibid., 180; 168:

   Quomodo idolum seu picture hæc spiritibus sioriis, qui resident in retina & in neruo, coniungatur, & utrum per spiritus intro in cerebri cauernas, ad animæ seu facultatis visoriæ tribunal sistatur, an facultas visoria, ceu quæstor ab Anima datus, è cerebri prætorio foras in ipsum neruum visorium & rerinam, ceu ad inferior subsellia descendens, idolo huic procedat obuiam, hoc inquam Physicis relinquo disputandum.

10. On Kepler's understanding of the nature of the soul (both human and otherwise), and in particular on the relation between bodily sensation and the soul in the production of knowledge, see Escobar, "Kepler's Theory of the Soul."
11. Descartes, *Dioptrics*, 166; *Oeuvres de Descartes*, vol. 6, 114–15:

    ainsi que quelques uns ont desia tres-ingenieusement expliqué, par la comparaison de celles qui paroissent dans une chamber, lors que l'ayant toute fermeé, reserué un seul trou, & ayant mis au deuant de ce trou un verre forme de lentille, on stend derriere, a certain distance, un linge blanc, sur qui la lumiere, qui vient des obiets de dehors, forme ces images. Car ils dissent que cete chamber represente l'œil; ce trou, la prunellel ce verre, l'humeur cristiline, ou plustost toutes celles des parties de l'œil qui causent quelque refraction; & le linge, la peau interieure, qui est compose des extremités du nerf optique.

    All further references to the *Dioptrics* will refer to the customary Adam and Tannery pagination.

12. Ibid., 130:

    Or, encores que cete peinture, en passant ainsi iusques au dedans de nostre teste, retiene tousiours quelque chose de la resemblance des obiets don't elle procede, il ne se faut point toutesfois persuader, ainsi que ie vous ay desia tantost assés fait entendre, que ce soit par le moyen de cete resemblance qu'elle face que nousles sentons, comme s'il y auoit derechef d'autres yeux en nostre cerueau, auec lesquels nous la pussions aperceuoir.

13. Ibid., 109. On the relation between the soul and the body in perception, see M. Wilson, "Descartes on the Origin of Sensation" and C. Wilson, "Descartes and the Corporeal Mind."
14. Locke, *Essay*, II.xi.17.
15. Ibid., IV.iii.6. The whole of this passage reads (emphasis original):

    We have the *ideas* of *matter* and *thinking*, but possibly shall never be able to know, whether any mere material being thinks, or no; it being impossible for us, by the contemplation of our own *ideas*, without revelation, to discover, whether omnipotency has not given to some systems of matter fitly disposed, a power to perceive and think, or else joined and fixed to matter so disposed, a thinking immaterial substance: it being, in respect of our notions, not much more remote from our comprehension to conceive, that GOD can, if he pleases, superadd to matter a faculty of thinking, than that he should superadd to it another substance, with a faculty of thinking.

The line of thought expressed in this passage played a particularly prominent role in the development of both English and French materialism. See Yolton, *Thinking Matter* and *Locke and French Materialism.*

16. Locke, *Essay*, IV.x.10.

17. See Stillingfleet, *Vindication of the Doctrine of the Trinity*; Stillingfleet, *Answer to Mr. Locke's Second Letter*; Locke, *The Works of John Locke*, vol. 4.

18. On the tension between mechanism and the doctrine of the immateriality of the soul in Locke, see Stuart, "Locke on Superaddition and Mechanism."

19. Leibniz, *New Essays* 141; *Sämtliche Schriften* 6.6, 144–45:

    Car non seulement nous recevons des images ou traces dans le cerveau, mais nous en formons encore de nouvelles, quand nous envisageons des idées complexes. Ainsi il faut que la toile qui represente nostre cerveau soit active et elastique. Cette comparaison expliqueroit tolerablement ce qui se passe dans le cerveau: mais quant à l'ame, qui est une substance simple ou Monade, elle represente sans etendue ces memes varieties des masses etenduës, et en a la perception.

20. For an analysis of Leibniz's arguments for the insufficiency of a physical mechanistic account of consciousness, see Seager, "The Worm in the Cheese."

21. Jonathan Crary has cut a similar path through the history of seventeenth-century reflections on the camera obscura in his *Technique of the Observer*. He argues there that "the camera obscura is inseparable from a certain metaphysic of interiority: it is a figure for both the observer who is nominally a free sovereign individual and a privatized subject confined in a quasi-domestic space, cut off from a public exterior world" (39). I find it more useful, however, to track the explicit metaphysical commitments individual authors maintain alongside their analyses of the camera obscura than to reconstruct "a certain metaphysic of interiority" that holds the key to the nature of seventeenth- and eighteenth-century visual observation as a whole.

22. See for example, Corr, "Christian Wolff and Leibniz."

23. Wolff, *Anmerckungen* 396:

    Hier sehen wir die Frucht davon / daß wir untersucht haben / wie es eigentlich zugehet / bewust ist / indem ich daraus zeige / daß kein Cörper / auch keine subtile Materie dencken kan / wie die Materialisten vorgeben. Und demnach gebe ich hier die Waffen in die Hand / damit man die Materialisten bestreiten kan / welche die Freyheit und Unsterblichkeit der Seele aufheben / und daher eine schädliche Meynung hegen.

24. See Israel, *Radical Enlightenment* 544–552.

25. Wolff, *Vernünfftige Gedancken von Gott* [*German Metaphysics*] §755: "Weil demnach diese Kraft der Grund ist von allem demjenigen, was veränderliches in der Seele vorgehet (§754); so bestehet in ihr das Wesen der Seele (§53)."

26. Ibid., §740:

    Wenn aber auch gleich eine Maschine oder ein Cörper vorhanden wäre, darinnen durch die Würckung des Lichtes und andere äusserliche Berührungen eine innerliche Bewegung erreget würde, dadurch eine subtile Materie in solche Ordnung gesetzet würde, daß sie den äusserlichen Cörper, von dem das Licht herkäme, oder der sie sonst auf eine andere Weise berührete, vorstellete; so würde doch noch ein merklicher Unterschied zwischen dieser Vorstellung und dem Gedancken der Seele seyn, dadurch sie sich eben diesen Cörper vorstellete. Denn in dem Cörper geschähe die Vorstellung in ihm; die Seele aber stellet sich alles als ausser ihr vor. Und die Ursache ist aus dem klar, was wir schon gesaget. Die Seele stellet sich die Sachen, daran sie dencket, als ausser sich vor, weil sie dieselben also von sich unterscheiden erkennet (§45, 730). Durch die Bewegung aber der Maschine kan nicht erhalten werden, daß sie diejenige Sache, die in ihr vorgestellet wird, gegen sich halt, und den Unterschied von sich zugleich vorstellet. Derowegen können die materialische Vorstellung der Dinge in einer Maschine nimmermehr zu Gedancken werden, man mag es auch anfangen, wie man will.

27. Ibid., §730.

28. See also, Knutzen, *Philosophische Abhandlung*, and Crusius, *Entwurf der Notwendigen Vernunft-Wahrheiten.*

29. See Leibniz, *Monadology*, 70.

30. Ibid.; *Die philosophischen Schriften*, vol. 6, part 2, 609: "on ne trouvera […] que des pièces, qui poussent les unes les autres, et jamais de quoi expliquer une perception."

31. See Brown, "German Interest in John Locke's 'Essay.'"

32. See, for example, Engfer, "Von der Leibnizischen Monadologie" and Dyck, "The Divorce of Reason and Experience."

33. Voltaire, *Philosophical Letters*, 41–46.
34. Wolff, *German Metaphysics*, §741.
35. For an account of the theological issues at work in the *Brief-Wechsel*, see Mulsow, "Säkularisierung in der Seelenlehre?"
36. *Brief-Wechsel*, 19 (emphasis original): "die Actiones, die der Seele zugeschrieben warden, heißen *intellectus* und *voluntas*, und warden insgemein inorganicae genennet; beyde aber gründen sich auf die *sensation*."
37. Ibid., (emphasis original):

    Der *Processus intelligendi* geschiehet folgender massen: Wenn das organum sensus sonderlich visus und auditus auf das objectum gerichtet wird, so geschehen unterschiedene Bewegungen in denen fibris cerebri, die, wie bekannt, sich allemahl an einem organo sensorio determiniren. Solche Bewegung in crebro ist mit der, da die radii ab objectis protensi auf unterschiedene Art auf das Album in der Camera obscura, auffallen, und eine gewisse Idee formiren einerley, welche Idee doch nicht realiter auf dem albo ist, sondern pro varia dimotione fibrillarum funicæ in oculo entstehet. Wie nun hier diese auf unterschiedene Art bewegt werden, so wird diese motus im Gehirn continuiret, also daß darinnen eben dergleichen Idee oder motus, wenn schon das objectum weg ist, formiret wird.

38. *Brief-Wechsel* [review].
39. Buddeus, "Programmate de Arabicorum Hæresi."
40. Thomasius, *Summarische Nachrichten* A more complete list of responses to the *Brief-Wechsel* can be found in the preface to the fourth edition of that text, 9.
41. Knutzen, *Philosophische Abhandlung*, 85.
42. See, for example, Wolff, *Vernünfftige Gedancken von den Würckungen der Natur*, §426. Similar passages are found in Wolff, *Anfangs-Gründe der Optick*, vol. 3, 955ff.
43. For an account of the ramifications of the identification of natural philosophy as a potential threat to metaphysics in early eighteenth-century German philosophy, see Ahnert, "Newtonianism in early Enlightenment Germany."

Bibliography

Ahnert, Thomas. "Newtonianism in Early Enlightenment Germany, c.1720–1750: Metaphysics and the Critique of Dogmatic Philosophy." *Studies in History and Philosophy of Science Part A* 35, no. 3 (2004): 471–491.

Brown, F. Andrew. "German Interest in John Locke's 'Essay,' 1688–1800." *Journal of English and Germanic Philology* 50, no. 4 (1951): 466–482.

Buddeus, Johann Franz. "Programmate de Arabicorum Hæresi." In *Dissertatio Theologicum syntagmaticum*. Jena, 1713.

Corr, Charles. "Christian Wolff and Leibniz." *Journal of the History of Ideas* 36, no. 2 (1975): 241–62.

Crary, Jonathan. *Technique of the Observer: On Vision and Modernity in the Nineteenth Century*. Cambridge, MA: MIT Press, 1990.

Crusius, Christian August. *Entwurf der Notwendigen Vernunft-Wahrheiten*. 3rd ed. Königsberg, 1766.

della Porta, Giambattista. *Magiae Naturalis Libri Viginti*. Hannover, 1619.

della Porta, Giambattista. *Natural Magick*. London, 1658.

Descartes, René. *Dioptrics*. In *The Philosophical Writings of Descartes*. 3 vols. Translated by J. Cottingham, et al. Cambridge: Cambridge University Press, 1985.

Descartes, René. *Oeuvres de Descartes*. Edited by C. Adam and P. Tannery. 11 vols. Paris: Vrin, 1964–74.

Dupré, Sven. "Inside the Kunstkammer: The Circulation of Optical Knowledge and Instruments at the Dresden Court." *Studies in History and Philosophy of Science* 40, no. 4 (2009): 405–420.

Dupré, Sven. "Playing with Images in a Dark Room: Kepler's *Ludi* inside the Camera Obscura." In *Inside the Camera Obscura: Optics and Art under the Spell of the Projected Image*, edited by W. Lefèvre, 57–79. Berlin: Max-Planck-Institut für Wissenschaftsgeschichte, 2007.

Dyck, Corey. "The Divorce of Reason and Experience: Kant's Paralogisms of Pure Reason in Context." *Journal of the History of Philosophy* 47, no. 2 (2009): 249–275.

Engfer, Hans-Jürgen. "Von der Leibnizischen Monadologie zur empirischen Psychologie Wolffs." In *Nuovi studi sul pensiero di Christian Wolff*, edited by S. Carbocin and L. Madonna, 193–215. Hildesheim: Olms, 1992.

Escobar, Jorge. "Kepler's Theory of the Soul: A Study on Epistemology." *Studies in History and Philosophy of Science* 39, no. 1 (2008): 15–41.

Gernsheim, Helmut, and Allison Gernsheim, *The History of Photography, 1685–1914: From the Camera Obscura to the Beginning of the Modern Era*. 2nd ed. New York: McGraw-Hill, 1969.

Hammond, John. *The Camera Obscura: A Chronicle*. New York: Hilger, 1981.

Israel, Jonathan. *Radical Enlightenment: Philosophy and the Making of Modernity 1650–1750*. Oxford: Oxford University Press, 2001.

Kepler, Johannes. *Ad Vitellionem Paralipomena*. Frankfurt, 1604.

Kepler, Johannes. *Optics: Paralipomena to Witelo, and Optical Part of Astronomy*. Translated by William H. Donahue. Santa Fe: Green Lion Press, 2000.

Knutzen, Martin. *Philosophische Abhandlung von der Immateriellen Natur der Seele*. Königsberg, 1744.

Leibniz, Gottfried Wilhelm. *New Essays on Human Understanding*. Translated and edited by. P. Remnant and J. Bennett. Cambridge: Cambridge University Press, 1996.

Leibniz, Gottfied Wilhelm. *Die philosophischen Schriften von Gottfried Wilhelm Leibniz*. Edited by C.I. Gerhardt. 7 volumes. Berlin: Weidmann, 1875–1890.

Leibniz, Gottfried Wilhelm. *The Principles of Philosophy, or, The Monadology*. In *Discourse on Metaphysics and Other Essays*. Edited by D. Garber and R. Ariew, 68–81. Indianapolis: Hackett, 1991.

Leibniz, Gottfried Wilhelm. *Sämtliche Schriften und Briefe*. Edited by the Deutsche Akademie der Wissenschaften zu Berlin. Berlin: Akademie-Verlag, 1923–.

Lindberg, David. "Continuity and Discontinuity in the History of Optics: Kepler and the Medieval Tradition." *History and Technology: An International Journal* 4 (1987): 431–448.

Locke, John. *An Essay Concerning Human Understanding*. Edited by P. Nidditch. Oxford: Oxford University Press, 1979.

Locke, John. *The Works of John Locke*. 2nd ed. 10 vols. London, 1823.

Marx, Karl, and Friedrich Engels. *Die Deutsche Ideologie*. In *Karl Marx and Friedrich Engels Historisch-Kritische Gesamtausgabe*. Edited by V. Adoratskij, vol. 5. 42 vols. Frankfurt: Verlag Detlev Auvermann, 1970.

Mulsow, Martin. "Säkularisierung in der Seelenlehre? Bibilizismus and Materialismus in Urban Gottfried Buchers *Brief-Wechsel vom Wesen der Seelen*." In *Säkularisierung in den Wissenschaften seit der frühen Neuzeit*. Edited by S. Pott and L. Danneberg, vol. 2, 145–173. Berlin: Akademie-Verlag, 2002.

Seager, William. "The Worm in the Cheese: Leibniz, Consciousness and Matter." *Studia Leibnitiana* 23, no. 1 (1991): 79–91.

Stillingfleet, Edward. *The Bishop of Worcester's Answer to Mr. Locke's Second Letter; wherein his Notion of Ideas Is prov'd to be inconsistent with it self, and with the Articles of the Christian Faith*. London, 1698.

Stillingfleet, Edward. *A Treatise in Vindication of the Doctrine of the Trinity: With an Answer to the late Socinian Objections against it from Scripture, Antiquity and Reason*. London: 1696.

Stuart, Matthew. "Locke on Superaddition and Mechanism." *British Journal for the History of Philosophy* 6, no. 3 (1998): 351–379.

Thomasius, Christian. *Summarische Nachrichten von auserlesenen, mehrentheils alten*. In *Thomasischen Bibliotheque vorhandenen Büchern*, vol. 30. Leipzig, 1716.

Voltaire. *Philosophical Letters; or, Letter Regarding the English Nation*. Edited by John Leigh. Translated by P. Steiner. Indianapolis: Hackett, 2007.

Wilson, Catherine. "Descartes and the Corporeal Mind: Some Implications of the Regius Affair." In *Descartes' Natural Philosophy*. Edited by S. Gaukroger, J. Schuster, and J. Sutton, 659–679. London: Routledge, 2000.

Wilson, Margaret. "Descartes on the Origin of Sensation." *Philosophical Topics* 19, no. 1 (1991): 293–323.

Wolff, Christian. *Anfangs-Gründe der Optick, Catoptrick, Dioptrick, und Perspectiv*. In *Der Anfangs-Gründe aller mathematischen Wissenschaften*, vol. 3. Halle, 1737.

Wolff, Christian. *Anmerckungen über die* Vernünfftige Gedancken von Gott, der Welt und der Seele des Menschen, auch alle Dinge überhaupt, *zu besserem Verstande und bequemerem Gebrauch derselben*. Frankfurt am Main, 1724.

Wolff, Christian. *Vernünfftige Gedancken von Gott, der Welt und der Seele des Menschen, auch alle Dinge überhaupt [German Metaphysics]*. 2 vols. Reprint, Hildesheim: Georg Olms, 2009.

Wolff, Christian. *Vernünfftige Gedancken von den Würckungen der Natur*. 4th ed. Halle, 1739.

Yolton, John. *Locke and French Materialism*. Oxford: Oxford University Press, 1991.

Yolton, John. *Thinking Matter: Materialism in Eighteenth Century Britain*. Minneapolis: University of Minnesota Press, 1984.

Zweyer Guten Freunde vertrauter Brief-Wechsel vom Wesen der Seelen. The Hague, 1713.

Zweyer Guten Freunde vertrauter Brief-Wechsel vom Wesen der Seelen, 4th ed. Amsterdam, 1723.

Zweyer guten Freunde vertrauter Brief-Wechsel vom Wesen der Seelen [review]. Deutsche Acta Eruditorum 10, no. 8 (1713): 862–881.

Striving Machinery: The Romantic Origins of a Historical Science of Life

Jessica Riskin

Stanford University, Stanford, CA, USA

A core principle of modern science is that one must explain natural phenomena without ascribing purposeful agency to them, without attributing the descent of a rock, for example, to its desire to reach the center of the earth. This scientific principle originated in the seventeenth century conjoined with a theological principle, the argument from design, which gave a monopoly on purposeful agency to a supernatural Designer, leaving behind a passive mechanical cosmos. The ban on appeals to agency in nature, and the passive mechanical world that it entailed, have been very successful as the predominant modern models of science, theology and the natural world. Nevertheless, from the first, they have inspired resistance as well as adherence, often in the same person (Isaac Newton, for instance, whose hesitations over the cause of gravity provided the Enlightenment with material to last the century). This essay considers an episode in the struggle over the presence or absence of agency in nature, and its results: the emergence of a historical science of life during the Romantic period.

The story should really begin this way: once upon a time, the poets conducted electrical experiments and rushed to attend chemistry lectures, while the physicists and physiologists offered their theories in verse. An intimacy between poetry and natural science was a defining characteristic of the Romantic Movement.[1] While practitioners of the natural sciences wrote poetry, reciprocally, poets and novelists busied themselves with electrical studies, flocked to physics demonstrations and pored over the latest results in physiology. Immanuel Kant offered formal grounds for this intimacy in his last major work, the *Critique of Judgment* (1790). Here he argued that living nature must be regarded as intrinsically "purposive" and that people were only able to apprehend it as such, in the first instance, by means of an act of aesthetic judgment, a feeling of pleasure or displeasure. Judgments in relation to natural objects, therefore, all began with an aesthetic response.[2]

Goethe, whose discovery of Kant's *Critique of Judgment* inaugurated "a wonderful period in my life," rejoiced in the union of science and poetry he found there.[3] Goethe was persuaded that his own efforts to combine science and poetry constituted a lone act of rebellion, remarking in frustration that "[n]owhere would anyone grant" the essential oneness of scientific and poetic knowledge.[4] He was mistaken. Natural philosophers of this period were by default also poets, often presenting their scientific findings in poetic form. They did tend, like Goethe, to suggest that their poetic approach to nature constituted a rebellion. If so, it was a large rebellion.

The rebellion defined itself by opposition to an ideal of non-poetic science: the rational account of a passive mechanical cosmos. The Romantic love affair between science and poetry constituted a search for an alternative approach to science, and in particular to the science of life.

From this search and the self-consciously poetic science it entailed came an understanding of the mechanisms of life in which matter and mechanism were active rather than, as in the classical mechanist tradition, passive and inert.[5] Classical mechanist science placed the locus of purpose and agency outside living nature in the hands of a supernatural Creator. This classical model was also essentially timeless, postulating that living entities received their forms once and for all, by an external agency, upon creation. The Romantic sciences of life ascribed living forms to an inherent agency acting over time, setting them in forward motion, enabling them to produce a history. A fundamentally historical, active-mechanist[6] science of life was accordingly the bastard offspring of the Romantic affair of science and poetry.

1.   The dilemma

The inability of the reigning model of mechanist science to account for living nature received its definitive assessment from Kant.[7] The dialectic between a mechanist rejection and a naturalist embrace of intrinsic purposefulness in natural phenomena shaped his philosophy from the beginning to the end and, partly through him, defined the preoccupations of a generation of Romantic poets and philosophers. Kant's first publication, for example, a work that his admirer and promulgator Samuel Taylor Coleridge later warmly recommended, was a defense of *vis viva*, or "living force." This was the notion by which the mechanist G.W. Leibniz had built the source of action into his world-machine rather than attributing it to an external source, distinguishing his inherently active form of mechanism from what he saw as the passive machinery of both Descartes's and Newton's cosmos.[8] In his first work, so admired by Coleridge, Kant embraced Leibniz's *vis viva*, although he also wrote that reason (but not fact or experience) went against such a notion of intrinsic, living force in the world machine.[9]

In *The Critique of Judgment*, Kant took on a related and seemingly insurmountable problem: to accommodate both the mechanist ban on ascribing purposefulness to natural phenomena and also contemporary accounts of living beings for which purposefulness was abidingly, indeed, increasingly crucial. The result was a work so tortuous it has moved some to allege that the philosopher was senile by the time he wrote it.[10] This essay advances a more charitable view: not senility but the same lifelong commitment to both mechanist science and an understanding of living nature as intrinsically purposeful can explain the convolutions of Kant's third *Critique*. Here, at the end of his career, Kant took on the core and most seismically active fault line in science and philosophy: the growing trench between understandings of life and of science.

Consider the contortionist view of living things that Kant presented in this final work.[11] He wrote that organisms demanded to be understood in terms of purposive action. They simply could not be conceived in any other way. Their parts must be seen as having "agency," as working individually and collectively to produce the whole organism, each part "existing *for the sake of the others*" and of the whole." But this did not mean that organisms necessarily were the results of purposeful action by their parts, merely that they could only be understood as such. A living creature thus appeared, though it was not necessarily so in fact, "*both cause and effect of itself*," an "*organized* and *self-organized* being."[12]

Kant drew a contrast with artificial machinery to define this inherently purposive, self-organizing mode of action apparently specific to organisms: whereas an artificial machine had only the power to move, with which it was endowed by some external agency, an organism had "a self-propagating formative power." Matter-in-motion could not explain this power, Kant thought. For with the advent of classical mechanism, matter had become definitively inert. "The possibility of living matter is quite inconceivable," Kant wrote. "The very conception of it involves a self-contradiction, since lifelessness, *inertia*, constitutes the essential characteristic of matter."[13] As noted above, this characterization of matter as fundamentally lifeless and inert was a central principle of classical mechanism, which evacuated action and agency from nature to the province of an external Engineer, leaving behind a passive material world. The contrast between this intrinsically passive world-machine and the notion of living beings as essentially active, became, we will see, a constant theme for Romantic authors.

Naturalists were thus caught on the horns of a dilemma, as Kant described it, "quite as unable to free themselves" from what he called "teleological" approaches to living beings – by which he meant an internal teleology, a purposeful agency within the natural forms themselves – as from the abiding principle of "general physical science" that precluded internal purposive agency in nature. "[E]ach mode of explanation excludes the other," and yet naturalists could renounce neither.[14] For Kant accepted the classical mechanist model of natural science, and yet he firmly rejected the argument from design, on which it rested. He thought it was contradictory to seek proofs of God's existence through natural science. Natural science could never uncover the purpose of nature itself, because such a purpose must lie outside of nature, beyond the purview of science.[15] In order to maintain the integrity of natural science, one had to treat the agency in nature as operating within nature itself, not externally imposed as in the argument from design. Otherwise "there will be no more nature. There will be only a God in the machine who produces the world's changes."[16]

Kant's dilemma, then, was how to reconcile the mechanist ban on agency in nature, which he embraced, with his own conviction that the argument from design was unintelligible: that one could only meaningfully understand the apparent purposiveness of living forms as intrinsic to themselves. His solution was to distinguish between how people understood organisms and how organisms actually were in themselves (which was anyway, he said, unknowable). The apparent purposiveness of organisms did not mean that these were in fact the results of internal, purposive action, but rather that our reason or "cognitive faculty" had to understand them as such.[17] Naturalists should therefore retain their methodological principle that all living forms originate in purposeful agency, but they should also regard this principle as "reflective" and "regulative" rather than "determining" and "constitutive." In this way, they might carry on seeking natural purposes while assuming no "underlying end," no actual "teleology."[18]

Organisms viewed from this as-if perspective, Kant hoped, lent natural science a legitimate basis for a teleology that would otherwise be "absolutely unjustifiable."[19] Mechanism and teleology, "thesis" and "antithesis," could coexist in science without contradiction as long as people treated these as "maxims of reflective judgement" or "regulative principles of investigation" rather than "constitutive principles."[20] One could speak "with perfect justice of the wisdom, the economy, the forethought, the beneficence of nature," but in doing so, one must never represent nature as an intelligent being, "for that would be absurd." On the other hand, neither must one portray nature as a lifeless, passive artifact. This would amount to placing an intelligent being "above nature as its architect," which Kant deemed "presumptuous" and, we have seen, contradictory.[21]

It was a quandary, but a productive one: if Kant's struggle over thesis and antithesis did not produce a clear synthesis, it did produce some considerable new possibilities. One was the principle that teleological judgments must be local and relative, operating only within the system of nature, rather than absolute. Kant offered the convergence of living and natural forms in the Arctic region as an example. The people living in the Arctic had found snow to protect their seeds from frost; reindeer to serve their needs for travel and communication; other arctic animals to provide sources of fuel, food and clothing; and the sea to bring them driftwood to build houses. It was a "truly marvelous confluence" of means to ends, the ends being "Greenlanders, Laplanders,

Samoyedes, Jakutes, and the like." However, why should human beings live in the Arctic at all? What larger purpose or benefit could there be? If all this natural utility were absent, it would never be missed.[22] A naturalist must note all this local suitedness of means to ends, and yet must leave a deliberate and necessary blank in the spot where an ultimate end might make sense of it all … or not.

Besides the subordination of teleology to a greater contingency, another powerful possibility to emerge from Kant's struggles to reconcile mechanism with teleology was the notion that the two approaches might one day come together in a single, genetic account of living beings. That is, Kant considered the possibility that mechanical causes might explain the purposiveness displayed by living forms, acting not in a single moment of construction, but through a process of "descent from a common parent." The fact that an enormous variety of species shared a single, underlying structural plan, Kant thought, suggested a "kinship" among them, like a great family whose "genesis" one could trace, the forms flowing from one another "by the shortening of one part and the lengthening of another, by the involution of this part and the evolution of that." Perhaps the apparent "purposiveness" of living beings had come about gradually through a process of genesis:

> the womb of mother earth as it first emerged, like a huge animal, from its chaotic state, gave birth to creatures whose form displayed less purposiveness, and […] these again bore others which adapted themselves more perfectly to their native surroundings and their relations to each other […].

With this idea of a genesis of new organisms over time, Kant wrote, "there gleams upon the mind a ray of hope, however faint that the principle of the mechanism of nature, apart from which there can be no natural science at all, may yet enable us to arrive at some explanation of organic life." In the next paragraph, Kant renounced this "ray of hope" for an account of living nature whose causes were purely mechanical in the sense of being non-purposive, finding that it merely pushed the purposiveness back a stage to the primordial mother earth. Nevertheless, he had introduced the notion of time as a possible force in the production of purposeful, natural, living mechanisms.[23]

A scientific mode of explanation that was at once mechanist and historical, operating over time and by means of various intrinsic, natural agencies: this was not, in fact, a new idea for Kant. Already in 1755, he had described the cosmos itself as arising "from the mechanical laws of matter striving to develop."[24] Here already an inner agency was the means by which natural mechanisms transformed and created their own history. This genetic account seemed to Kant to hold out the best hope of uniting mechanical and final causes with the "least possible expenditure of the supernatural" in comparison with the leading contenders. First among these contenders was *occasionalism*, in which God acted directly to shape each organized being on the occasion of its birth. Second was the theory that went in contemporary natural history by the name of *evolution* (not to be confused with the later meaning of "evolution"): the Creator had acted in advance, pre-forming every organism and nesting the homunculi generation within generation.[25]

In preference to both of these, Kant chose *epigenesis*: the Supreme Cause had endowed organized beings themselves with the ability to reproduce. He commended Johann Friedrich Blumenbach, whose theory of epigenesis provided Kant's model, for having acknowledged both the purposiveness of life and the mechanist dictates of science in framing his theory. In Blumenbach's view, each generation of organisms following the first, propelled by a "formative impulse" in matter itself, mechanically constituted the next. [26] His hesitation between mechanism and teleology led Kant to favor an epigenetic account of living beings, an account that operated in terms of self-organization rather than externally imposed design, and made the "purposiveness" of living structures central to every explanation, but in which teleology was subordinated to a greater contingency. It was a process driven by ubiquitous but limited agency. Struggling to reconcile mechanism and teleology, Kant arrived at a view of life that was fundamentally historical.

Several years later, Goethe announced his own embrace of a genetic approach to living forms, regarding the stages of the creation of life as a "progression of uninterrupted activity."[27] His *Metamorphosis of Plants* (1790) had already exemplified the genre. It presented a minutely detailed account of the transformations of the material parts of plants in growth. The driving force in this account was each plant's ability to "express its vitality" by continually making and remaking its parts.[28] Elsewhere, Goethe described this as a force of "intensification [...] a state of ever-striving ascent."[29] Blumenbach, we have seen, likewise assigned the definitive role to a "formative impulse," a kind of striving agency. A living being, Blumenbach wrote, was the result of unorganized matter taking on "a particular action." This action, which constituted the life of the organism and continued throughout its duration, was distinct from other animal capacities such as sensibility. Blumenbach called it a "nisus": a striving.[30]

A mechanical striving impelled the emergence and development of living beings also according to Jean-Baptiste Lamarck, author of the discipline of biology and professor of natural history at the *Muséum national d'histoire naturelle* in Paris. When Lamarck coined the term *biologie* in 1802, he defined the distinctive subject area of his new field in terms of this vital striving.[31] An intrinsic "force of life," he observed, drove "animate machines," plants and animals, not only to compose themselves, but to elaborate their organization over time. The process began with the most rudimentary form of life, an "animated point" to which Lamarck gave the Leibnizian name *monade*. Organisms developed and grew purely as a result of their own movements, specifically the movements of fluids within them. Plants and animals were the sole beings on the planet to form this way, using materials of their own composition. In addition to the inner force of composition and complexification, higher animals also responded to their environments by will, forming habits that gradually transformed them. Accordingly, every sort of living being had arisen from inner agencies: the vital action of fluids within the animate machinery acting in endlessly varying circumstances over an "incalculable series of centuries."[32]

Lamarck was convinced that such a process was the only way to account for sentient life. If each creature owed its organization to a "force entirely exterior and foreign" to it, then instead of being animate machines, animals would have been "totally passive machines." They would never have had "sensibility or the intimate sentiment of existence that follows from it," nor the power to act, nor ideas, nor thought, nor intelligence. In short, they would not have been alive.[33]

The notion that living beings produced themselves by their own agency was widely but not universally accepted. Lamarck's colleague and critic, the naturalist and zoologist Georges Cuvier, was prominent among those who rejected it.[34] Moreover, he rejected it on the grounds that ascribing agency to natural phenomena might make good poetry but never good science. Alas, poor Lamarck! It was Cuvier who wrote his eulogy, which he read to the Academy of Sciences in November 1832, three years after Lamarck's death. Rarely can a eulogy have offered fainter praise. Cuvier observed that no one had found Lamarck's theory of life "dangerous enough to merit attacking." It hinged upon the "arbitrary" supposition "that desires, efforts, can engender organs," an idea that might "amuse the imagination of a poet" but could never persuade a true anatomist.[35] And yet Cuvier himself defined life as an activity: the faculty of "enduring" through give and take, assimilating substance from one's surroundings and rendering substance back.[36] Even Cuvier, who rejected as "poetry" the idea of ascribing agency to natural phenomena, understood life as a form of activity.

By the turn of the nineteenth century, a living being in scientific, philosophical and literary understanding had become, in essence, an agent. An agent, in turn, was a thing in constant, self-generated motion and transformation of material parts. Living agency took the form of a responsive "striving," a capacity to bring about developmental change over time and in response to external circumstances: in short, to produce a history. It therefore demanded a kind of understanding that was at once mechanist, in the sense that it resided in interactions of material parts, and diachronic, operating over time. "Nature is a line in constant and continuous evolution," wrote Coleridge.[37] The science of living nature must take the form of history.

2. The dilemma dramatized

Kant's genetic approach to the phenomena of life, divided between a mechanist model of science and a "purposive" model of living beings, became a touchstone for the generation of poet-philosophers working in the first decades of the nineteenth century. "The writings of the illustrious sage of Koenigsberg," wrote Coleridge, "took possession of me as with the giant's hand." Kant's works, he judged, had shaped his thinking more than any other, had "invigorated" and "disciplined" his understanding, and he returned to Kant over the years with "undiminished delight and increasing admiration."[38]

Coleridge made it his mission to bring Kant to his compatriots.[39] William Wordworth, Thomas Carlyle, and in America, Ralph Waldo Emerson and Edgar Allan Poe encountered the sage of Koenigsberg through Coleridge.[40] As he proselytized, he dwelt especially upon the third *Critique*.[41] The dilemma that Kant had struggled to describe and overcome was the focus of Coleridge's writing. Rather than working to resolve it, he dramatized it. Descartes's mechanist system, Coleridge wrote, was "a lifeless Machine whirled about by the dust of its own Grinding," a reduction of "the living fountain of Life" to "Death." In Coleridge's judgment, living organs were different from artificial machines in that, rather than being composed of parts, they actively assimilated foreign matter into themselves: "As the unseen Agency weaves its magic eddies, the foliage [eaten by an Ox or Elephant] becomes indifferently the Bone and its Marrow, the pulpy Brain, or the solid Ivory." *Agency* was the key word in Coleridge's understanding of living nature. He rejected the Cartesian-mechanist approach as having excluded "life and immanent activity from the visible Universe." In Newtonian physics, Coleridge perceived "the necessity of an active power, of positive forces present in the Material Universe," and he lamented the natural-theological identification of these forces with God.[42]

The argument from design left nature inert and God indistinguishable from gravitational force. Coleridge preferred the "dynamic spirit" he saw at work in contemporary physical science, such as the electromagnetic chemistry of Humphrey Davy and Hans Christian Oersted, which found active forces and tendencies at work throughout matter. Surely, Coleridge thought, these dynamic sciences had dealt a "mortal blow" to scientific mechanism. They had proven that a living being was not a particular material structure but a "distinct and individualized Agency" expressing itself through successive combinations of particles.[43]

As a child, Mary Shelley, the creator of Frankenstein's monster, the leading hypothetical man-machine of the Romantic period, inhaled these principles and preoccupations with the air she breathed. Coleridge was a good friend of her father, the novelist and radical social theorist William Godwin, and Shelley knew him well from childhood. As an adult, she remembered having hidden beneath the parlor sofa with her half-sister during a gathering one summer evening shortly before her ninth birthday to hear Coleridge croon out the *Rime of the Ancient Mariner*.[44]

The evening conversations that gave rise to *Frankenstein* (1818) took place at the Geneva villa of George Gordon, Lord Byron during the rainy summer of 1816, when the author was 19, and they touched upon the latest theories of life.[45] Percy Shelley, with whom Mary Shelley had eloped two years earlier, was interested in the work of the French doctor and physiologist Pierre-Jean-Georges Cabanis, one of the leading contemporary proponents of machinery as a model of animal and human life.[46] Cabanis wrote that the brain was an organ for producing thought just as the stomach digested and the liver filtered bile.[47] His model of living machinery was however intrinsically active and sentient rather than brute and inert: sensation spread throughout the "living machine" by the constriction and relaxation of the nerves.[48] Living machinery needed "to feel and to act: and life is that much more whole, when all the organs feel and act strongly."[49]

One evening at the villa, the group discussed some experiments that had been performed by Erasmus Darwin. The creator of a mechanical talking head, Darwin was a prolific and popular naturalist who discussed zoology and natural history in poetry as well as prose. He was interested in the artificial production of lifelike entities and, indeed, of life itself. The experiments in question were reported, like Darwin's talking head, in the "philosophical notes" to a poem entitled *The Temple of Nature*, published posthumously in 1802.[50] Darwin claimed to have produced life – or rather, triggered life's production of itself – by spontaneous generation. Shelley referred to the spontaneous generation experiments: Darwin, she said, had locked a noodle in a glass case until it began to move on its own. The actual experiments involved a paste of flour and water left to putrefy in a closed container, yielding "animalcules called eels, vibrio anguillula" that displayed "wonderful strength and activity."[51]

Alongside Erasmus Darwin, another figure hovered over Shelley's story. He was Sir Humphry Davy, the son of a Cornish woodcarver who had risen to become one of Britain's most prominent natural philosophers. Davy, another acquaintance of Shelley's father, was the chemical lecturer at the Royal Institution and, like everybody, a poet. His approach to the subject of "Life's warm fountains,"[52] equal parts lyrical and experimental, included research into "the conversion of dead matter into living matter."[53]

Darwin and Davy together contributed a crucial element of the story of *Frankenstein*: they were leading proponents of a widely-held theory that the "living principle, or spirit of animation, which resides throughout the body" was a sort of "electric fluid."[54] The idea of "animal electricity," also known as "galvanism" after the man who had proposed it just over a decade earlier, was another topic of conversation at Byron's Geneva villa on the rainy night in question. The Bolognese anatomist Luigi Galvani had reported in 1791 that he could make the leg of a dissected frog jump by applying electric sparks to its nerves. He had surmised that animal tissue contained a vital force, which he named "animal electricity" by analogy with the "natural electricity" generated by lightning and the "artificial electricity" produced by friction in an electrostatic generator. Galvani believed animal electricity was secreted by the brain and conducted by the nerves and acted as the medium of both sensation and muscular motion.[55] The torpedo fish and electric eel, which produced shocking electrical discharge, provided additional support for this view, and commanded much attention, again at once poetic and philosophical. "The tropic eel, electric in his ire," Darwin rhymed, "alarms the waves with unextinguish'd fire."[56]

As a student at Oxford, Percy Shelley had kept electrical equipment in his rooms and liked to demonstrate his electrostatic generator to guests by having them turn the crank while he drew off the fire, perched on a glass-footed stool, "so that his long, wild locks bristled and stood on end."[57] During the evening conversations at Byron's villa, he and the others wondered aloud whether artificial electricity might be used to reanimate a corpse.[58]

They were able to cite experimental data. In a London anatomy theater in 1803, Galvani's nephew, Giovanni Aldini, had used an electrical battery to cause the corpse of a hanged criminal to grimace and twitch its muscles.[59] An Edinburgh doctor, Andrew Ure, had repeated the experiment in 1818 with "truly appalling" results. "The scene was hideous," recalled a witness, including an episode of apparent "laborious breathing" on the part of the corpse.[60] Ure wrote that "several of the spectators were forced to leave the apartment from terror or sickness, and one gentleman fainted." In both cases, the experimenters were persuaded that "vitality might, perhaps, have been restored" if they had known how to manage it just right.[61]

In the night following these discussions at Byron's villa, Mary Shelley was visited by a horrible vision: Frankenstein kneeling beside his monster as it comes hideously to life, then fleeing in terror, falling into a troubled sleep and awaking to find the monster gazing upon him "with yellow, watery, but speculative eyes."[62] In the midnight reverie that was the germ of *Frankenstein*, the defining feature of the finished novel was already in place: the conflict between dead matter and living agency.

Matter, we have seen, had become antithetical to life: passive, inert. The surgeon and physiologist Richard Saumarez described matter this way in his *New System of Physiology* (1799), a book Coleridge greatly admired. The "Principle of Life" according to Saumarez was a power of organization that, passing from a state of dormancy into one of "energy and action," could "overcome" the "passivity of common matter." Deprived of this living principle of organization, Saumarez wrote, the matter of an organism was "as imbecile and inert as the shoe without the foot."[63]

The Romantic poet-philosophers who took over the question of living machinery in the first years of the nineteenth century carried the reasoning one step farther. In their hands, inanimate matter, which Saumarez had described as the shoe without the foot, became the dead and severed foot itself. A horrified fascination with the juxtaposition of "dead" matter and living agency worked at the heart of the Romantic understanding of the nature of life, which was inseparably poetic, moral and scientific.

In his popular 1802 "Discourse on Chemistry," studied not only by Mary Shelley but by many other Romantic writers including Coleridge and William Wordsworth, Humphry Davy used the phrase "dead matter" and similar ones – "dead nature," the "dead state" – on almost every page.[64] This was not Davy's idiosyncrasy, but a standard way of speaking. "The matter that surrounds us," the London doctor William Lawrence, Percy Shelly's own physician, told audiences at his much-discussed public lectures on the nature of life in 1814 and 1815, "is divided into two great classes, living and dead."[65] Rather than contrasting life with non-life — the inanimate — the Romantics set life up against death: what was not alive was dead. Frankenstein's monster represented the central dilemma of contemporary science, according to which all living beings were constituted by an inherent agency and yet made out of dead matter.

That matter was dead, the opposite of life, and that life was a form of activity, the continual effort to constitute oneself from and against dead matter, were the Romantic principles that informed the founding of biology as a discipline. Life was the struggle against extinction, "the sum of the functions that resist death," as the French surgeon and physiologist Marie-François-Xavier Bichat defined it.[66] Erasmus Darwin versified, "Life clings trembling on her tottering throne."[67] Lamarck, in a manuscript sketch of the book he planned to write to inaugurate his new science entitled "Biology, or considerations on the nature, the faculties, the developments and the origins of living bodies," began by dividing nature into two parts: "brute bodies" and "living bodies." This division, Lamarck wrote, was "infinitely distinct," with no "intermediary" between the brute and the living. A living body was "a natural body limited in its duration, organized in its parts […] possessing what we call life, and subject necessarily to lose it, that is, to succumb to death," at which point it must be re-classed among the brute bodies.[68] In addition to these two sorts of bodies, Lamarck announced two opposing forces to govern them: one a force of composition and life, the other a force of destruction and death.[69]

The effortful activity of life, the striving agency, Lamarck emphasized, was ultimately doomed.[70] His colleague and fellow-traveler, Étienne Géoffroy Saint-Hilaire, described the situation of life in similarly combative terms. Saint-Hilaire was the author of a theory broadly sympathetic to Lamarckism, in which species transformed by the direct impingement of the environment. He described this process as an "engagement of actions and reactions." The "battle," Saint-Hilaire wrote, must always favor the forces of organization over disorganization as long as "the machine is not definitively totally disorganized."[71]

Life could triumph on a grander scale, if not in any individual case. Erasmus Darwin made the point in poetry: "Organic forms with chemic changes strive, / Live but to die, and die but to revive."[72] The living, organizing power by which organisms produced themselves from "senses, feelings and conceptions," wrote the Prussian philosopher and poet Johann Gottfried Herder, did not perish with an individual's death. Even in the "dissolved machine" of a dead flower the power remained "active."[73] Erasmus Darwin agreed: "The births and deaths contend with equal strife / And every pore of Nature teems with Life."[74] Redefined in terms of their duel with dead matter, the vital powers and striving impulses of the eighteenth century took on heroic capital letters and became the "Vital Power,"[75] the "World Spirit."[76]

The institutional establishment of physiology, like biology, occurred in the midst of these phi-losophical-literary-scientific-aesthetic developments. The notion of a generalized, circulating living agency, larger than the life of any given organism, connected physiology with a tradition in physics that had arisen from Leibniz's "living force." The new physics that emerged from *vis viva* centered upon an active force within nature on which all motion depended. During the eight-eenth and early nineteenth centuries, Emilie du Châtelet, Lazare and Sadi Carnot, Gaspard Monge, John Smeaton and others worked the idea of living force into an energistic approach to physics and engineering.[77]

Physiologists, beginning especially with the German Johannes Müller and later his students, Emil du Bois Reymond and Hermann von Helmholtz, began to understand living agency and sen-tience in terms of energies and, later, energy.[78] Quoting Kant, Müller wrote that living matter con-tained "a principle constantly in action," which "adapted" the parts of an organism to one another, perhaps a "vital energy." Müller explained sensation itself, and in particular its differentiation, in terms of energies specific to each nerve.[79] Cabanis similarly supposed that the brain exerted its control over the rest of the "living machine" by means of its "energy and activity."[80]

Like the older ideas of a striving impulse in living beings – Blumenbach's *nisus*, Lamarck's *pouvoir de vie* – the idea of a vital energy incorporated action and purpose into the machinery. But while the earlier forms of vital agency had constituted a categorical distinction between living beings and dead matter, energy reconnected animate with inanimate nature. Energy was not a primitive feature of living substance but the currency of its engagement with dead matter, and moreover, this engagement was not specific to organisms: "The animal machine resembles every other machine, the action of which necessitates the destruction of some material," wrote Müller.[81]

Moving forces acted throughout inorganic and organic nature alike, according to Helmnoltz, and all originated in the sun. All moving forces were interconvertible forms of the same essential "activity": "whenever the capacity for work of one natural force is destroyed, it is transformed into another kind of activity."[82] It was a cosmic circuit: sunlight enabled plants to grow and produce the fuel and nutriment for animals to "burn" in their lungs, while the products of this combustion became the plants' nutriments taken from air, water and soil: carbon, hydrogen, nitro-gen. The whole process originated in the sun, and therefore "all force, by means of which our bodies live and move, finds its source in the purest sunlight."[83]

The living agency of organisms was integral to a general living agency of nature itself. The poets had arrived there before the physiologists. "O! the one Life within us and abroad," Coler-idge rhapsodized,[84] while Erasmus Darwin explained, "With finer links the vital chain extends / And the long line of Being never ends."[85] To live was now to transcend, not from matter into spirit, but from the individual into the universal. It was a form of "transcendental materialism," in Anson Rabinbach's aptly oxymoronic phrase: a materialism that assumed, not a reductive sameness in nature, but instead a dynamic "unity of all material being" in the form of interconvertible forces and, ultimately, of energy.[86] "Be it," wrote Herder, "that we know nothing of our soul as pure spirit: we desire not to know it as such. Be it, that it acts only as an organic power: it was not intended to act otherwise."[87] Electricity, magnetism, heat, mechanical and chemical forces, and life were all forms of a single entity, energy. They were all modes of one another, convertible into one another, and so living creatures were participants in the life of nature itself. "That what you see *is* blood, *is* flesh, is itself the work […] of the invisible Energy."[88]

Not only life but also consciousness and sentience were forms of dynamic participation, in this case in the greater sentience of Nature itself, "A motion and a spirit, that impels / All thinking things, all objects of all thought, / And rolls through all things."[89] Our own "machine," wrote Herder, was "a growing, flourishing tree," and so it "feels even with trees; and there are men, who cannot bear to see a young tree cut down or destroyed."[90] According to Erasmus Darwin, Mind likewise characterized all Life: even flowers could entertain "ideas" and "passions."[91] Looking into one's own mind, one looked "into the Mind of Man,"[92] and also into the mind of all plants and animals too: "And what if all of animated nature / Be but organic Harps diversely framed, / That tremble into thought, as o'er them sweeps / Plastic and vast, one intellectual breeze."[93]

How to revoke the monopoly on agency that the founders of modern, mechanist science had assigned to God? How to bring the inanimate, clockwork cosmos of classical mechanist science back to life while remaining as faithful as possible to the core principles of the scientific tradition? A movement of poets, physiologists, novelists, chemists, philosophers and experimental physicists – often combined in the same person – struggled with this question. Their struggles brought the natural machinery of contemporary science from inanimate to dead to alive once more, and in so doing, produced two major developments.

The first was a genetic approach to life whose proponents thought that by tracing the developments of limited agents working in particular contexts over periods of time, they might reconcile the demands of mechanism with the appearance of living purpose. In other words, they placed their hope in a form of explanation that might best be named historical. The second development was the idea that organisms, understood as living machines, could transcend the limits of their own machinery without leaving the realm of material nature. It was an attempt to rescue Frankenstein's monster from his isolation without giving him a soul.

The possibility the Romantics arrived at, through a dramatic collaboration of science and poetry, was the possibility of a rigorously, exhaustively natural science: one in which the divine Clockmaker ceded his monopoly to inherent agencies operating over time and across space, always within the continuum of nature.

Notes

1. On the intimacy of natural philosophy and poetry, see Lawrence, "The Power and the Glory," 589–595; Levere, "Coleridge and the Sciences," 295–306; King-Hele, "Romantic Followers," Ch. 11. Robert J. Richards has mapped the union of poetry, philosophy and natural science in the German Romantic movement in *The Romantic Conception of Life*. Denise Gigante, in *Life: Organic Form and Romanticism*, and Alan Richardson, in *British Romanticism and the Science of Mind*, have done the same for the English Romantics.
2. Kant, *Critique of Judgment*, 24–25, 28.
3. Goethe, "The Influence of Modern Philosophy," 29.
4. Goethe, "History of the Printed Brochure" (1817), 171–172.
5. I use the term "classical mechanism" to refer to a specific form of mechanist science and philosophy established and espoused from the latter seventeenth century by Cartesians and others such as Robert Boyle, who insisted upon a strict separation of matter and force, and upon the fundamental inactivity of matter itself. Others who described themselves as "mechanists" – such as G.W. Leibniz and his

followers and fellow-travelers – meant something very different by it. This is why I find it important to distinguish "classical" mechanism from mechanism in general, which included a variety of views.

6. On the role of mechanist science in the culture of Romanticism, and specifically on the falsity of the opposition between mechanism and Romanticism, see Tresch, *The Romantic Machine*, especially Ch. 1. Tresch argues that the idea of an opposition between mechanism and Romanticism was a conceit of the early twentieth century.

7. Timothy Lenoir has influentially characterized Kant's complicated stance with regard to the science of living beings as "teleomechanism." See Lenoir, *Strategy of Life*, Ch. 1. Robert Richards has more recently disagreed with Lenoir's account, arguing that Kant excluded biology from the realm of science. See Richards, *Romantic Conception of Life*, 229–237. Here I am reading Kant's *Critique of Judgment* against the background of the animal-machine tradition with its escalating contradiction between understandings of living forms as intrinsically purposeful and a mechanist model of science that precluded such ascriptions of purposefulness to natural phenomena. In this context it seems to me that Kant's account of the study of life is unclassifiable either as science or non-science, teleological, mechanist, or both at once. Rather, it addresses the contradiction itself and seeks to encompass all of the conflicting positions.

8. Because of the central role of gravitational force in the Newtonian system, some commentators from the seventeenth century onward have seen Newton's physics as intrinsically active in contrast with Cartesian cosmology. For a recent representation of this view of Newtonianism, see Dear, *Intelligibility of Nature*, Ch. 1, §4. As Dear points out, Newton did invoke "active principles" in his last major work, the *Opticks*. See Newton, *Opticks*, 398.

9. Kant, *Gedanken*; Coleridge, *Aids to Reflection*, 394–395 fn..

10. See, e.g., Scruton, *Kant*, 97.

11. To any philosophers, especially Kantians, who might be reading this: I read as a historian, not as a philosopher. My main purpose is not to demonstrate Kant's influence on the Romantic Movement, or on nineteenth-century life sciences, nor is it to arrive at a rigorous Kantian program by interpreting his writings so as to eliminate any apparent tensions or contradictions. I am not interested in trying to free Kant's ideas from the messiness of historical context. Rather I aim to situate his thinking, including its tensions and contradictions, in time and place, to see what it signifies regarding the intellectual world in which he was working, and the one we have inherited.

The *Critique of Judgment* has been the subject of a great deal of philosophical analysis and debate, but rather less historical consideration (important exceptions are the works of Timothy Lenoir and Robert Richards mentioned in note 7, above). I have studied the philosophical literature in this area and it has informed my own reading, but in a trans-disciplinary and therefore indirect way. Philosophers read very differently from historians. Philosophers' primary purpose in reading Kant, or any philosopher, is to define a philosophical approach of their own in keeping with his principles. They therefore seek ways to "rescue" and "defend" key aspects of what he wrote, to resolve tensions and ambiguities, to solve apparent contradictions, to arrive at something they feel able to endorse. As a historian, in contrast, I am reading for the whole of what Kant wrote in a given text, including – indeed, especially – the tensions and ambiguities, because these reflect the preoccupations of the world in which he was working.

For recent philosophical discussions of Kant's understanding of the role of teleology and mechanism in the sciences of life, see the works listed below. These offer ways to resolve the central tension of the *Critique of Judgment*: the conflict between the requirement of contemporary mechanist science that scientific explanations attribute no intrinsic purposefulness to natural phenomena, and the apparent purposefulness of living forms. For my (historian's) purposes, these philosophical readings of Kant serve to confirm the presence and importance of this central tension, since what I am interested in is the tension itself, and in the fault line it represents in contemporary science, not in finding a philosophical resolution to it. See Steigerwald, *Kantian Teleology and the Biological Sciences*; Breitenbach, "Teleology in Biology," 31–56; Ginsborg, "Kant's Biological Teleology and its Philosophical Significance"; Ginsborg, "Kant on Aesthetic and Biological Purposiveness," 329–360; Ginsborg, "Lawfulness Without a Law," 37–81; Ginsborg, "Kant on Understanding Organisms as Natural Purposes," 231–258; Ginsborg, "Oughts Without Intentions"; Guyer, "Organisms and the Unity of Science," 259–281; and McLaughlin, *Kant's Critique of Teleology*.

12. Kant, *Critique of Judgment*, §s 62–68, quoted passages in §64, Academy Edition [hereafter AE] 371 and §65, AE 374–375.

13. Kant, *Critique of Judgment*, §65, AE 374; §73, AE 395.

14. Kant, *Critique of Judgment*, §66, AE 376.

15. Kant, *Critique of Judgment*, §85, AE 436–441. On Kant's rejection of the argument from design, see also *Der einzig mögliche Beweisgrund*, especially Fünfte – Siebente Beträchtungen; and §68, AE 381, where he argues that the argument from design is a vicious circle.
16. Kant, *Universal Natural History*, 115 [first published in German as *Allgemeine Naturgeschichte*, 146: "Es wird in der That alsdenn keine Natur mehr seyn; es wird nur ein Gott in der Maschine die Veränderungen der Welt hervor bringen."] See also Kant, *Critique of Judgment*, §78, AE 411–412.
17. Kant, *Critique of Judgment*, §§66, 72, 78, 81, quoted passage from §81, AE 421.
18. Kant, *Critique of Judgment*, §§62, 65, 67, 71, 73, quoted passages from §62, AE 364 and §65, AE 375.
19. Kant, *Critique of Judgment*, §65, AE 375.
20. Kant, *Critique of Judgment*, §§70–71, AE 387–389.
21. Kant, *Critique of Judgment*, §68, AE 382.
22. Kant, *Critique of Judgment*, §63, AE 369.
23. Kant, *Critique of Judgment*, §80, AE 418–420.
24. Kant, *Universal Natural History*, 94 ["aus den mechanischen Gesetzen der zur Bildung strebenden Materie," *Allgemeine Naturgeschichte*, 110].
25. See Maienschein, "Epigenesis and Preformationism."
26. Blumenbach, *Über den Bildungstrieb*; Kant, *Critique of Judgment*, §81, AE 424; Kant – Johann Friedrich Blumenbach, 5 August 1790, in Guyer and Wood, *Correspondence*, 354.
27. *Genetishe Behandlung*: Goethe, "Vorarbeiten zu einer Physiologie der Pflanzen," 303–304. Published in partial English translation as "Excerpt from Studies for a Physiology of Plants," 73–75.
28. Goethe, *The Metamorphosis of Plants*, ¶113.
29. Goethe, "A Commentary on the Aphoristic Essay 'Nature,'" 6.
30. Blumenbach, *An Essay on Generation*, 61. For an analysis of the nature and status of Blumenbach's *nisus* in relation to contemporary notions of vital forces, see Larson, "Vital Forces," 235–249.
31. Lamarck, *Hydrogéologie*, 8, 188. For "biologie," see also Lamarck, *Histoire naturelle*, 49–50; Lamarck, *Recherches sur l'organisation*, vi, 186, 202; Lamarck, *Philosophie zoologique*, xviii; and Lamarck,"Biologie, ou considérations sur la nature," a manuscript plan for a never-written book. Lamarck was not the only person to coin the term: several authors arrived at it independently around the same time. See Corsi, "Biologie," 37–64.
32. Lamarck, *Philosophie zoologique*, Vol. 2: 95, 127; Lamarck, *Histoire naturelle*, 50, 134; Lamarck, *Hydrogéologie*, 188. On Lamarck's "ceaseless tendency" of living beings to compose and complexify themselves, a "continually active cause," see also *Philosophie zoologique*, Vol. 1: 132; Vol. 2: 69, 100, 101, 104. For "monade," see Vol. 1: 285; Vol. 2: 67, 212. "Animated point" is in *Discours d'ouverture prononcé*, 16. On Lamarck's relations to Leibniz and the possibly Leibnizian origins of his term "monade," see Canguilhem, "Note sur les rapports," 188 (for Maupertuis's role in transmitting the Leibnizian monad into theories of life); Smith, "Leibniz's Hylomorphic Monad," 24; and Burkhardt, *The Spirit of System*, 233, n. 36.
33. Lamarck, *Philosophie zoologique*, Vol. 2: 310–311.
34. For analyses of Cuvier's denigration of Lamarck, see Gould, "Foreword"; and Rudwick, *Georges Cuvier*, 83.
35. Cuvier, "Eloge de M. de Lamarck," i–xxxi, on p. xx.
36. Cuvier, *Le Règne animal*, Vol. 1: 7.
37. Coleridge, *Aids to Reflection*, 257.
38. Coleridge, *Biographia Literaria*, 264.
39. Coleridge, *Biographia Literaria*, 273.
40. See Micheli, *The Early Reception*, Ch. 3: "Samuel Taylor Coleridge and Kant"; and Edwards, *The Statesman's Science*, 144.
41. Robinson, *Diary, Reminiscences and Correspondence*.
42. Coleridge, *Aids to Reflection*, 393–397, 399, 401.
43. Ibid., 389–392.
44. See Seymour, *Mary Shelley*, 58.
45. Shelley, Introduction to *Frankenstein*, Third Edition, 170, 171.
46. Richardson, *British Romanticism*, 17.
47. Cabanis, *Rapports*, Vol. 1: 128.
48. Ibid., 118.
49. Ibid., 243.
50. Darwin, *The Temple of Nature*, 62–64. The talking head is reported in Additional Note XV on page 98.
51. Shelley, "Introduction to Frankenstein," 171; Darwin, *Temple of Nature*, note 12.

52. Davy, "The Sons of Genius," 1:26 (ln. 97).
53. Davy, "Discourse Introductory," 2: 311–326, at ¶3.
54. Darwin, *Zoonomia*, §2, part 2, ¶1–2. See also Darwin, *Botanic Garden*, Part I, Canto I, ln. 363 ff; *Temple of Nature*, Additional Notes, 12–13, 74–89; Abernethy, *Introductory Lectures*, 5: no. 130; Humboldt, *Expériences sur le galvanisme*.
55. Galvani, *Commentary*.
56. Darwin, *Temple of Nature*, Canto III, lns. 111–112.
57. Hogg, *The Life of Percy Bysshe Shelley*, 1:56.
58. Shelley, Introduction to Frankenstein, 171–172.
59. Aldini, *An Account*.
60. "Horrible Phenomena! – Galvanism," in *The Times*, 11 February 1819, 3; see also *The Examiner*, 15 February 1819, 103; and Keddie, *Anecdotes Literary and Scientific*, 3–4.
61. Ure, "An Account of Some Experiments," 290; see also Golinksi, "The Literature of the New Sciences"; and Sleigh, "Life, Death and Galvanism," 219–248.
62. Shelley, Introduction to *Frankenstein*, 172.
63. Saumarez, *A New System of Physiology*, Vol. 2: 8. For Coleridge's admiration of this work, see Coleridge, *Biographia Literaria*, Ch. 9 and fn. 31.
64. Davy, "Discourse."
65. Lawrence, *Lectures*, 57.
66. Bichat, *Recherches*, 2.
67. Darwin, *The Botanic Garden*, Part I, Canto I, ln. 368.
68. Lamarck, "Biologie," 10–11.
69. Lamarck, *Mémoires de physique*, 248–249; see also *Recherches*, ¶817, 289.
70. Lamarck, *Recherches*, ¶818, 289–290.
71. Saint-Hilaire, *Philosophie anatomique*, Vol. 1: 208–209.
72. Darwin, *Temple of Nature*, Canto II, lns. 41–42.
73. Herder, *Outlines of a Philosophy*, 59, 109.
74. Darwin, *Temple of Nature*, Canto IV, lns. 379–80.
75. Coleridge, "On the Passions," 2: 1442.
76. [Anima Mundi] Abernethy, *Introductory Lectures*, 51.
77. The principal primary texts for the emergence of energy conservation include Mayer, "Bemerkungen," an early formulation of the law of energy conservation with a physiological foundation; Helmholtz, *Über die Erhaltung der Kraft*; and Reymond, *Über die Lebenskraft*, 1:1–26. For a primary account of the development of the principle of energy conservation, see Mach, History and Root of the Principles of the Conservation of Energy. Important secondary treatments include Kuhn, "Energy Conservation," 321–356; Cardwell, *From Watt to Clausius*; and Smith, Science of Energy. On Helmholtz, see also Bevilacqua, "Helmholtz's Ueber die Erhaltung."
78. Johannes Müller first presented his doctrine of specific nerve energies in *Zur vergleichenden Physiologie*. For an overview of the emergence of ideas about energy in physiology, see Rothschuh, *History of Physiology*, Ch. 6. For an analysis of the instrumental connections between Helmholtz's work in physics and in physiology, see Brain and Wise, "Muscles and Engines."
79. Müller, *Elements of Physiology*, 27, 31–35, 712, 714, 719.
80. Cabanis, *Rapports*, Vol. 2: 423–24.
81. Müller, *Elements of Physiology*, 285.
82. Helmholtz, "On the Conservation of Force," 124.
83. Helmholtz, "On the Interaction of the Natural Forces," 37, 38.
84. Coleridge, "The Eolian Harp," ln. 27.
85. Darwin, *Temple of Nature*, Canto II, lns. 19–22.
86. Rabinbach, *The Human Motor*, 92. Rabinbach uses the phrase "transcendental materialism" specifically in connection with the theory of energy conservation, which made energy the common basis of all things, and the corresponding social and technological concepts of work, labor power and industry.
87. Herder, *Outlines*, 113.
88. Coleridge, *Aids to Reflection*, 393.
89. Wordsworth, "Lines Composed," lns. 101, 102, *Complete Poetical Works*.
90. Herder, *Outlines*, 99.
91. Darwin, *Zoonomia*, 2: no. 129, 44.
92. Wordsworth, "The Recluse," ln. 793, *Complete Poetical Works*.
93. Coleridge, "The Eolian Harp," lns. 44–47.

Bibliography

Abernethy, John. *Introductory Lectures, Exhibiting Some of Mr. Hunter's Opinions Respecting Life and Diseases, Delivered before the Royal College of Surgeons, London, in 1814 and 1815*. London: Longman, 1823.

Aldini, Giovanni. *An Account of the Late Improvements in Galvanism*. London: Cuthill and Martin, 1803.

Bevilacqua, Fabio. "Helmholtz's Ueber die Erhaltung der Kraft: The Emergence of a Theoretical Physicist." In *Hermann Von Helmholtz and the Foundations of Nineteenth-Century Science*, edited by David Cahan, Ch.7. Berkley and Los Angeles: University of California Press, 1993.

Bichat, Marie-François-Xavier. *Recherches physiologiques sur la vie et la mort*. Edited by François Magendie. Paris: Bechet jeune, 1822.

Blumenbach, Johann Friedrich. *An Essay on Generation*. Translated by A. Crichton. London: T. Cadell, Faulder, Murray and Creech, 1792. Originally published as *Uber den Bildungstrieb* (Göttingen: Johann Christian Dieterich, 1789).

Brain, Robert M., and M. Norton Wise. "Muscles and Engines: Indicator Diagrams and Helmholtz's Graphical Methods." In *The Sciences Studies Reader*, edited by Mario Biagioli, Ch. 4. New York: Routledge, 1999.

Breitenbach, Angela. "Teleology in Biology: A Kantian Approach." *Kant Yearbook* 1 (2009): 31–56.

Burkhardt, Jr., Richard W. *The Spirit of System: Lamarck and Evolutionary Biology*. Cambridge, MA: Harvard University Press, 1995.

Cabanis, Pierre-Jean-Georges. *Rapports de physique et du moral de l'homme*. Paris: Caille et Ravier, 1815 [1808].

Canguilhem, Georges. "Note sur les rapports de la théorie cellulaire et de la philosophie de Leibniz." In *La connaissance de la vie*. Paris: J. Vrin, 1998.

Cardwell, D.S.L. *From Watt to Clausius: The Rise of Thermodynamics in the Early Industrial Age*. London: Heineman, 1971.

Coleridge, Samuel Taylor. *Aids to Reflection in the Formation of a Manly Character on the several grounds of Prudence, Morality and Religion*. London: Hurst, Chance & Co., 1831 [en2nd ed.]).

Coleridge, Samuel Taylor. *Biographia Literaria; Or, Biographical Sketches of My Literary Life and Opinions*. New York: William Gowans, 1852 [1817].

Coleridge, Samuel Taylor. "The Eolian Harp." In *Selected Poetry*, edited by H. J. Jackson, 27–29. Oxford: Oxford University Press, 2009.

Coleridge, Samuel Taylor. "On the Passions" (1828). In *Shorter Works and Fragments*, edited by H.J. Jackson and J.R. de J. Jackson. London: Routledge, 1995.

Corsi, Pietro. "Biologie." In *Lamarck: Philosophe de la nature*. Edited by Pietro Corsi, Jean Gayon, Gabriel Gohau and Stéphane Tirard, 37–64. Paris: Presses universitaires de France, 2006.

Cuvier, Georges. "Eloge de M. de Lamarck, lu a l'Académie des sciences, le 26 novembre 1832." In *Memoires de l'Académie Royale des Sciences de l'Institut de France*, vol. XIII, i–xxxi. Paris, 1835.

Cuvier, Georges. *Le Règne animal distribué d'après son organization*. Brussels: Louis Hauman, 1836 [1816]).

Darwin, Erasmus. *Botanic Garden; A Poem, in Two Parts [...] with Philosophical Notes*. London: J. Johnson, 1791.

Darwin, Erasmus. *The Temple of Nature; or, the Origin of Society: A Poem, with Philosophical Notes*. London: Jones and Co., 1825 [1802].

Darwin, Erasmus. *Zoonomia, or the Laws of Organic Life*. London: J. Johnson, 1794–96.

Davy, Humphry. "Discourse Introductory to a Course of Lectures on Chemistry" (1802). In *The Collected Works of Sir Humprhy Davy*, edited by John Davy, 2:311–326. London: Smith, Elder, 1839–40.

Davy, Humphry. "The Sons of Genius." In *The Collected Works of Sir Humphry Davy*, edited by John Davy, 1: 24–27. Bristol: Thoemmes Press, 2000.

Dear, Peter. *The Intelligibility of Nature: How Science Makes Sense of the World*. Chicago: University of Chicago Press, 2006.

Edwards, Pamela. *The Statesman's Science: History, Nature and Law in the Political Thought of Samuel Taylor Coleridge*. New York: Columbia University Press, 2004.

Fulford, Tim, ed. *Romanticism and Science, 1773–1833*. London: Routledge, 2002.

Galvani, Luigi. *Commentary on the Effects of Electricity on Muscular Motion*. Translated by Margaret Glover Foley and edited by I. Bernard Cohen. Norwood: Burndy Library, 1953 [1791].

Gigante, Denise. *Life: Organic Form and Romanticism*. New Haven: Yale University Press, 2009.

Ginsborg, Hannah. "Kant on Aesthetic and Biological Purposiveness." In *Reclaiming the History of Ethics: Essays for John Rawls*, edited by Andrews Reath, Barbara Herman, and Christine Korsgaard, 329–360. Cambridge: Cambridge University Press, 1997.

Ginsborg, Hannah. "Kant on Understanding Organisms as Natural Purposes." In *Kant and the Sciences*, edited by Eric Watkins, 231–258. Oxford: Oxford University Press, 2001.

Ginsborg, Hannah. "Kant's Biological Teleology and its Philosophical Significance." In *A Companion to Kant*, edited by Graham Bird, Ch. 29. Oxford: Blackwell, 2006.

Ginsborg, Hannah. "Lawfulness Without a Law: Kant on the Free Play of Imagination and Understanding." *Philosophical Topics* 25, no. 1 (1997): 37–81.

Ginsborg, Hannah. "Oughts Without Intentions: A Kantian Perspective on Biological Teleology." In *Kant's Theory of Biology*, edited by Ina Goy and Eric Watkins. Berlin: De Gruyter, forthcoming.

Goethe, Johann Wolfgang von. "A Commentary on the Aphoristic Essay 'Nature.'" 24 May 1828. In *Scientific Studies (Goethe: The Collected Works*, Vol. 12), edited and translated by Douglas Miller, 6–7. Princeton: Princeton University Press, 1995.

Goethe, Johann Wolfgang von. "Excerpt from Studies for a Physiology of Plants." In *Scientific Studies (Goethe: The Collected Works*, Vol. 12), edited and translated by Douglas Miller, 73–75. Princeton: Princeton University Press, 1995.

Goethe, Johann Wolfgang von. "History of the Printed Brochure" (1817). In *Goethe's Botanical Writings*, edited and translated by Bertha Mueller, 170–176. Woodbridge, CT: Oxbow Press, 1989.

Goethe, Johann Wolfgang von. "The Influence of Modern Philosophy." In *Scientific Studies (Goethe: The Collected Works*, Vol. 12), edited and translated by Douglas Miller, 28–30. Princeton: Princeton University Press, 1995.

Goethe, Johann Wolfgang von. *The Metamorphosis of Plants [Versuch die Metamorphose der Pflanzen zu erklären*, 1790]. Translated by Douglas Miller and edited by Gordon L. Miller. Cambridge, MA: MIT Press, 2009.

Goethe, Johann Wolfgang von. "Vorarbeiten zu einer Physiologie der Pflanzen" (1797). In *Werke*: II. Abtheilung 6. Band, 303–304. Weimar, 1891.

Golinksi, Jan. "The Literature of the New Sciences." In *The New Cambridge History of English Literature: The Romantic Period*, edited by James Chandler. Cambridge: Cambridge University Press, forthcoming.

Gould, Stephen Jay. "Foreword." In *Georges Cuvier: An Annotated Bibliography of his Published Works*, edited by Jean Chandler Smith. Washington, DC: Smithsonian, 1993.

Guyer, Paul. "Organisms and the Unity of Science." In *Kant and the Sciences*, edited by Eric Watkins, 259–81. Oxford: Oxford University Press, 2001.

Guyer, Paul, and Allen W. Wood, eds. *The Cambridge Edition of the Works of Immanuel Kant: Correspondence*. Cambridge: Cambridge University Press, 1999.

Helmholtz, Hermann von. "On the Conservation of Force" (1862–63). Translated by Edmund Atkinson. In *Science and Culture: Popular and Philosophical Essays*, edited by David Cahan, Ch. 5. Chicago: University of Chicago Press, 1995. Originally published as *Über die Erhaltung der Kraft: Eine physikalische Abhandlung*. Berlin: Reimer, 1847.

Helmholtz, Hermann von. "On the Interaction of the Natural Forces" (1854). Translated by Edmund Atkinson. In *Science and Culture: Popular and Philosophical Essays*, edited by David Cahan, 18–45. Chicago: University of Chicago Press, 1995. Originally published as *Über die Erhaltung der Kraft: Eine physikalische Abhandlung*. Berlin: Reimer, 1847.

Herder, Johann Gottfried. *Outlines of a Philosophy of the History of Man*. Translated by T. Churchill. New York: Bergman, 1966. Originally published as *Ideen zur Philosophie der Geschichte der Menschheit*. 1784.

Hogg, Thomas Jefferson. *The Life of Percy Bysshe Shelley*. London: J.M. Dent and Son, 1933 [1832].

Humboldt, Alexander von. *Expériences sur le galvanisme et en général sur l'irritation des fibres musculaires et nerveuses*. Paris, 1799.

Kant, Immanuel. *Critique of Judgment*. Translated by James Creed Meredith and edited by Nicholas Walker. Oxford: Oxford University Press, 2007 [1790].

KantmImmanuel. *Der einzig mögliche Beweisgrund zu einer Demonstration des Daseyns Gottes [The One Possible Basis for a Demonstration of the Existence of God]*. Königsberg: Kanter, 1763.

Kant, Immanuel. *Gedanken von der Wahren Schätzung der lebendigen Kräfte* [Thoughts on the True Estimation of Living Forces]. 1747.

Kant, Immanuel. *Universal Natural History and Theory of the Heavens*. Translated by Ian Johnston. Virginia: Richer Resources, 2008. Originally published in German as *Allgemeine Naturgeschichte und Theorie des Himmels* (Königsberg und Leibzig: Johann Friederich Petersen, 1755).

Keddie, William, ed. *Anecdotes Literary and Scientific*. London: Charles Griffin, 1863.

King-Hele, Desmond. "Romantic Followers: Wordsworth, Coleridge, Keats and Shelley." In *The Essential Writings of Erasmus Darwin*, edited by Desmond King-Hele, Ch. 11. London: MacGibbon & Kee, 1968.

Kuhn, Thomas S. "Energy Conservation as an Example of Simultaneous Discovery." In *Critical Problems in the History of Science*, edited by Marshall Clagett, 321–356. Madison: University of Wisconsin Press, 1957.

Lamarck, Jean-Baptiste. "Biologie, ou considérations sur la nature, les facultés, les développements et d'origine des corps vivants" (c. 1809–1815). *Muséum national d'histoire naturelle*, Bibliothèque centrale. Ms 742, tome I.

Lamarck, Jean-Baptiste. *Discours d'ouverture prononcé le 21 floréal an 8*. Paris: Déterville, 1801.

Lamarck, Jean-Baptiste. *Histoire naturelle des animaux sans vertèbres*. Paris: Déterville, 1815–1822.

Lamarck, Jean-Baptiste. *Hydrogéologie, ou Recherches sur l'influence qu'ont les eaux sur la surface du globe terrestre*. Paris: Chez l'Auteur, 1802.

Lamarck, Jean-Baptiste. *Mémoires de physique et d'histoire naturelle*. Paris: chez L'auteur, 1797.

Lamarck, Jean-Baptiste. *Philosophie zoologique*. Paris: Dentu, 1809.

Lamarck, Jean-Baptiste. *Recherches sur les causes des principaux faits physiques*. Paris: Maradan, 1794.

Lamarck, Jean-Baptiste. *Recherches sur l'organisation des corps vivans*. Paris: Maillard, 1802.

Larson, James L. "Vital Forces: Regulative Principles or Constitutive Agents? A Strategy in German Physiology, 1786–1802." *Isis* 70, no. 2 (June 1979): 235–249.

Lawrence, Christopher. "The Power and the Glory." In *Romanticism and the Sciences*, edited by Andrew Cunningham and Nicholas Jardine, 589–595. Cambridge: Cambridge University Press, 1990.

Lawrence, William. *Lectures on Physiology, Zoology and the Natural History of Man*. London: J. Smith, 1823.

Lenoir, Timothy. *The Strategy of Life: Teleology and Mechanics in Nineteenth Century German Biology*, Studies in the History of Modern Science 13. Dordrecht: D. Reidel, 1982.

Levere, Trevor. "Coleridge and the Sciences." In *Romanticism and the Sciences*, edited by Andrew Cunningham and Nicholas Jardine, 295–306. Cambridge: Cambridge University Press, 1990.

Mach, Ernst. *History and Root of the Principles of the Conservation of Energy*. 1871.

Maienschein, Jane. "Epigenesis and Preformationism." In *The Stanford Encyclopedia of Philosophy (Spring 2012 Edition)*, edited by Edward N. Zalta. http://plato.stanford.edu/archives/spr2012/entries/epigenesis/.

Mayer, Julius Robert. "Bemerkungen über die Kräfte der unbelebten Natur." In *Annalen der Chemie und Pharmazie*, Bd. 42 (1842).

McLaughlin, Peter. *Kant's Critique of Teleology in Biological Explanation*. Lewiston, NY: Edwin Mellen Press, 1990.

Micheli, Giuseppe. *The Early Reception of Kant's Thought in England: 1785–1805*. London: Routledge, 1999 [1931].

Müller, Johannes. *Elements of Physiology*. Translated by William Baly and edited by John Bell. Philadelphia: Lea and Blanchard, 1843. Originally published as *Handbuch der Physiologie des Menschen für Vorlesungen*, 2 Vols. Coblenz: Verlag von J. Hölscher, 1837–1840.

Müller, Johannes. *Zur vergleichenden Physiologie des Gesichtssinnes des Menschen und der Thiere, nebst einem Versuch über die Bewegung der Augen und über den menschlichen Blick*. Leipzig: C. Cnobloch, 1826.

Newton, Isaac. *Opticks, or A Treatise of the Reflections, Refractions, Inflections & Colors of Light*. New York: Dover, 1952 [1st edition 1706]).

Rabinbach, Anson. *The Human Motor: Energy, Fatigue, and the Origins of Modernity*. Berkeley: University of California Press, 1992.

Reymond, Emil du Bois. *Über die Lebenskraft* (1848). In *Reden von Emil du Bois-Reymond in zwei Bänden*, edited by Estelle du Bois-Reymond. Leipzig: Veit & Comp, 1912.

Richards, Robert J. *The Romantic Conception of Life: Science and Philosophy in the Age of Goethe*. Chicago: University of Chicago Press, 2002.

Richardson, Alan. *British Romanticism and the Science of Mind*. Cambridge: Cambridge University Press, 2001.

Robinson, Henry Crabb. *Diary, Reminiscences and Correspondence*. London: Macmillan and Co., 1869.

Rothschuh, Karl E. *History of Physiology*. Edited and translated by Guenter B. Risse. New York: Huntington, 1973. Originally published in German as *Geschichte der Physiologie* (1953).

Rudwick, M.S.J. *Georges Cuvier, Fossil Bones, and Geological Catastrophes: New Interpretations of Primary Texts*. Chicago: University of Chicago Press, 1997.

Saint-Hilaire, Étienne Géoffroy. *Philosophie anatomique*. Paris: J.-B. Baillère, 1818.

Saumarez, Richard. *A New System of Physiology*. London, 1799.

Scruton, Roger. *Kant: A Very Short Introduction*. Oxford: Oxford University Press, 2001.

Seymour, Miranda. *Mary Shelley*. London: John Murray, 2000.

Shelley, Mary. Introduction to *Frankenstein*, Third Edition (1831), by Mary Shelley and edited by J. Paul Hunter, 169–173. New York: Norton, 1996.

Sleigh, Charlotte. "Life, Death and Galvanism." *Studies in History and Philosophy of Biological and Biomedical Sciences* 29C (1998): 219–248.

Smith, Crosbie. *The Science of Energy: Cultural History of Energy Physics in Victorian Britain*. London: Heinemann, 1998.

Smith, Justin Erik Halldór. "Leibniz's Hylomorphic Monad." *History of Philosophy Quarterly* 19, no. 1 (January 2002): 21–42.

Steigerwald, Joan, ed. *Kantian Teleology and the Biological Sciences*, special issue of *Studies in the History and Philosophy of Science, Part C: Studies in the History and Philosophy of the Biological and Biomedical Sciences*, Vol. 37, issue 4 (2006).

Tresch, John. *The Romantic Machine: Utopian Science and Technology After Napoleon*. Chicago: University of Chicago Press, 2012.

Ure, Andrew. "An Account of Some Experiments Made on the Body of a Criminal Immediately after Execution, with Physiological and Practical Observations." *Journal of Science and the Arts* 6 (1819): 283–294.

Wordsworth, William. *The Complete Poetical Works*, edited by John Morley. London: Macmillan, 1888.

Sensibility and Organic Unity: Kant, Goethe, and the Plasticity of Cognition

Dalia Nassar

University of Sydney, Sydney, Australia

In 1796 Friedrich Schiller famously declared that there are two kinds of poets, those who "will *be* nature" and those who "will *seek* lost nature."[1] He called the former "naïve," identified them with ancient writers, and described their works as more concrete and sensuously immediate. The latter he termed "sentimental" poets, poets of the modern era, whose estrangement from nature went hand in hand with their greater emphasis on reflection and freedom. For Schiller, however, Goethe presented a strange paradox: a modern poet who was nonetheless naïve.

The notion that Goethe's poetry and his approach to the natural world in general are "naïve" has stuck, and become the accepted view of Goethe as both poet and thinker. Indeed, Goethe seems to have agreed with his friend's characterization, writing some years later that while Schiller "preached the gospel of freedom," he, Goethe, "defended the rights of nature" (MA 12, 97).[2] In turn, Goethe was often critical of philosophical abstractions, because they had no sense for the concrete, and even declared himself to lack possession of the "organ" necessary for philosophy (MA 12, 94).

However, in spite of Goethe's self-proclaimed incapacity for philosophical reflection, there is ample evidence to the contrary. Not only did he seriously engage with Spinoza, Kant, Schelling, and Hegel, but he was also in dialogue with some of the most influential thinkers of the time, including Jacobi, Herder, and Niethammer. Most significantly, his encounter with Schiller did not – as might appear – result in a rejection of philosophy or a refusal to undertake critical enquiry. The opposite was the case: Goethe and Schiller's famous 1794 meeting prompted Goethe to offer more systematic explications of his methodology and undertake further study of Kantian philosophy.

Nonetheless, Goethe's views were decisively different from those of the philosophers who surrounded him, and this difference concerned the role of sensibility in knowledge. In his *Maxims and Reflections*, Goethe writes that "we are adequately equipped for all our genuine earthly needs if we will trust our senses, and develop them in such a way that they continue to prove worthy of our confidence" (MA 17, 918). And again, he remarks that "the senses do not deceive; it is judgment that deceives" (MA 17, 917). In deep contrast to his contemporaries, who were largely concerned with establishing pure forms of thought, elaborating their relationships, and, as Fichte put it, offering a "pragmatic history of the spirit," Goethe was convinced that sensible knowledge must be incorporated into philosophy, and more strikingly, that sensibility provides the foundation for all knowledge.[3]

It is thus not surprising to note that Goethe's criticism of philosophy revolved around what he considered to be a misunderstanding of sensibility and a tendency toward abstraction. German philosophy, he repeatedly remarked, lacked a sense for sensibility. Or, as he put it in the *Conversations with Eckermann*,

> in German philosophy there were still two great things to be done. Kant composed the *Critique of Pure Reason*, through which an infinite amount has occurred. However, the circle is not yet closed. Someone capable, someone significant, is needed to write the critique of *sensibility* [*Sinne*] and human understanding, and then, if this is done well, we would have nothing more to wish from German philosophy. (MA 19, 244)[4]

Goethe's claim here can be read in two different ways. On the one hand, it can mean that Kant offered a critique of reason, and now someone must offer a critique of sensibility and understanding. On the other hand, it can imply the more interesting and compelling claim, namely, that Kant's critique *made evident the need for a more comprehensive investigation of sensibility and understanding*. I consider this second interpretation to be more compelling, because it takes account of Kant's accomplishment in a more convincing way. After all, the *Critique of Pure Reason* was not simply an investigation of the faculty of reason, but also of sensibility and the understanding. Thus, for Goethe to claim that Germans have not yet produced a critique of sensibility and understanding seems hard to fathom. By contrast, the claim that Kant did not offer an *adequate* account of sensibility and understanding – and thus calls us to produce one – makes quite a bit more sense. But how exactly are we to understand this claim, and in what ways does it relate to Goethe's own project and his emphasis on sensibility? In the following, I want to answer this question.

My argument is two-fold. First, I want to illustrate that in his attempt to create a space for organisms (i.e., living beings) within his system, Kant reveals both a deficiency and a tension in his earlier conception of experience and suggests (albeit entirely implicitly) that experience is much more plastic than he had previously argued.[5] Goethe picks up on Kant's suggestive insights and develops his theoretical account of knowledge in light of them. He discerns an affinity between Kant's approach in the *Critique of Judgment* and his own, specifically with regard to the structure of organisms and the teleological principle or purposiveness. He also comes to see that any attempt to understand organic beings involves a methodological difficulty, which Kant pointed to but did not resolve. Nonetheless, Kant's findings spurred Goethe to develop a methodology that sought to resolve the tension that Kant had uncovered.

My aim is thus to trace a "leading thread" from the *Critique of Judgment* to Goethe that involves a shift from a conceptual framework, in which a priori concepts furnish necessity and thereby science, to a framework in which sensible experience plays a far more significant and determining role in the formation of knowledge. Although this shift was not enacted by Kant, his elaboration of organic unity or organisms paved the way for this transformation. By considering both the methodological difficulties that Kant encounters in his attempt to articulate the structure of organisms and Goethe's response to these difficulties, my goal is to locate a specific trajectory in the history of nineteenth-century philosophy, in which empirical experience and sensibility play a far more significant role than otherwise acknowledged.

1. The challenge of thinking organism in the *Critique of Judgment*

Kant is most well known as a transcendental idealist, who developed a regressive methodology, which begins with the pure concepts of the understanding and seeks to justify them by demonstrating their necessity for experience.[6] Thus, although sensibility plays a significant role in his epistemology, it cannot offer any cognitive insight without the pure concepts of the understanding, for, as Kant famously put it, the intuitions given through the pure forms of sensibility are on their own meaningless.[7] Rather, to gain meaning, and moreover, achieve objective validity, they must be determined by the pure concepts of the understanding.[8]

By contrast, Kant's concern in the *Critique of Judgment* is not with developing and justifying the pure concepts of the understanding. Rather, his goal is to offer a richer account of experience – one which can adequately portray and explicate the diversity of the natural world. Because his concerns in the third *Critique* are decisively different from those of the first, his starting point is also different. Instead of beginning with the pure forms which structure our experience, Kant begins with the wealth of experience, and notes the inherent inability of the pure concepts to grasp it. Thus in the Introduction he writes:

> In spite of all the uniformity of things in nature in accordance with the universal laws […] the specific diversity of the empirical laws of nature together with their effects could nevertheless be so great that it would be impossible for our understanding to discover in them an order that we can grasp, to divide its products into genera and species in order to use the principles for the explanation and the understanding of one for the explanation and comprehension of the other as well, and to make an interconnected experience out of material that is for us confused (strictly speaking, only infinitely diverse and not fitted for our power of comprehension). (AA 5: 185)[9]

In the *Critique of Pure Reason*, Kant laid out the a priori structures of experience, which determine nature according to universal laws. In so doing, however, he left "the specific diversity of the empirical laws of nature" underdetermined. That is to say, the specific character of a thing, its individual structure, was not (could not be) determined by the universal laws of nature and experience. Thus, what distinguishes an individual, Kant explicates in the first *Critique*, is its spatial location (A264/B320). This is because all objects of external intuition must be given through the pure form of space, such that the a priori distinguishing mark of an object – what grants it individuality – is its location in space. This, however, leaves the specificity or particularity of the object underdetermined. Furthermore, spatial determination alone cannot non-arbitrarily determine something as an individual with particular properties. For, along the series of space-filling parts we do not know where to "stop" and distinguish a thing as a unified being or event. What would be the criterion by which to distinguish which set of parts (i.e., properties) counts as an object, and which set of parts does not? What, in other words, allows us to discern parts as not mere space-filling matter, but as participating in an object or event?

The inability to determine the particular – to recognize the *necessity* of an object's properties and determine the object's *distinctiveness* or *particularity* – was not a problem for Kant until the *Critique of Judgment*, and for good reason. In previous work, Kant was not concerned with classifying and ordering empirical nature or with distinguishing the structures of living beings. Instead, his goal was to elaborate the necessary and universal structures of experience, and thereby nature. These structures, as he argues as early as *The Only Possible Basis for the Proof of God's Existence* (1763), describe only one of the two orders of nature, namely the order that functions according to mathematical physical laws. The other order, which he identifies with organic or living beings, functions independently of these laws, and is therefore "contingent" (AA 2: 107.14–22). In the *Metaphysical Foundations of Natural Science* (1786), Kant reiterates this view by distinguishing "*proper* science" as the domain in which "certainty is apodictic," and contrasting it to "cognition that can contain mere empirical certainty" (AA 4: 468). Apodictic certainty, he elaborates, is achievable only through mathematics: "In any special doctrine of nature there can be only as much *proper* science as there is *mathematics* therein" (AA 4: 470). This means that entities which appear to function independently of the mathematical physical laws are "contingent" and thus irrelevant from the perspective of proper science.

In the *Critique of Judgment*, then, Kant turns to precisely that realm (or order of nature) which he had previously sidelined. Whatever his motivations might have been, one thing is certain: Kant realized that within the framework laid out in the *Critique of Pure Reason*, certain entities and therefore certain aspects of experience remained underdetermined and unintelligible or, as he puts it in the third *Critique*, "inexplicable." The goal of the third *Critique* is to make these entities and experiences intelligible – that is to say, to grant *necessity* to what is otherwise *contingent*. In order to do so, Kant invokes the principle of purposiveness. The question is: why does Kant invoke purposiveness in order to make these special entities explicable? The answer to this question lies in Kant's conceptions of unity and matter.

In the *Critique of Judgment* Kant distinguishes "material unity" from what he calls a "determinate unity." "Matter," Kant writes, is "a multitude of things, which *by itself can provide no determinate unity of composition* [...]" (AA 5: 377) and adds that "if the cause is sought merely in *matter*, as an *aggregate* of numerous substances *external* to one another, the unity of the principle for the intrinsically purposive form of its formation is entirely lacking" (AA 5: 421). While a material unity is an aggregate composed of substances that are only "externally" related, a "determinate unity" is internally related through a "purposive form." To grasp Kant's distinctions, it is necessary to understand what he means by matter.

In his pre-critical writings, Kant distinguishes material and non-material (i.e., spiritual) entities in terms of their activity and entailing unity. Matter is essentially space-filling and thus impenetrable. This means that it exerts a force on other material beings, such that they cannot occupy the same space. Matter, in other words, has repulsive force.[10] For this reason, Kant goes on, material entities are determined by their location in space, and material unities are composed of parts which happen to share the same space. The activity and unity of matter stands in contrast to "internal activity," which involves spontaneity (AA 2: 327–8). Thus, Kant maintains, "the principle of life," which requires that a thing have "an inner capacity to determine itself," can only be found in "an immaterial nature" (AA 2: 327). Put differently, the capacity for spontaneity, generation, and reproduction cannot be attributed to matter because material beings only exhibit "external" activity – i.e., activity determined by their location in space.

This basic idea remains throughout Kant's later writings. Thus in the *Mrongovius Metaphysics* he claims that "all matter is lifeless, has no faculty for determining itself, and the principle of life is something other than matter. For every matter remains in motion or at rest until it is altered by something else. Matter thus has mere receptivity or passivity. The principle of life, however, is spontaneity or the faculty of determining oneself from inner principles" (AA 29: 913).[11] In the *Metaphysical Foundations*, Kant similarly maintains that "matter, as mere object of outer senses, has no other determinations except those of external relations in space, and therefore undergoes no change except by motion" (AA 4: 543). For this reason, he concludes, matter is essentially "lifeless" (AA 4: 544). Life belongs only to substances that determine themselves or act in accordance with an internal principle (ibid.).

The key difference between material unities and non-material unities (non-living and living beings respectively) thus concerns the nature of the activity in which each participates. Living beings exhibit an internal activity, i.e., an activity that cannot be reduced by location in space or the laws of motion. For this reason, life is the realm of contingency, the realm that functions independently of the mathematical physical laws. But how exactly do these living beings function, and what are the characteristics that distinguish them from non-living matter? In other words: what kind of activity and unity do living beings display that non-living beings do not?

On the basis of Kant's conception of matter, there are at least three answers to this question. First, given that a material unity is a unity of parts that are merely spatially distinct – i.e., their distinction is simply determined by their spatial difference – it follows that the *qualitative diversity* of the parts, i.e., their specific function within the unity, plays no role in material unity. In other words, the *particularity* of the parts, their *necessity* within the unity (why *these* properties and not others), is left undetermined (i.e., contingent). Second, because these internal differences are irrelevant to material unity, the unity itself must be *extrinsic* to the distinctive parts and their relations. It is an external unity in the sense that the unity has nothing to do with the internal differences (with the *particularity* of the parts). Finally, a "material whole," as Kant puts it, is composed of independently existing entities, such that it is "a product of the parts and of their forces and their capacity to combine by themselves," that is to say, it is explicable through the independent activities of its parts and not on account of their necessary relations with one another (AA 5: 408).

In contrast, a "determinate unity" with "an intrinsic purposive form" must involve internal relationality – the differing functions and qualities of the parts play a fundamental role in the formation of the unity. Thus, it is an *internally* differentiated unity, a unity that is inseparable from the distinctive functions and qualities of its parts. This implies, furthermore, that the different parts are only possible in relation to one another, and their differences are constitutive of their relations – their differences are, in other words, necessary rather than contingent. From this it follows that a determinate unity is not explicable through the independent activities of its parts, since its parts cannot exist independently of one another.

The aim of the second part of the third *Critique* is to explicate the structure of this so-called determinate unity and investigate our ability to grasp it, in spite of its apparently contingent character. The aim is, in other words, to invoke a principle that would be able to discern necessity *between* the parts and recognize how the parts *inherently* and thereby *necessarily* relate to one another. This principle, Kant maintains, is purposiveness.

In his earlier writings Kant had distinguished the two realms of nature, and argued that only the realm that is governed by the laws of physical mechanism can be considered proper science. In the third *Critique* he explicitly connects this realm to the discursive character of our intellect, contending that it is because of the way in which we cognize and experience the world that certain entities are (for us) undetermined and thereby contingent.[12] Specifically, he explains that because our intellect is discursive, it proceeds analytically from the universal to the particular, wherein the particular is subsumed under the universal concept. This means that it cannot grasp the properties of a particular object as necessary – i.e., grasp why this object is (must be) composed of these properties and not others. In other words, the discursive intellect cannot grasp the *particularity* of the particular (the particular *as* particular), and thereby leaves it underdetermined, or, as Kant puts it, "contingent." He writes, "this contingency is quite naturally found in the *particular*, which the power of judgment is to subsume under the *universal* of the concepts of the human understanding; for through the universal of *our* (human) understanding the particular is not determined, and it is contingent in how many different ways distinct things that nevertheless coincide in a common character can be presented to our perceptions" (AA 5: 406).

This means that we cannot grasp a unity that is composed of internally differentiated and inherently connected parts – i.e., a unity in which the parts are *necessarily* related to one another and the whole. Rather, the only unity the discursive intellect can grasp is composed of externally related parts, which are independent of one another and the whole, such that the unity between part and whole (particular and universal) is purely contingent. In other words, the discursive intellect can only grasp a material unity.

In spite of this, Kant maintains that we can invoke a principle – namely purposiveness – in order to make explicable (and thereby grant necessity to) these otherwise contingent and underdetermined unities. Now, while it is clear that Kant needs to invoke a principle that does not reduce all relations to external relations and all activity to motion in space (i.e., the mechanical principle), it is not clear why he turns to purposiveness specifically. Indeed, Kant's turn to purposiveness seems to be based on a disjunctive argument, with a hidden major premise: *either* mechanism *or* teleology. Not mechanism, therefore, teleology.

Kant's argument is that the idea of purposiveness is based on an analogy between human activity (as guided by ends) and the activity of organisms. The principle of purposiveness, then, does not specifically tell us that there are *actual* beings in the world that act purposively (i.e., according to final causes), but rather helps us (by analogy) to make sense of experiences that are otherwise unintelligible. The exact relation between purposiveness and these unintelligible experiences remains, however, unclear. That is to say: to what extent is the principle of purposiveness related to our actual experience of organisms and their structure?

Some commentators suggest that it tells us very little. Hannah Ginsborg, for instance, argues that the experience of organisms is an experience of "contingency," wherein certain entities appear not to coincide with mechanical laws, and are therefore "contingent."[13] Thus, the *experience* of organisms is – on its own – entirely negative: it does *not* fit into the structure of experience and is thus left undetermined, contingent. Purposiveness, in turn, is invoked to make this otherwise inexplicable experience intelligible. This means, however, that the principle of purposiveness is ultimately distinct from the reality of organisms and our experience of them – or, as Peter McLaughlin puts it, "the concept of natural purpose is not introduced as a synonym for the organism."[14] There is, in other words, a difference between our *experience* of organisms (whatever that may be) and the concept of natural purpose. The concept is invoked purely analogically in order to make these contingent experiences intelligible.

It is understandable why the principle of purposiveness is conceived as ultimately distinct from the structure (and our experience) of organisms. After all, purposiveness is not an empirical concept that is gained through experience; rather, it is an a priori principle of the faculty of judgment (AA 5: 185). In addition, purposiveness is not a pure concept of the understanding, insofar as it is not deduced from the table of judgments and thus cannot be schematized. This means that purposiveness has a solely analogical status, and, as such, cannot be ascribed to these contingent experiences in any constitutive sense.

Yet, it is not entirely clear that Kant considered the analogy with human activity to be an ultimate justification for invoking the principle of purposiveness, for, as he writes, "strictly speaking, the organization of nature is [...] not analogous with any causality that we know" (AA 5: 375). Furthermore, he distinguishes purposiveness from other ideas of reason, insofar as the objects of purposiveness are, as he puts it, "given to us in nature." He writes:

> In the remark, we have adduced special characteristics of our cognitive faculty (even the higher one) which we may easily be misled into carrying over to the things themselves as objective predicates; but they concern ideas for which no appropriate objects can be given in experience, and which could therefore serve only as regulative principles in the pursuit of experience. It is the same with the concept of a natural end, as far as the cause of the possibility of such a predicate is concerned, which can only lie in the idea; but the *consequence that answers to it (the product) is after all given in nature* [doch in der Natur gegeben], *and the concept of a causality of the latter, as a being acting in accordance with ends, seems to make the idea of a natural end into a constitutive principle of nature; and in this it differs from all other ideas.* (AA 5: 405; emphasis added)

Purposiveness *differs from all other ideas* in that it can be applied to objects which are "given" to us in nature. Or, as Kant puts it toward the end of the *Critique of Judgment*, the concept of a natural end "can never be given a priori but only through experience [*nicht a priori, sondern nur durch die Erfahrung gegeben*] [...]" (AA 5: 476).

Similarly, Kant describes the idea of purposiveness as "occasioned [*Veranlassung*]" by experience. Thus, in Section 66, he speaks of the principle in the following way: "As for what occasions it, this principle is of course to be derived from experience, that is, experience of the kind that is methodically undertaken and is called observation [*Dieses Prinzip ist zwar seiner Veranlassung nach von Erfahrung abzuleiten, nämlich derjenigen, welche methodisch angestellt wird und Beobachtung heißt*]" (AA 5: 376). This seems to point to a stronger relation between the concept of purposiveness and our experience of the structure of organisms. In other words, the analogical function of purposiveness does not play a purely heuristic role – an *as if* characterization that is not based on or "occasioned" by the actual experience. Rather, the concept of purposiveness appears to bear a strong relationship to experience and is appropriately applied in relation to methodical observation.

Kant emphasizes that while there are three different concepts of purposiveness, only one of them makes something intelligible that is otherwise unintelligible. This notion of purposiveness, which he terms *internal purposiveness*, applies to a "special class" of objects, namely organisms, and makes them explicable (AA 5: 382). In contrast, formal and relative purposiveness reveal useful relationships, without, however, being necessary in order to explicate the structure of the objects under consideration.

The unity of geometrical figures exhibits formal purposiveness because a geometrical figure – such as a circle – can offer solutions to a host of problems, and is therefore useful. For this reason, it is a kind of purpose. However, Kant notes, the usefulness of the circle is something that I introduce to it, i.e., through my own way of representing something externally (in space). This means, he goes on, that "I am not instructed empirically about this purposiveness by the object, and consequently do not need for this purposiveness any particular end outside of me in the object" (AA 5: 365). In other words, the useful or purposive character of a circle has to do with my specific capacity for intuition, and with the way in which I put the circle to use. There is nothing in the circle itself (in the concept of the circle) that would require me to put it to this use; the concept of the circle is thus not equivalent to its use or purpose. Furthermore, while it adds useful knowledge to my understanding of a geometrical figure, the concept of purpose in this instance does not actually render it intelligible.

Means-ends relations within nature (such as ecosystems or habitats) exhibit relative purposiveness, because they bring about useful or advantageous relations. As such, however, they are not necessary. Kant provides the example of the environment created by the receding of the sea in northern Europe to explain what he means. The sandy soil deposits left behind, which were useless for cultivation, were particularly advantageous for pine trees. Does this mean that the effect or end (the growth of pine trees) determined the cause (the recession of the sea)? In other words, was the sea acting in order to bring about the pine trees? Kant's response is twofold. First, he maintains that although in many environments the confluence of advantageous elements working toward one end is admirable, one cannot judge these relations teleologically. This is because the cause (the receding of the sea) would have to be grounded in the idea of an advantage for pine trees. For this to be the case, however, we would have to assume that pine trees *must* exist, such that the sea *must act to bring them about*. Clearly, there is no such imperative. Second, the action of the sea can be explained through physical mechanism alone. In other words, we do not need to think of an end (the growth of pines) in order to understand the receding of the sea. The movement of the sea is explicable through the laws of motion.[15]

Importantly, in both these cases, Kant emphasizes that the relationships that are revealed through the application of the concept of purposiveness are not "necessary." In the geometrical figure, he explains, purposiveness is something that I *introduce*, such that the purposive relations are not necessary to the object under consideration. Similarly, the relationships within an ecosystem, while useful, do not exhibit necessity: the parts of an ecosystem can conceivably exist independently of the other parts, i.e., in a different ecosystem. This is not the case with internal purposiveness which specifically applies to organisms.

Internal purposiveness, Kant begins, should not be thought of in terms of use, advantage, or a final goal of nature, but rather as "internal form." He writes that "to judge a thing to be purposive on account of its internal form [*innere Form*] is entirely different from holding the existence of such a thing to be an end of nature [...]," and he then adds that to determine ends "far exceeds all of our teleological cognition of nature; for the end of the existence of nature itself must be sought beyond nature" (AA 5: 378). By contrast, he continues, "the internal form of a mere blade of grass can demonstrate its merely possible origin in accordance with the rule of ends in a way that is sufficient for our human faculty of judging" (ibid.). The question is: in what way is this internal form "purposive," or, why does Kant invoke purposiveness in order to distinguish and articulate this internal form? The answer to this question lies in the specific structure of the organism as a living being.

Kant distinguishes two important characteristics of an organism. First, each of its parts must be connected in a necessary fashion to the proper function of the whole. Thus, all the parts act in accordance with an underlying idea or organizing principle. Importantly, this character obtains not only for organisms, but also for any structure that is developed in accordance with a final goal or end – such as a machine. On this point alone, then, an organism is not unique.

Second, a living unity must not be externally imposed (as in the case of the machine, for instance) but must be internal to each of the parts. This means that the parts cannot exist independently of one another, but rather, as Kant puts it, the parts "reciprocally produce each other" (AA 5: 373). Unlike the parts of a machine, then, the parts of an organism *produce* and *sustain* one another. For this reason, the organism is "cause and effect of itself" (AA 5: 370). It is "both an *organized* and *self-organizing* being" (AA 5: 374).

But what does it mean for every part to be both cause and effect? Kant's claim is that the organism exhibits a very particular *causal* structure, in which cause and effect are interchangeable. This clearly differs from efficient causality, in which cause and effect are distinctive and the cause necessarily precedes the effect (AA 5: 372). For in the organism, it is not only the future that is determined by the past – i.e., the effect determined by the cause – but also the past is determined by the future – the cause is determined by the effect. After all, in the same way that the formation of the fruit presupposes the formation of the flower, so also the possibility of the fruit is implied in the development of the flower. In other words, the movement forward is always accompanied by a movement backward. It is here, in the causal structure of the organism, that the necessity of the relations between the organism's parts becomes evident. For the parts to be both cause and effect means that they can only exist *in and through* one another; they do not exist otherwise. For this reason, the unity between them is not imposed from without – on the basis of their spatial location – but is internal. They are what they are – they function in a particular way – only because they stand in these particular relationship. The whole (unity) and the parts are thus absolutely interdependent and inseparable.

From this several things become clear: first, the internally differentiated unity, which Kant calls a "determinate unity," exhibits a specific causal structure that cannot be determined by the mechanical principle and efficient causality. The principle of purposiveness is invoked in order to make sense of causal relationships that appear to be otherwise unintelligible. In other words, the principle of purposiveness provides us with a causal model that can illuminate the necessary relationships in an organism. Thus the notion of purpose makes sense of an experience of necessary relationships, which appear – from the perspective of the universal laws of experience – contingent.

Now one might disagree with my interpretation, and argue that the causal structure that is specific to the principle of internal purposiveness cannot be identified with organisms (or with our experience of these "contingent" entities), since, as McLaughlin puts it, purposiveness is not synonymous with organisms. Rather, the causal structure is a heuristic tool that Kant deploys in order to make contingent or inexplicable experiences explicable. Thus, purposiveness simply tells us about ourselves, about the way we judge.

Additionally, one might argue that purposiveness as a concept or principle does not concern *temporal* structures at all, but rather is an idea of reason that concerns change or motion that is determined by a final goal. As such, it has nothing to do with what is given to sensibility or the structure of experience.[16] In other words, purposiveness is a concept that is ultimately separable from the experience of organisms. It does not tell us anything about the "internal form" of organisms; it does not articulate a specific (temporal) structure that is occasioned in experience. Rather, purposiveness is an idea of reason, which we develop and employ when – in the face of certain, mysterious experiences – we cannot employ mechanical principles.

Yet one is left to wonder why it is that we find ourselves compelled to apply non-mechanical principles to specific entities. Why, furthermore, does Kant differentiate between three kinds of purposiveness, arguing that only internal purposiveness concerns necessary relationships? In other words, an organism is determined by relationships which are qualitatively different from relationships found in other natural entities. In turn, relationships must be experienced as *necessary*, otherwise Kant would not have distinguished them from either formal or relative purposiveness or emphasized that they are not introduced by the knower.

The distinctive character of organisms – what differentiates them from other purposive entities – is the fact that their parts reciprocally determine one another. It is this characteristic that makes the relationship between the parts necessary. Lacking a structure of reciprocal determination, in which the cause and effect are interchangeable, necessity would not be achieved, and internal purposiveness would not be distinguishable from, for instance, relative purposiveness. Thus, it is the specifically *causal structure* of the organism that distinguishes it from other purposive entities, and that grants to internal purposiveness necessity. The unity of an organism is inextricably linked to a particular kind of causality and a distinctive temporal order – one that clearly differs from successive space-time.

This helps to illuminate Kant's claim that the concept of purpose differs from all other ideas of reason because its objects are given in experience. For what is given in experience is a particular causal structure that is not reducible to efficient causality. Thus, purposiveness – as the principle that illuminates this causal structure – is not entirely separable from what is given in experience. Rather, it is the conceptual tool through which a *very specific* (rather than merely "contingent") experience is brought to light. This means that the causal relationship that underlies purposiveness is fundamentally connected to our experience of organisms, such that it is in experience and through our interpretation of this experience, that we recognize a distinctive causal structure.

This line of reasoning has important implications. In the *Critique of Pure Reason*, Kant explained that sensibility provides the pure forms of space and time, which determine how we receive the sensibly given. The pure form of time is sequence in space, which means that our experience of time is necessarily successive. Furthermore, in the Transcendental Deduction, Kant argued that the first synthesis occurs when the manifold is run through successively. Prior to this, nothing is actually given to intuition.[17] In other words, an experience of a non-successive temporal structure, such as the causal structure of the organism, cannot be "given" to intuition.[18] Furthermore, and as elaborated above, the procedure of the discursive intellect dictates that only material-mechanical unities can be grasped. While the latter point more specifically eliminates the possibility of *knowing* organisms – although in light of Kant's cognitive account of experience, this is not its only implication[19] – the former point eliminates the possibility of *experiencing* organisms at all. After all, their causal structure implies a temporal structure that cannot be "given" to intuition.

Now if, as I have argued, Kant's notion of purposiveness is much closer to experience than otherwise thought, then it seems that we can *actually experience* something like a purposive causality, i.e., a non-successive causality. This means that our experience is not – as Kant had implied – limited to successive causality and ultimately material-mechanical unities. Rather, experience appears to be much more malleable and able to adjust to what is before it – and thereby grants us *positive* insight into organisms, rather than the purely negative notion of contingency (i.e., organisms as not reducible to mathematical physical laws).

Kant, however, did not pursue these suggestive claims. Nonetheless, his account of organisms paves the way for a new framework for understanding living beings and our cognitive ability to grasp them. Specifically, Kant's insight into the temporal structure of the organism leads to two important results. First, that the structures of nature *are not* the same as the a priori structures of our experience (as delineated in the first *Critique*). This means that we can no longer identify nature with the necessary structures of our cognition, and ultimately, we must grant to nature independence from our own cognitive faculties. Second, in spite of an obvious incongruity between our cognitive structures and organic beings, we have some experience of the structure of organisms. In this way, Kant invites his readers to consider *how* it is possible to experience entities whose structures differ from our own. The very fact that we can recognize them means that our cognitive faculties are much more plastic than Kant had allowed. It is this plasticity of cognition that Goethe recognized, and sought to develop.

2. Goethe and the plasticity of cognition

In his essay "Intuitive Judgment [*Anschauende Urteilskraft*]," Goethe poignantly remarks that an essential problem with Kant's methodology concerns the way in which he established the limits of knowledge. By setting limits, Goethe argued, Kant was also, and necessarily, transgressing them. He writes:

> In my effort to utilize, if not actually master, the Kantian doctrine, it sometimes occurred to me that the worthy man was proceeding roguishly and ironically, at one point appearing to set narrow limits for our cognitive capacity and at another beckoning us furtively beyond them […] Our master thus restricts his thinkers to reflective and expository judgment, sternly forbidding determinative judgment; but after driving us sufficiently into a corner and even bringing us to despair, he suddenly decides in favour of the most liberal interpretations and allows us to make what use we will of the freedom he has in some measure vouchsafed for us. (MA 12, 98)

Goethe's critique, which Hegel later levelled against Kant's methodology, clearly applies to the question of organisms. For in order to draw the limits of knowledge, Kant offers an account of what is "beyond our cognition," leaving the reader to wonder how *he* (Kant) was able to determine these inaccessible structures. In the case of the *Critique of Judgment*, this problem is more obvious, in that Kant appears to claim that through careful observation we can experience entities that are beyond our experiential limits.

For Goethe, however, this was not the only reason that Kant's framework appeared perplexing. The very thing that Kant had denied – cognition of organic beings – Goethe believed himself to have achieved. Thus, he goes on, "had I myself not ceaselessly pressed forward to the archetype, though at first unconsciously, from an inner drive; had I not even succeeded in evolving a method in harmony with Nature? What then was to prevent me from courageously embarking upon the adventure of reason, as the old gentleman of Königsberg himself calls it?" (MA 12, 99).

This last statement offers a good summary of Goethe's understanding of the Kantian system, and of his own approach to the problem. In Kant's writings, Goethe found much to praise; yet, he felt compelled to go beyond the limits that Kant had set – at first without realizing it because he was unfamiliar with Kant's work, and then later, after studying critical philosophy, by giving more thought to methodological and epistemological questions. Nonetheless, for Goethe, the Kantian problems were largely, although not exclusively, theoretical. His aim was to make explicit the methodology that he had already implicitly employed. For this reason, Goethe did not proceed –

as Kant did – to provide the necessary structures of experience *as such*, but rather he sought to identify the character of specific experiences and thereby understand what is involved in making a *particular* experience possible.

Goethe agreed with Kant that there is a "gap" between idea and experience. However, while Kant explained the gap in terms of a *general* inadequacy between the particular sensible and the universal concept, and only hinted at its connection to differences in temporal structures, Goethe saw the gap as *specifically* temporal. He outlines the problem as follows:

> This difficulty of *connecting* idea and experience presents obstacles in all scientific research: the idea is independent of space and time, while scientific research is bound by space and time. In the idea, then, simultaneous elements are intimately bound up with sequential ones, but our experience always shows them to be separate; we are seemingly plunged into madness by a natural process which we are to conceive of in idea as both simultaneous and sequential. (MA 12, 99–100)

While in the idea, successive and simultaneous are "intimately connected," in experience they are "always separated." But what exactly do these terms mean, and how is it possible – if at all – to overcome the gap between idea and experience?

Before answering this question it is important to distinguish what Goethe means here by *idea*. He does not imply a concept of the understanding, nor does he mean an idea of reason. Rather, and in line with Kant's findings, Goethe's idea denotes the organizing principle of an organism and its temporal structure. The question for Goethe thus is: how are we to grasp this organizing principle if its temporal structure is, as Kant implies, contrary to the structure of our experience?

However, unlike Kant, Goethe does not seek to determine the structures that make experience possible without reference to a particular experience. Rather, he proceeds by distinguishing the character of specific experiences, and discerning the different elements that are involved in these (much repeated and re-examined) experiences.

He begins by asking the question: what does it take to grasp a living organism? Or, how is it that I am able to grasp living beings? First, he considers what takes place in the act of observing. Observation involves distinguishing different parts and thus seeing them as distinct from – rather than in relation to – one another. However, in observing an organism, I become aware that this kind of isolated view is in fact inaccurate. My observation, then, does not simply reveal to me the different parts, but also signals to me the fact that these parts do not develop in isolation from one another, but rather in relation to one another. In observing a plant, for instance, I notice that the parts appear in sequence, from the stem to the leaf to the calyx to the flower, etc., such that they are temporally connected to one another. Furthermore, I notice that this temporal development is not only sequential but also simultaneous. A stem does not first grow, and is then followed by a leaf. Rather, leaves develop simultaneously with the stem.

However, while this exhausts what I *immediately* see before me, it does not actually *explain* what is taking place, i.e., it does not explain growth. I want to be careful here so as to avoid confusion. The point is not to explain *why* it is the case that plants develop both simultaneously and successively. This is not Goethe's goal, nor was it Kant's. Rather, the aim it to explain *how* the parts relate to one another *both* successively and simultaneously. It is thus not enough simply to *note that* the parts relate to one another in this way, but also to *grasp how* these parts relate to one another, and thus grasp growth.

But how is this to be done? For Goethe this involves the work of the imagination, precisely because it is only through the imagination that I can recreate in my mind what takes place in nature, and thereby perceive the simultaneous and successive developments at once. He describes the process as follows: I must "consider all phenomena in a certain developmental sequence and attentively follow the *transitions* forwards and backwards. Only in this way do I finally arrive at the living view of the whole, from which a concept is formed that soon will merge with the idea along an ascending line" (LA 1/8, 74).

Here we have two steps.[20] First, through the use of the imagination, I am able to present before me the transitions between the parts that I would otherwise not perceive. I am thus able to grasp a *continuity* between them: I see how each of the parts relates to the others both successively – as in the case of a fruit that succeeds a flower – and simultaneously – as in the case of a leaf and stem. This way of observation led Goethe to his notion of metamorphosis, and his view that plant development is nothing other than the bringing forth of "one part through the other," wherein the parts present "the most diverse forms through modification of a single organ" (MA 12, 29, no. 3). Each part, one can say, reflects the *history* of the plant – manifesting what preceded it and anticipating what is to come after it – and as such contains within it the whole plant.

This leads directly to the second step. After all, the goal is not simply to arrive at an understanding of the continuity between the parts and see how each part is a metamorphosis of the one that preceded it, but also to grasp the unified activity of the plant. For only in this way can one see all the parts as interrelated members of a living process. But what does it mean to grasp the unified activity, or the *underlying unity* of the distinctive parts? For Goethe this means nothing less than transforming what is given to perception and imagination into an idea.[21] He explains this transformation as follows:

> If I look at the created object, inquire into its creation, and follow this process back as far as I can, I will find a series of steps. Since these are not actually seen together before me, I must visualize them in my memory so that they form a certain ideal whole. / At first I will tend to think in terms of steps, but nature leaves no gaps, and thus, in the end, I will have to see this progression of uninterrupted activity as a whole. I can do so only by dissolving the particularity without destroying the impression itself. (WA 2/6, 303–4)[22]

Importantly, the idea here is not a static or general concept that is divested of difference and particularity. It is also not something that is imposed upon the sensibly given by the understanding. Rather, the idea emerges through an engagement with the sensibly given, and is, as Goethe puts it, an impression of the whole that does not destroy the particular. It must preserve insight of the different parts and their relations – the continuity between them – and thus grasp the differences *within* the unity. The aim is, after all, to gain insight into an internally differentiated unity.

As I have laid it out, for Kant the key problem in the encounter with living beings arose out of an incongruity between the temporal structures of our experience and those of the organism, such that it is theoretically impossible for us to have an experience of an organic unity. This incongruity is connected to a variety of incongruities – between the general and particular, between necessity and contingency – which all result from the basic incongruity that underlies the Kantian project, namely that between sensibility and the understanding.

Goethe's claim is that by beginning with perception and imagination, and developing ideas from out of what is perceived, the gap between idea and experience is overcome. Instead of commencing with the necessary conditions of experience as such, Goethe commences with (repeated and re-examined) particular experiences and asks what is involved in them. In the case of living beings, it was apparent to him that the only way we can actually distinguish living unities from mechanical unities was by grasping growth. This did not mean, however, offering an abstract explanation of the mechanism of growth, but rather overcoming the gap between successive and simultaneous that emerges from observing the plant. In other words, *understanding* means above all *remaining with what is perceived and seeking to make it meaningful and coherent.*

What exactly is implied in Goethe's approach? First, it implies a transformation in both thinking and perceiving, such that they are no longer incongruous. Thinking must become perceptive, and perceiving must become thoughtful. Or, as Goethe puts it, "my thinking is not separate from objects [...] the elements of the object, the perceptions of the object, flow into my thinking and are fully permeated by it [...] my perception itself is a thinking, and my thinking a perception" (MA 12, 306). Only in this way do we achieve a necessary "plasticity" in our thinking. For, Goethe elaborates, "if we want to arrive at a living intuition of nature, we must become as flexible and quick as the examples that nature gives us [...]" (MA 12, 13).

Goethe described his method as a "delicate empiricism, which makes itself utterly identical with the object" (MA 17, 823). This identity requires a transformation in the knower – a transformation that takes place on two levels.[23] On the one hand, the knower actively seeks to make her thinking identical with her perceiving – and thus shifts the balance in her cognition, so that it is not the concepts that determine and grant meaning to an inchoate sensibly given, but rather, thought and ideas emerge from and in light of what is perceived. On the other hand, perceiving must itself strive to become identical with what is before it; it too must achieve a certain plasticity, so as to be able to glean the dynamic, living character of an organic unity. This double transformation leads to what Goethe calls the "eye of the mind," that is, a thinking that emerges out of and is identical with perception (LA 1/9, 138).

Goethe's method clearly differs from that of the transcendental idealist. The idealist imposes upon nature the structures of the mind, and, from there, seeks to determine the laws of nature as the laws of experience. By contrast, Goethe sought to transform the structures of thought and perception so that they accord with the structures of nature.

Yet, as I have tried to show, Goethe's methodology was not naïve, and developed directly of Kantian insights. In his attempt to offer a richer conception of nature and elaborate the structure of organisms, Kant arrived at conclusions which called for further investigation into our cognitive faculties and their ability to grasp living beings. Specifically, Kant's insights into the kind of *unity* at work in organisms led to two important results. First, Kant showed that certain beings in nature exhibit structures which fundamentally differ from our own. This meant that we can no longer identify nature *with the a priori structures of our cognitive faculties* – as Kant had done in the first *Critique*. Rather, it appears that we must grant to nature an independence from these a priori structures. Second, in spite of an incongruity that results from the discursive nature of our intellect – one which limits our ability to grasp organic unities – Kant maintains that we have some experience of living beings. This experience, in turn, implies a distinctive causal structure and occasions a search for an adequate principle. In this way, Kant suggestively invited his readers to consider how it is possible for us to experience entities whose structures differ from our own. The very fact that we can recognize them meant that cognition is much more malleable and plastic than Kant had allowed. It also implied, as Goethe elaborated, that we can transform our cognitive capacities so that they become more adequate to what is before them.

With this in mind, we can briefly return to Goethe's remark, that German philosophy still lacked a philosophy of sensibility. Whether or not Goethe himself furnished or attempted to furnish this philosophy is a matter for another paper. What we can now appreciate is how the third *Critique* provided the seeds, even if unintentionally, for a philosophy of sensibility. That is to say, the *Critique of Judgment* made evident the need to rethink the nature of cognition, specifically, the relation between sensibility and understanding. For if we can experience certain non-mechanical unities, then the only question remaining is *how*. Goethe sought to answer this question by developing a methodology that placed perception at the centre. The goal, he repeatedly maintained, is to transform thought so that it becomes an organ of perception. Or, as he put it, "every new object, well contemplated, opens up a new organ of perception within us" (HA 13, 39).

Funding

The research and writing of this article was made possible through the support of the Australian Research Council DECRA Grant [DE120102402].

Notes

1. *Schillers Werke* vol. 20, 427.
2. All references to Goethe's works will be made in the body of the text and are as follows:
   MA: Johann Wolfgang Goethe, *Sämtliche Werke nach Epochen seines Schaffens* (Münchner Ausgabe).
   HA: Johann Wolfgang Goethe, *Werke* (Hamburger Ausgabe).
   FA: Johann Wolfgang Goethe, *Sämtliche Werke. Briefe, Tagebücher und Gespräche* (Frankfurter Ausgabe).
   LA: Goethe, *Die Schriften zur Naturwissenschaft.*
   WA: *Goethes Werke* (Weimarer Ausgabe).
3. Fichte, *Gesamtausgabe* 1/2, 364.
4. See also MA 17, 805.
5. See note 12 below. In the following, I will be working with the view – espoused by Henry Allison – that the categories are necessary *for all* experience, such that experience is necessarily cognitive. I agree with Allison because, as I see it, this is the only way that the B Deduction can succeed. Allison argues that the categories are necessary to provide structural unity to sensations – and it is precisely in doing this that they gain their objective validity, and the Deduction is successful. See Allison, *Kant's Transcendental Idealism*, 193ff. More recently, Michael Olson has persuasively argued for a similarly strong interpretation of the B Deduction, disagreeing with the contrasting interpretation given by Beatrice Longuenesse's *Kant and the Capacity to Judge*. See Olson, "Kant's Transcendental and Metaphysical Idealism."
6. See Ameriks, *Interpreting Kant's Critiques* and "Kant's Transcendental Deduction as a Regressive Argument."
7. The exact status of sensibility in the *Critique of Pure Reason* has long been a topic of debate, and already a point of contention during Kant's time. Reinhold in 1798 argued that the dualism that underlies Kant's distinction between sensibility (as passive and receptive) and understanding (as active and spontaneous) is deeply problematic and a unified conception of the faculties must replace Kant's heterogeneous conception. For a good summary of the recent debates on sensibility in the first *Critique*, see Manning, "The Necessity of Receptivity: Exploring a Unified Account of Kantian Sensibility and Understanding."
8. Thus Kant writes that "the manifold in a given intuition is necessarily subject to the categories" (B143).
9. All references to the *Critique of Judgment* will be made in the body of the text and are as follows:
   AA: Kant, Immanuel. *Gesammelte Schriften.*
   Reference to the *Critique of Pure Reason* will adhere to the A/B pagination.
10. See for instance *Dreams of a spirit-seer elucidated by dreams of metaphysics*, AA 2: 322.
11. See also *Volckmann Metaphysics* in *Lectures on Metaphysics*, AA 28: 441. I am grateful to Michael Olson for pointing out these passages to me.
12. Kant identifies cognition and experience in the first *Critique*, such that *all experience must be cognitive*, i.e., depends on the synthesis of the understanding and the employment of the categories. Thus, when we speak of something being beyond the limits of experience, we also mean that it is falls outside of the parameter of the categories, and vice versa, when we speak of something as being incognizable, we imply that it is outside of the limits of experience. The identification of experience and cognition in this sense is made clear in the second edition of the Transcendental Deduction, where Kant writes that "everything that may ever come before our senses must stand under all laws that arise *a priori* from the understanding alone" (B 160) and "all synthesis, through which even perception itself becomes possible, stands under the categories" (B 162) and "all possible perception, hence everything that can ever reach empirical consciousness, i.e., all appearances of nature […] stand under the categories" (B 164–5).
13. Ginsborg, "Kant on Understanding Organisms as Natural Purpose." Elsewhere Ginsborg argues that purposiveness must be understood as "conformity to normative law," which is to say that teleological judgment is a judgment of what something ought to be, in accordance with a normative standard. See Ginsborg, "Kant on Aesthetic and Biological Purposiveness." This conception of purposiveness, however, does not adequately account for the significant difference that Kant draws between natural

organisms (which are purposive) and geometrical figures or other means-ends relations which would indeed fit under the rubric of "conforming to normative law" but which Kant does not designate as purposive. See my discussion of these differences above.

14. McLaughlin, *Kant's Critique of Teleology in Biological Explanation*, 46.

15. My view is that purposiveness specifically implies final causality (and not formal causality) and must therefore be understood as concerning the extent to which the effect or end determines the cause, such that an object or an event can be thought of as purposive only when the effect (end) fully determines the cause.

16. That temporality plays a significant role in the third *Critique* and is a key distinguishing mark of organisms has not been adequately noted in the literature. Zuckert is an important exception to this, and has made a very strong case for the significance of temporal structures in both parts of the *Critique of Judgment*. She has, moreover, made the important argument that "objective time" as presented in the first *Critique* cannot adequately account for the processes that are at the heart of teleological judgments (Zuckert, *Kant on Beauty and Biology*, 15–16 and 136–138). However, she does not consider how this claim affects the relationship between the concept of purposiveness and the character or structure of our experience – i.e., she does not consider the fact that organisms, although they do not fit within the matrix of objective time, nevertheless make their "appearances" within our experience – and thus does not draw the (to my mind) necessary conclusion that the third *Critique* furnishes a significant challenge to the notion of experience elaborated in the first *Critique*. If the temporal structures explicated in the first *Critique* can only establish mechanical and efficient causality, and are not adequate to account for the temporal structures that underlie teleological processes, then we must consider how it is possible for us to have any experience or occasion to experience non-mechanical beings. This leads to the question regarding the relation between sensibility and the understanding. As noted above, in the first *Critique*, the spatio-temporal structures are determined by the successive synthesis of apprehension, which implies that sensibility is determined by the operations of the understanding. The account of temporality given in the third *Critique* however implies that sensibility may be more independent of the operations of the understanding – and may even itself play a formative role in these operations than previously thought.

17. In the B Deduction Kant argues that the receptivity of intuition on its own cannot account for the unity of the temporal structure of intuition since unification "presupposes a synthesis which does not belong to the senses but through which all concepts of space and time become possible" (B 161n). In other words, the spatio-temporal unity that is necessary for any perception is *not* provided by the receptivity of intuition, but rather by the synthesizing activity of the understanding through the synthesis of apprehension.

18. The relation between the categories and sensation – a topic which Kant discusses in Section 26 of the second part of the B Deduction (the "transcendental deduction") – is complex and controversial. It revolves around the question of whether the objects of sensation are necessarily (i.e., automatically) structured by the categories, or whether the human intellect must exercise some intentionality in order to provide them with structural unity. See note 5 above.

19. See note 12 above.

20. While I largely follow Eckart Förster's interpretation of Goethe's epistemology (see note 21 below), I emphasize two aspects of Goethe's relation to (interpretation of) Kant and transcendental philosophy, which Förster does not discuss. First, Goethe recognizes that the problem with grasping organisms as elaborated (albeit only implicitly) by Kant specifically concerns the *temporal* structure of natural ends and thus concerns the relationship between sensibility and the understanding. This, in turn, directly relates to Goethe's critique of German philosophy as having not yet produced an adequate critique of sensibility. What Goethe realized is that Kant had himself transgressed the limits of transcendental philosophy – as elaborated in the first *Critique* – by articulating a causal structure that is neither reducible to physical-mechanical explanation or knowable by the discursive intellect. Second, Goethe thematized Kant's "transgression" by elaborating the plasticity or malleability of experience, such that what appears to be unknowable within the framework of the first *Critique*, is "given" in experience in the third *Critique*.

21. Eckart Förster emphasizes that in order to perceive the idea of the plant, it is necessary not only to grasp the transitions between the parts, but also to grasp these transitions *at once*, and only then does the perception *become* an idea. See *Die 25 Jahre der Philosophie*, 263.

22. See also FA 1/24, 102.

23. Frederick Amrine offers a detailed account of the transformation of the scientist through observing and knowing nature. See "The Metamorphosis of the Scientist."

Bibliography

Allison, Henry. *Kant's Transcendental Idealism*. New Haven: Yale University Press, 2004.

Ameriks, Karl. *Interpreting Kant's Critiques*. Oxford: Oxford University Press, 2003.

Ameriks, Karl. "Kant's Transcendental Deduction as a Regressive Argument." *Kant-Studien* 69 (1978): 273–287.

Amrine, Frederick. "The Metamorphosis of the Scientist." *Goethe Yearbook* 5 (1990): 188–212.

Fichte, Johann Gottlieb. *Gesamtausgabe der Bayerischen Akademie der Wissenschaft*. Edited by R. Lauth, H. Jacob, and H. Gliwitsky. Stuttgart-Bad Cannstatt: Frommann-Holzboog, 1964–2012.

Förster, Eckart. *Die 25 Jahre der Philosophie*. Frankfurt: Klostermann, 2011.

Ginsborg, Hannah. "Kant on Aesthetic and Biological Purposiveness." In *Reclaiming the History of Ethics: Essays for John Rawls*, edited by Andrews Reath, Barbara Hermann, and Christine M. Korsgaard, 329–360. Cambridge: Cambridge University Press, 1996.

Ginsborg, Hannah. "Kant on Understanding Organisms as Natural Purpose." In *Kant and the Sciences*, edited by Eric Watkins, 231–254. Oxford: Oxford University Press, 2001.

Goethe, Johann Wolfgang von. *Die Schriften zur Naturwissenschaft*. Edited by D. Kuhn et al. Weimar: Hermann Bölhaus Nachfolger, 1947.

Goethe, Johann Wolfgang von. *Goethes Werke* (Weimarer Ausgabe). Edited by P. Raabe et al. Weimar: Hermann Böhlau, 1887–1919.

Goethe, Johann Wolfgang von. *Sämtliche Werke* (Frankfurter Ausgabe). Edited by H. Birus et al. Frankfurt: Deutscher Klassik Verlag, 1985–.

Goethe, Johann Wolfgang von. *Sämtliche Werke nach Epochen seines Schaffens* (Münchner Ausgabe). Edited by K. Richter et al. Munich: Carl Hanser, 1985–98.

Goethe, Johann Wolfgang von. *Werke* (Hamburger Ausgabe). Edited by E. Trunz et al. Hamburg: Christian Wegner Verlag, 1949–1971.

Kant, Immanuel. *Gesammelte Schriften*. Edited by Preußische Akademie der Wissenschaft. Berlin: de Gruyter, 1900–.

Longuenesse, Beatrice. *Kant and the Capacity to Judge*. Princeton: Princeton University Press, 1998.

Manning, Richard N. "The Necessity of Receptivity: Exploring a Unified Account of Kantian Sensibility and Understanding." In *Aesthetics and Cognition in Kant's Critical Philosophy*, edited by Rebecca Kukla, 61–84. Cambridge: Cambridge University Press, 2006.

McLaughlin, Peter. *Kant's Critique of Teleology in Biological Explanation: Antinomy and Teleology*. Lewiston: E. Mellen Press, 1990.

Olson, Michael. "Kant's Transcendental and Metaphysical Idealism." PhD diss., Villanova University, 2013.

Schillers Werke. *Nationalausgabe*. Edited by Norbert Oellers, at the request of the Stiftung Weimarer Klassik and Schiller-Nationalmuseums in Marbach. Stuttgart: Metzler, 2001.

Zuckert, Rachel. *Kant on Beauty and Biology: An Interpretation of the* Critique of Judgment. Cambridge: Cambridge University Press, 2007.

"Je n'ai jamais vu une sensibilité comme la tienne, jamais une tête si délicieuse!": Rousseau, Sade, and Embodied Epistemology

Henry Martyn Lloyd

University of Queensland, St. Lucia, Australia

Introduction: Rousseau, Sade, and the site of engagement

Rousseau preceded Sade: Rousseau (1712–1778) published most of his major works in two remarkably fecund years, 1761–1762[1]; Sade (1740–1814) published most of his major texts between 1791 and 1801[2]; thus there are roughly 30 years separating the two. We know that Sade owned Rousseau's major works and Sade mentions Rousseau as an important author, calling *Julie, or the New Héloïse* a "sublime book" which will "never be bettered."[3] Yet the two *oeuvres* are startlingly different, especially in their affects. In fact they seem to be the exact opposite of one another. So it is startling and perhaps somewhat controversial to claim that the Sadean *oeuvre* is in fact highly proximate to Rousseau's. This is what I shall do in this paper. More specifically, I shall argue that Sade's *oeuvre* constitutes a series of precise engagements with Rousseau on many different levels, including at the level of fundamental epistemology.

In addressing the relationship between Rousseau and Sade I do not seek to deemphasise the very substantial relationships between Sade and other key figures in his intellectual context. While I will discuss aspects of Sade's thought that are drawn from Condillac and d'Holbach, much has also been written about other figures in his context from whom he drew a great deal: Helvétius and La Mettrie are perhaps the most obvious examples.[4] Sade's *oeuvre* has most often, and most naturally, been read in the context of the "Radical" or "Libertine" Enlightenment. While much is left to be said here, this paper seeks to reconstruct the relationship between Sade and perhaps the most famous critic of the "Libertine" Enlightenment. The most obvious proximity between Rousseau and Sade is in their epistolary novels: between *Julie, or the New Héloïse* and Sade's now little-read *Aline et Valcour.*[5] In contrast, this paper will focus on questions of philosophical anthropology and theories of embodied epistemology, notions which are imbricated with – which in an ontological sense may be said to underpin – their respective literary projects.[6] At this level Rousseau and Sade agree on what they disagree on, and to do this a very great deal of agreement is first required.

Sade's *Philosophy in the Bedroom* (1795) is the tale of the initiation into libertinage of the young and virginal Eugénie by a trio of libertines led by irrepressible philosopher-hero Dolmancé. The text, in the style of much of Sade's writings, is made up of philosophical harangues interspersed with sections of typically pornographic narrative. In purely narrative terms this format is slightly awkward, and Sade typically smoothes the potentially jarring transitions from "philosophy" to "pornography" by having the philosophy serve in a very real sense as fore-play[7]: "Dear God," Eugénie declares after Dolmancé has explained to her the defects of charity and benevolence, "how your discourses inflame me!"[8] And later, following an extended discourse on the particular cruelty of women, Eugénie, incited by the speech to masturbation, calls out: "Oh Christ! You drive me wild! See what your [fucking] speeches do! [*Voilà l'effet de vos foutus propos!*]"[9] The response from Mme de Saint-Ange, one of the trio of libertines, is here significant and in a quite narrow sense it will be the object of my inquiry in this paper: "Adorable creature, never have I beheld a sensibility like yours, never so delightful a mind! [*je n'ai jamais vu une sensibilité comme la tienne, jamais une tête si délicieuse!*]"[10] I shall, in the first part of this paper, discuss the meaning of the word "sensibility" by outlining aspects of the broader discourse of sensibility within which this term operates. In the second part I shall return again to this term and broaden the discussion of the first half: I shall examine the relationship between the broader discourse of sensibility and the period's more narrowly construed sensationist epistemology and I shall address the question of various *types* of sensibility and their location in the body. It is on this ground that Sade's engagement with the epistemology of his period takes place: the body of sensibility, the affective body, is very literally the *site* of Sade's engagement with Rousseau.

The discourse of sensibility: from sensation to moral sense

In Sade philosophy *itself* serves as pornography (or at least as foreplay): the discourses literally move or stimulate his characters.[11] Unprecedented as it may appear, this *type* of response ought to be familiar to readers of eighteenth-century literature: novels of the period are littered to the point of cliché with characters being "moved" in various ways. We may take Diderot's "Éloge de Richardson" as explanatory. Lauding Richardson's *Pamela* (1740) and *Clarissa* (1748), in many ways the prototypes of the English sentimental novel and widely read and influential in France, Diderot writes:

> All that Montaigne, Charron, Rochefoucauld and Nicole put into maxims, Richardson has put into action. […] A maxim is an abstract and general rule of conduct which we are left to apply ourselves. It does not leave any sensible image in our mind: but the one who acts does so visibly. We put ourselves in his place, we become impassioned for or against him; we join with him in his role if he is virtuous; we turn away indignantly if he is unjust and vicious.[12]

Emphasising the highly emotive or affective manner in which the reader of Richardson responds to the text, Diderot continues:

> O Richardson! Whether we wish it or not, we play a part in your works, we intervene in the conversation, we approve, we apportion blame, we admire, are irritated and respond indignantly […] [In reading] my heart was in a state of permanent agitation. How good I was! How just I was! How satisfied I was with myself! When I had been reading you, I was like a man who had spent the day doing good.[13]

Diderot's "Éloge" serves as a justification for the period's philosophical novel: literary philosophy itself is *effective* insofar as it *affects* the subject, either fictive or real.

In the period it is not just for moral philosophy that this occurs but also for traditional metaphysical questions. Specifically for this paper, we may note that Eugénie's response to Dolmancé utilises a trope similar to that used in key aspects of the works of Rousseau. We can take as but one example the "Profession of Faith of a Savoyard Vicar," a largely self-standing tract inserted into *Emile* and a very important point in Rousseau's *oeuvre* as it is a "rare piece of technical philosophy."[14] I will return to some of the details of the "Profession" in the second half of this paper. Here, I want to note the reaction of the tutor to the vicar's speech. After listening to the profession, the narrator says: "The good priest has spoken with vehemence. He was moved, and so was I. I believed I was hearing the divine Orpheus sing the first hymns and teaching men the worship of the gods."[15] "Movement" in Rousseau is a good deal more reserved than in Sade: for Rousseau, time and meditation is required before the effect on the heart is known, thus the narrator's assent is not given immediately; this is in contrast to the way in which the Sadean characters generally respond. Yet the tutor declares:

> I will carry your discourse with me in my heart. I must meditate on it. If after taking careful council with myself, I remain as convinced of it as you are, you will be my final apostle and I shall be your proselyte unto death.[16]

This response illustrates the same principle as can be seen in Sade. That is, in Rousseau the effect of the Vicar's speech is literally measured by its impact on the sensibility of the heart; when Eugénie describes Dolmancé's speech with the adjective *foutu*/fucking she is also describing a literal impact. The power of the speech, the correctness of the sentiments expressed in it, are evidenced by the affect that they produce in the listener, or, in the terminology of the period, on the listener's sensibility; in fact the use of the term "sensibility" in Sade is a key indicator of the way that the Sadean text and Rousseauvian text "agree" about the terms of their disagreement.

For both Sade and Rousseau sensibility is the key epistemological operator: the term is highly charged in the context of eighteenth-century literature and philosophy. Diderot's *Encyclopédie* defines sensibility as:

> SENSIBILITY, (Morality) Delicate and tender disposition of the soul that makes it easily moved, touched.
>
> The sensibility of the soul […] imparts a kind of wisdom about propriety, and it goes farther than the penetration of the mind alone. […] Reflection can make a man of honour; but sensibility makes a man virtuous. Sensibility is the mother of humanity and of generosity; it increases worth, it helps the spirit, and it incites persuasion.[17]

This short definition of *moral* sensibility is linked to a much longer and more detailed *medical* article on the same subject written by Henri Fouquet.[18] Here sensibility is equated with the faculty of sensing in the living body: this is the realm of vitalist medicine, a movement particularly associated with the faculty of medicine at Montpellier.

It is hard to overestimate the influence of medicine on the French Enlightenment and on the *philosophes*; for the *Encyclopédie*, "the enlightenment truly *was* a medical matter."[19] Particularly for the 1765 volumes, medicine specifically meant the theories of the *médecins philosophes* of Montpellier vitalism.[20] In brief, the Vitalists' influence began when, determined to undermine the "ordinary" medicine of their day, Bordeu, Venel, and Barthez moved to Paris in the late 1740s and 1750s. Going "to school alongside Diderot, d'Holbach, and Rousseau at the Jardin Royal," they loosely joined forces with the *philosophes*, "Bordeu in particular [making] a powerful impression on the Encyclopaedist circle."[21] By the mid-eighteenth century Montpellier vitalists were active in Parisian medical journalism and publishing, in the court, and in the salons, particularly d'Holbach's. Although they never "sought to lead the *philosophes* in their campaigns against religious and philosophical tradition […] there can be no doubt that they left their mark on the Holbachian coterie."[22]

The bulk of Fouquet's article is concerned with observable phenomena, yet he begins with three pages, described by him as "metaphysical" and "speculative," that constitute a clear example of what was properly philosophical about the project of the *médecins philosophes*.[23] The breadth of the speculative concept elucidated in the article is quite astonishing and helps to explain, or at least illustrate, the power of the idea for the period. For Fouquet sensibility is:

> The faculty of feeling, the sensitive principle, or the feeling even of the parts, the base and the preserving agent of life, animality *par excellence*, the most beautiful, the most singular phenomenon of nature.[24]

Diderot, elsewhere in the *Encyclopédie*, defines sensibility simply as that which opposes death;[25] sensibility here is simply equated with life. There are two key aspects to Fouquet's medical concept. In the first instance sensibility is passive: it is the power to receive impressions.[26] The more narrow epistemological idea of sensations is then incorporated into its fold and so Fouquet's article incorporates the much shorter articles on sense and on sensation,[27] articles that constitute a relatively orthodox presentation of Locke and Condillac's sensationist epistemology.

I will return to sensationism in the second part of this paper and discuss Sade's particular use of it. My point here is narrower and is important, though a full explication of this point is outside the scope of this paper.[28] A theory of knowledge construed narrowly, or as epistemology in our contemporary sense, is, in the thought of the period, not *in itself* foundational, but is taken to be a particular instance within a broader medical anthropology. One example must suffice to elucidate the point: Fouquet's article is consistent with a self-standing text of similar theme, Antoine Le Camus's *La Médicine de l'esprit* (1769).[29] Le Camus, named *docteur régent* of the conservative Paris faculty of medicine in 1745 and appointed to the Chair of Surgery in 1766, shows in this text the extent to which Montpellier Vitalism had by the 1760s penetrated French medical thought.[30] The text clearly illustrates what it was to be a *médecin philosophe* and the extent to which the introduction of the sensing or sensitive body to the problem of knowledge allowed embodied epistemology to progressively become a central concern for philosophical medicine.[31] Like Fouquet, Le Camus begins by surveying the metaphysical foundations of medical theory, focusing particularly on the understanding and the will, and on causes in general, including the physical causes, which influence the mind.[32] Commencing with a brief introduction on understanding ("the general faculty of knowing [*connaître*]"),[33] the text rapidly arrives at the first substantive chapter, "De la Sensibilité & des Sensations."

> Before knowing, it is necessary to feel; before feeling, it is necessary to be sensitive. It is thus necessary to speak of sensibility before examining the sensations, which are the origin of our knowledge. A difficult subject, but worthy of research by any *Philosophe*. While one need not go out of oneself to grasp it, one must have pondered on the whole of nature to treat it pertinently.[34]

Sensibility is the "force of all our knowledge [*connaissances*], just as it was the source of all our passions."[35] And so for Fouquet, where the first key aspect of sensibility is passivity, the second is activity: sensibility is "the impulse which carries us towards objects, or moves us away from them."[36] Importantly, for Fouquet the difference between passive and active sensibility is not real but is found in the imagination alone: there is only one singular power which is both active and passive. In this idea resonates in one of the most important ideas of the philosophy of the French Enlightenment: "one should never separate the idea of the physical from the idea of the moral."[37] It is worth briefly noting that in unifying activity and passivity in the single power of sensibility, the *médecins philosophes* are resolving what Lisa Shapiro has described as a tension in Locke between a conception of experience as passive, instrumental, or "disembodied," and a conception of affective or "immersed" responses.[38] That is, sensibility is a general property of living beings and becomes a "unifier" which brings together the active properties, including those traditionally ascribed to the mind, with the passive or instrumental properties of the body.[39] As the ontological basis of the ability to be affected, sensibility incorporates the entirety of the human affective life: the power of the body to sense passively (sight, sound, touch, etc.) is unified with, and has the same ontological status as, the active power of the body to respond (anger, pity, joy, etc.).

At least in the French context, sensibility provides the metaphysical foundation for those particularly eighteenth-century phenomena: theories of moral sense. Referencing Francis Hutcheson, the *Encyclopédie* defines moral sense in terms commensurate with this understanding of the body:

> Moral sense: the name given […] to this faculty of our soul which promptly distinguishes in certain cases moral good and evil by a kind of sensation and taste, independently of the reasoning and the reflexion.
>
> It is what the other moralists call *moral instinct*, feeling, type of tendency or natural inclination which carries us to approve certain things as good or laudable, and to condemn of others as bad and blameable, independently of any reflexion.[40]

The manner in which this article establishes moral sense as a sensation that operates independently of reason or reflection is highly significant. Moral sense here is unified with the evidence of the senses more narrowly construed: theories of moral sense are a version of "empiricism."[41] Again, a brief excursion must suffice to elucidate the point: Jean Senebier's *L'Art d'observer* (1775), a text that "arguably represents the formalised sum of the eighteenth century art of observation."[42] The text is, in the main, a detailed manual of natural philosophy devoted to questions of induction, analogical reasoning and the analytic method, general laws of nature, and the nature and use of hypothesis. However, as the fifth and final section of the text, "the art of observation [as] creator of the sciences and the arts," makes clear, observation is not a skill restricted to just natural philosophy.[43] Observation is also fundamental for the arts[44] and to morality, with the moral sense located in the sentiments of the heart.[45] The existence of a fundamental complicity between aesthetics and morality is a central feature of eighteenth-century moral sense theory. The point is worth stressing: there is no clear ontological distinction in this period between someone who is an acute observer of physical phenomena, a doctor who feels or senses a patient's fever for example, or an observer of moral phenomena, a moralist who feels or senses outrage at the plight of a beggar (or, to return to Diderot, of Richardson's Clarissa). The period makes a philosophical virtue of conjoining what contemporary philosophy would likely understand to be two radically distinct categories. This understanding of moral sense underpins the sentimental novel and Diderot's "Éloge de Richardson."[46]

It is within the parameters constructed by the eighteenth century's discourse of sensibility, and with this shared understanding of the body of sensibility, that Sade's principled engagement with Rousseau took place.

It is easy to separate Sade and Rousseau on the basis of their metaphysics. Sade takes his materialism from the "Radical" Enlightenment, particularly from d'Holbach, and it has generally been held that materialism is the key element of Sade's philosophy.[47] Rousseau argues vehemently against materialism and for the existence of an immaterial soul which can survive the death of the body.[48] And Fouquet too professes belief in a "rational and immortal soul."[49] But to separate them on these grounds is to put the philosophical cart before the horse and it obscures the very great amount that Sade and Rousseau have in common: Rousseau has a sensationist epistemology and a version of moral sense theory, and it is on the basis of this that he establishes his metaphysics and not the other way around.[50] Sade also has a sensationist epistemology, but using it he argue for materialism.[51] Here it is the case that the theory of knowledge is serving as first philosophy. Thus Sade's engagement with Rousseau is at this point based on a broad agreement that it is sensibility which is of fundamental importance, and based on a very specific disagreement on exactly what counts in terms of sensibility. What they are in disagreement about is exactly what sort of sensibility ought to be given epistemic precedence. For Rousseau it is the heart; for Sade it is not.

Rousseau's knowing heart – Sade's knowing body

I want to return to *Philosophy in the Bedroom* and to the quote I used to begin: Mme de Saint-Ange says of her star student: "never have I beheld a sensibility like yours, never so delightful a mind! [*je n'ai jamais vu une sensibilité comme la tienne, jamais une tête si délicieuse!*]"[52] The Grove Press translation of "*tête*" as "mind" is awkward if not completely erroneous: in contemporary usage *tête* would generally translate into English as "head"; however, it may also be taken as "face," more usually the correlate of *visage*, and also, although much less often, it may be taken as "mind," usually the correlate of *esprit*. This latter usage is quasi-metaphorical, a usage evidenced in English expressions such as "empty-headed." Thus the translation here of *tête* as "mind" is not exactly *wrong* so much as very misleading; rendering it accurate brings Sade's engagement with Rousseau into sharp focus. Sade specifically does not use the word *esprit*, a word which, while remaining somewhat ambiguous in the same way as has the word "soul/*âme*" generally carries with it a dualist heritage which opposes it to body or to "corporeal existence."[53] In the first instance then the use of *tête* rather than *esprit* can be taken to be indicative of Sade's materialism, but there is more to it than this. *Tête* opposes *cœur*, head opposes heart, and I argue this is Sade's intended meaning in using the word.

The question of the head *vis-à-vis* the heart has had a long history continuing at least since the Stoics, a history which has centred on the question of where the centre of the person lies. For Plato the heart was the seat of *noûs*; pre-Cartesian scholastic philosophy generally held the heart to be the seat of intelligence, knowledge, *and* sensitivity. For Descartes, though the heart is affected by the passions, so too are other parts of the body (including the legs); the seat of the soul, and so of reason and the will, was in the brain.[54] The *opposition* between the heart, as the seat of intuition, and the head, as the seat of reason, is largely established by Pascal.[55] Although the specifics of his understanding differ, Fouquet continues the tradition of opposing the head or brain as a centre of reason, and the heart, which, while associated with the "vascular system," is also one of the premier centres of sensibility.[56] And so Jaucourt's article locates moral sense in the "movement of the heart," movement which operates independently of reflection: that is, the sensibility of the heart is the centre of morality and is opposed to the sensibility of the head, or rationality.[57] It is on the question of primacy of the *cœur* or the *tête* that Rousseau and Sade engage.

Rousseau's "Profession of Faith of a Savoyard Vicar" begins with the vicar saying that he will reveal what he thinks in the simplicity of his heart;[58] Rousseau ought to be read here as positioning himself very carefully *vis-à-vis* the question of what sensibility means. The vicar continues:

> Taking the love of truth as my whole philosophy, and as my whole method an easy and simple rule that exempts me from the vain subtlety of arguments, I pick up again on the basis of this rule the examination of the knowledge that interests me. *I am resolved to accept as evident all knowledge to which in the sincerity of my heart I cannot refuse my consent*; to accept as true all that which appears to me to have a necessary connection with this first knowledge; and to leave all the rest in uncertainty without rejecting it or accepting it and without tormenting myself to clarify it if it leads to nothing useful for practice.[59]

This is the key point: in a period which has rejected innate ideas, and which understands that "we are only assured of our existence by our sensations," it is for Rousseau the sensations of the heart which have epistemic primacy even in matters of metaphysics.[60] Using this as his starting point the vicar then goes on to argue for a dualist metaphysics using an argument to first cause, and to argue for the existence of an immortal soul.[61]

Sade's response to this is direct, though, as is usually the case within his philosophical "system," ambidextrous. Firstly, by reducing the pleasure/pain binary in favour of an epistemology of intensity he confuses the clear trajectory of sensationist thought; this has the effect of disrupting the theories of moral sense which rely on sensationist anthropology. Secondly, he argues that the heart cheats and misleads and that the head ought to take precedence in such conflict as does exist between the two centres of sensibility. I shall deal with these two movements individually before addressing, in concluding, their interaction.

Sade's engagement with Rousseau presupposes that both take sensationism and vitalist anthropology as foundational. Sensationism is a widespread presumption in the thought of the period and is a foundational premise at least of Diderot, d'Holbach, and Helvétius. But it is Condillac who systematises and formalises it as an epistemology/psychology. Briefly: Condillac's *Treatise on the Sensations* (1754) outlines an epistemology which attempts to eliminate what he took to be the faculty of rationality from Locke's thought.[62] Condillac does this by using an elaborate philosophical fiction, imagining a statue-man to show that mind can arise from mere physical sensations and hence that there is only one faculty, that of sensation. By being drawn to pleasure and pushed away from pain, embodied sensations lead, in the statue, to the arising of mind and to the passions. Interestingly for the history of philosophy, which usually privileges sight,[63] Condillac privileges touch.

For his part, Sade, taking Condillac seriously, makes the rather simple observation that what we might call the sexual body, in terms of touch, is the most sensitive.[64] Sade also makes the point that pleasure and pain are not simply at two ends of a mutually exclusive binary as they are for Condillac.[65] For Condillac it is "impossible for us to suffer pain without wishing immediately not to suffer it":[66] this is the single drive, the "mainspring" behind the arising of mind in the statue. Hence, for Condillac pleasure and pain alone determine the scope of the statue's knowledge.[67] He is quite clear that the statue is driven *from* pain *to* pleasure: this is the simple sensationist trajectory. However, Condillac does note, somewhat parenthetically, that pleasures can become painful at least insofar as boredom is a pain (or a discomfort at least); hence, if the statue finds a continuous source of pleasant sensations it will not remain satisfied (and thus become motionless) but will eventually become bored.[68] Sade, developing this idea and making it central to his thought, notes conversely that pain becomes pleasure. Inducting Eugénie into the art of sodomy, Dolmancé notes that "occasionally, the woman suffers, if she is new, or young; but, totally heedless of the pangs which are soon to change to pleasures, the fucker must be lively and drive his engine ahead."[69] And so a few pages later when Dolmancé does sodomise Eugénie, her pain quickly morphs to the most extreme pleasure. Thus in the first instance, the Sadean subject is often drawn to pain, knowing it will transform into pleasure; it is hard to read many pages of Sade without coming across either a statement or an illustration of this principle. But in the second instance, pleasure is taken in pain itself: the Sadean philosopher-heros are just about as happy to be whipped bloody as they are to whip, a point worth making explicit as this fact tends to be occluded by the overhasty equation of "sadism," in the contemporary meaning established by Krafft-Ebing, with the Sadean *oeuvre*.[70] Sade then confuses the simple trajectory of sensationist epistemology, a point I will return to.

It often appears that Sade privileges the experience of pain. This idea is also found in Condillac who remarks, simply and plausibly, that in touch "the statue is more exposed to pain than with the other senses."[71] The statue learns more through pain than pleasure. But again an over-hasty association of Sade with "sadism" is unhelpful: at a deeper level what remains in Sade after his confusion of pleasure and pain is a principle of the intensity of sensation. Pain is thus justified not on account of its *painfulness*, but on account of its *intensity*, the natural correlate of *sensibility*. That is, vitalist anthropology privileges the subject with the greatest sensibility: they are more receptive to passive sensations and so are the most astute observers. In a period which holds that knowledge only arises through the senses, the greater the sensibility, the better able it is to provide knowledge.[72] Highly sensitive people are the most responsive too; for theories of moral sense, the most *sensitive* subject is the most *moral* subject. Cultivating (and managing) acute sensibility is an obsession of the period; again we can note the importance of the novel of sensibility. The natural correlate of this is that intensity of sensation ought to be privileged too insofar as intense sensations are better able to affect. That this is the case is made quite clear by d'Holbach's metaphysics.

D'Holbach is an atheist and an arch-materialist, and Sade adopts both of these aspects of his thought. For d'Holbach movement is the essential property of matter and so "all is in movement in the universe."[73] Movement is of two types: the gross movements of entire bodies easily evident to us, and the internal movement hidden within those bodies. This latter movement accounts for our intellectual faculties:

> That is to say, all the modes of action attributed to the soul, may be reduced to modifications, to the qualities, to the modes of existence, to the changes produced by the motion of the brain, which is visibly in man the seat of feeling – the principle of all his actions. These modifications are to be attributed to the objects that strike on his senses; of which the impression is transmitted to the brain, or rather to the ideas which the perceptions cause by the actions of those objects on his senses have there generated, and which it has the faculty to reproduce.[74]

Motion follows laws which are chiefly those of attraction and repulsion: the influence of Newton is evident even if the application is idiosyncratic. The laws of motion associated with a given body constitute the *essence* of that body: "a heavy body must necessarily fall [...] [and] a sensible body must naturally seek pleasure and avoid pain."[75] Each body is moved by its own laws to conserve its own being. Human beings are moved in each instant to do what pleases them.[76] More significantly for this paper – and given that for d'Holbach too the physical and the moral cannot be separated – attraction and repulsion for him also mean sympathy, antipathy, and what "moralists" call love, hate, friendship, and aversion. This is how d'Holbach explains human social arrangements. D'Holbach is a sensationist and has in his thought a simple trajectory grounded in pleasure and pain. However, it is the metaphysics that *supports* this binary which is central to Sade's epistemology and which is all that is left after Sade has disrupted the sensationist trajectory.

> The first faculty we behold in the living man, that from which all his others flow, is *feeling* [*sentiment*] [...] If we wish to define to ourselves a precise idea of it, we shall find that feeling is a particular manner of being moved peculiar to certain organs of animated bodies, occasioned by the presence of a material object that acts upon these organs, and which transmits the impulse of shock [*ébranlemens*] to the brain. [...] Every *sensation*, then, is nothing more than the shock [*secousse*] given to the organs; every perception is this shock [*secousse*] propagated to the brain: every idea is the image of the object to which the sensation and the perception is ascribed. From which it will be seen, that if the senses are not moved, there can neither be sensations, perceptions, nor ideas.[77]

(Note that *ébranlements*, perhaps: "rattles or shakes," and *secousses*, perhaps: "jolts," are both being translated here as "shocks." In addition to these terms Sade also uses *choc* where d'Holbach tends not to.) It is then the single notion of movement and the delivery of "shocks" which is foundational in d'Holbach. An idea having *impact* here ought to be taken quite literally: d'Holbach, in explaining the operation of the imagination writes: "That is how poetry, calculated to render nature more touching, pleases us."[78] Sade says almost exactly the same thing both about the imagination and about the touching of ideas.[79] Thus it is not hard, following his confusion of the pleasure/pain binary, to see how Sade can understand sensation in terms of intensity. Of cruel pleasures, Sade notes:

> It is purely a question of exposing our nervous systems to the most violent possible shock [*choc*]; now, there is no doubt that we are much more keenly affected by pain than by pleasure: the reverberations that result in us when the sensation of pain is produced in others will essentially be of a more vigorous character, more incisive, will more energetically resound in us, will put the animal spirits more violently into circulation […] pain must be preferred, for pain's telling effects cannot deceive, and its vibrations are more powerful.[80]

The Sadean epistemology privileges intensity of sensation: it privileges the sexual body as the most sensitive and pain as able to provide the most intense shocks, as being best able to affect the nerves. So when Dolmancé says that whores are the "only authentic philosophers" we do not *just* need to understand this in a non-literal sense: there is a sense in which, behind the hyperbole, he is being philosophically very serious.[81]

Sade is not a systematic thinker: to say this is not *per se* to criticise him, as systematicity was not in his period necessarily taken to be a philosophical virtue; this is particularly the case insofar as his genre of choice is the philosophical novel, the *roman philosophique*. And so it is useful to speak of the various "movements" of Sade's thought: he is ambidextrous. The move to complexify the pleasure/pain binary and to privilege the intensity of sensation is one movement of his thought. And of course this more strictly epistemological/metaphysical movement has a moral aspect which directly attacks the moral philosophy of his period: theories of moral sense, including Rousseau's, are grounded in a clean motivational trajectory from pain to pleasure. I have outlined here Sade's response to, and his own version of, sensationist thought. But moral sense theories are predicated on a sense of empathy as I have shown, and Sade moves against this as well: as I have noted, sensationist epistemology sits within broader discourses of sensibility, and at this level operates what I am calling the second movement of Sade's epistemology.

Where Rousseau entreats the reader to listen to their heart, Sade responds directly.[82] Though Sade's position on the heart is itself somewhat ambivalent – there are times when it is positioned as reliable[83] – his general position is that the heart's sensibility misguides and misleads. Dolmancé says to Eugénie:

> Never listen to your heart, my child; it is the most untrustworthy guide we have received from Nature; with greatest care close it up to misfortune's fallacious accents; far better for you to refuse a person whose wretchedness is genuine than to run the great risk of giving to a bandit, to an intriguer, or to a [plotter]: the one is of a very slight importance, the other may be of the highest disadvantage.[84]

Idiosyncratically for a Sadean text one of the libertine heroes, Le Chevalier, here argues with Dolmancé in what ought to be understood in some sense to be the (admittedly atheistic) presence of Rousseau in the text. Le Chevalier urges Eugénie,

> [Never] slay the sacred voice of Nature in your breast: it is to benevolence it will direct you despite yourself when you extricate from out of the fire of passions that absorb it the clear tenor of Nature. Leave religious principles far behind you – very well, I approve of it; but abandon not the virtues sensibility inspires in us.[85]

In a typically "empiricist" response Dolmancé chastises Le Chevalier telling him he is "wanting in experience," experience which would "dry out" his heart. To this Le Chevalier counters that "it is not from the mind that remorse comes; rather, [it is] from the heart's issue, and never will the intellect's sophistries blot out the soul's impulsions."[86] This is exactly Rousseau's argument. Dolmancé returns that the heart deceives as it is "never anything but the expression of the mind's miscalculations; allow the latter to mature and the former will yield in good time."

> I don't know what the heart is, not I: I only use the word to denote the mind's frailties. One single, one unique flame sheds its light on me: when I am whole and well, sound and sane, I am never misled by it; when I am old, hypochondriacal, or pusillanimous, it deceives me; in which case I tell myself I am sensible, but in truth I am merely weak and timid. Once again Eugénie, I say it to you: be not abused by this perfidious sensibility; be well convinced of it, it is nothing but the mind's weakness; one weeps not save when one is afraid, that is why kings are tyrants.[87]

Unsurprisingly at this point Eugénie declares Dolmancé the winner of the debate, Dolmancé caps off his "victory" with a short speech in praise of causing pain to others and finding himself with an erection he incites Mme de Saint-Ange to fart in his face and they all fuck: where for Rousseau the vicar's speech excited the tutor's moral sense, here the speech excites Eugénie's (and perhaps the reader's) libertine passions.

I do not want to give the impression, however, that sensibility in Sade operates just in simple head-or-heart terms; the discourse of sensibility is far more complex than this. This complexity is not just a feature of Sade: it is a feature of Montpellier vitalism and of Rousseau. So while "sensibility" in Sade sometimes means "moral sensibility" (often associated with the affects of the heart) it also means a more general sensibility associated with "the animal spirits" and synonymous for Sade with the general capacity for excitation or arousal, particularly of the sexual kind. As I have shown, Eugénie is particularly talented in these terms and that is why she is such a precocious student. In this aspect sensibility is a power which must be cared for, nurtured, cultivated, or developed. Elsewhere in *Philosophy in the Bedroom*, Eugénie asks Dolmancé, "might not charity and benevolence bring happiness to some sensitive souls?"[88] Dolmancé's response is multi-faceted, including several quasi-utilitarian arguments aimed at showing the harm to the greater good of giving alms. It is the conclusion that is of interest here:

> Nature has endowed each of us with a capacity for kindly feelings [*portion de sensibilité;* lit: a share of sensibility]: let us not squander them[/it] on others. What to me are the woes that beset others? Have I not enough of my own without afflicting myself with those that are foreign to me? May our sensibility's hearth warm naught but our pleasures! Let us feel it when it is to our advantage; and when it is not, let us be absolutely unbending. From this exact economy of feeling, from this judicious use of sensibility, there results a kind of cruelty which is sometimes not without its delights.[89]

And somewhat predictably, Eugénie responds, "Dear God, how your discourse inflames me!" The point is that the cultivation of the right *kind* of sensibility is a matter of careful training or habituation. Sade's *chef d'œuvre*, the enormous philosophical novel *Juliette*, is the story of just this kind of training: a specific training in libertinage which is not *just* a question of the *place* of sensibility, that is of having the head rule the heart (though this is certainly a major theme of the novel). This too fits with the broader discourse of sensibility which sees the power of sensibility itself as needing to be cared for, care which is usually expressed in medical terms; this is particularly evident in Rousseau's obsession with the careful management of bodily sensibility, an aspect of his thought which has been studied at length.[90]

Finally, just as it is not evenly distributed within individuals, sensibility is not evenly distributed *between* individuals. In fact the difference between Justine and her sister Juliette may be described simply in terms of their sensibility. So for Sade the particular cruelty of women can be attributed to the "excessive sensibility of women's organs."[91] Women's extreme sensibility comes from their extreme delicacy, and

> the extremes to which it drives them are [refinements of this delicacy]: this delicacy, so finely wrought, so sensitive to impressions, responds above all, best and immediately to cruelty; it awakens in cruelty, cruelty liberates it.[92]

In bringing this aspect of sensibility to light I have shown how the movement of Sade's thought that I have described as his epistemology of intensity meets here with the discourse of sensibility. It is through the particular cultivation of their given sensibility, not allowing morality to weaken or distract them, that the Sadean philosopher-hero can best match their particular affectivity with the most intense sensations. The philosopher-hero, the most sensible of persons and armed with the most cultivated sensibility, seeks the most urgent or violent shocks: this is Sade's epistemology of the body.

Conclusion

In this paper I have portrayed Sade's engagement with Rousseau as a very specific one which takes place on the grounds of eighteenth-century epistemology; I have described the theory of knowledge here as being first philosophy. Yet I have also shown how stating this is slightly disingenuous: epistemology in this period is not a discrete field as it is in its contemporary sense, but rather a highly diverse field (or set of fields) which incorporates much, particularly in late eighteenth-century France, where it incorporates or is incorporated by medical anthropology.[93] Sade's engagement with Rousseau is thus both broad and narrow: narrow insofar as Sade disrupts the pleasure/pain binary and argues for the primacy of the head over the heart, broad insofar as morality is absolutely central to Rousseau and Sade's epistemology – it is the sensibility of the *virtuous* heart which leads to truth for Rousseau, to error for Sade. And the contemporary reader cannot but notice the theological metaphysics which Rousseau relies upon and which Sade critiques. Rousseau's and Sade's positions on virtue here are critical and interrelate with their epistemologies. While I have mentioned these issues, I have largely avoided directly addressing them here.

The fact that Sade "subverts" the "sentimental tale" has been noted:[94] Richardson's novel, about which Diderot wrote in such enraptured terms is, after all, entitled *Pamela: Or, Virtue Rewarded* (1740), and Sade's novels entitled *Justine or The Misfortunes of Virtue* (1791) and *Juliette or the Prosperities of Vice* (1801). So when Diderot writes of *Clarissa*:

> Who would not like to be Clarissa, despite all her misfortunes? Often I have said in reading it: I would give readily my life to resemble her; I would prefer to be dead than to be [Lovelace].[95]

Sade responds to this in much the same vein as Voltaire does to Leibnitz's Optimism: he mocks. There is, however – and this is what I hope to have started to show – a serious philosophical engagement here too, an element not present in *Candide*. For Sade, Rousseau and Diderot have misunderstood the lessons of nature through a fault in their epistemic apparatus, that is, in their sensibility. Where Sade's response to Rousseau may be read in literary terms as subversion, it ought to be read in philosophical terms as a seriously considered counter-position.

Acknowledgements
I would like to thank Peter Cryle, Stephen Gaukroger, Anik Waldow, and Rebecca Young.

Notes

1. *Julie, ou la nouvelle Héloïse* (1761); *Émile, ou de l'éducation* (1762); *Du contrat social* (1762).
2. *Justine, ou les Malheurs de la vertu* (the second version of *Justine*, 1788, published 1791); *La Philosophie dans le boudoir* (1795); *Histoire de Juliette, ou les Prospérités du vice* (1797–1801). *Les cent vingt Journées de sodome, ou l'École du libertinage* (1785, published 1904), while perhaps the most (in)famous of all Sade's texts, it is, in terms of the presentation of Sade's philosophical "system," less representative than the 1791–1801 texts on which this paper will be based.
3. Lever, *Catalogue de La Coste*, 2:618–619; Sade, "Reflections on the Novel," 105.
4. For example, see Deprun, "La Mettrie et l'immoralisme sadien," 127–132; and Warman, *Sade*.
5. *Aline et Valcour, ou le Roman philosophique* (1788, published 1795).
6. For further, more detailed discussion of the relationship between the period's philosophical anthropology and the prevailing literary or aesthetical forms see Lloyd, "Discourse of Sensibility."
7. See Warman, *Sade*.
8. Sade, "Philosophy in the Bedroom," 217; Sade, "La Philosophie dans le boudoir," 34. This response by Eugenie is repeated identically elsewhere: see Sade, "Philosophy in the Bedroom," 217.
9. Sade, "Philosophy in the Bedroom," 257; Sade, "La Philosophie dans le boudoir," 72.
10. Sade, "Philosophy in the Bedroom," 257; Sade, "La Philosophie dans le boudoir," 72.
11. "Sometimes it is as pleasant to discuss as to undergo [sensations]; and when one has reached the limit of one's physical means, one may then exploit one's intellect." Sade, *Juliette*, 60; Sade, "Histoire de Juliette," 234.
12. Diderot, "Éloge de Richardson," 211–227.
13. Ibid.
14. Rousseau, *Emile, or On Education*, 266–313; O'Hagan, *Rousseau*, 83.
15. Rousseau, *Emile, or On Education*, 294.
16. Ibid.
17. Jaucourt, "Sensibilité, (Morale)," 15:52.
18. Fouquet, "Sensibilité, Sentiment (Médecine)," 15:38–52.
19. Vila, *Enlightenment and Pathology*, 80.
20. For more on Montpellier Vitalism, see Rey, *Naissance et Développement du Vitalisme en France*, 38:2–3; Wolfe and Terada, "Animal Economy," 540; Reill, *Vitalizing Nature in the Enlightenment*; Gaukroger, *Collapse of Mechanism and Rise of Sensibility*, 387–420; Kaitaro, "Can Matter Mark the Hours?," 583; Wolfe, "Introduction: Vitalism without Metaphysics?"
21. Williams, *Cultural History of Medical Vitalism*, 124–138.
22. Ibid., 147.
23. Fouquet, "Sensibilité, Sentiment (Médecine)," 15:40.
24. Ibid., 15:38.
25. Diderot, "Epicuréisme ou Epicurisme," 5:782.
26. "Une propriété qu'ont certaines parties de percevoir les impressions des objets externes." Fouquet, "Sensibilité, Sentiment (Médecine)," 15:38.
27. "Sens est une faculté de l'ame, par laquelle elle apperçoit les objets extérieurs." "Sensations (Métaphysique)," 15:24; "Les sensations sont des impressions qui s'excitent en nous à l'occasion des objets extérieurs." "Sensations (Métaphysique)," 15:34.
28. For a fuller explication, see Lloyd, "*Sensibilité*, Embodied Epistemology, French Enlightenment."
29. Le Camus, *Medecine de l'esprit*. The first edition of the text was published in 1753.
30. Vila, *Enlightenment and Pathology*, 81. See also Rey, *Naissance et Développement du Vitalisme en France*, 252–255.
31. See Vila *Enlightenment and Pathology*, 44; Suzuki, "Anti-Lockean Enlightenment?," 336–337. Suzuki argues that Locke becomes heavily influential on medical discourses in the late eighteenth century though not earlier. See also Vermeir and Deckard, "Philosophical Enquiries into the Science of Sensibility," 9, 12.
32. Le Camus, *Medecine de l'esprit*, 1:10.
33. Ibid., 1:15.
34. Ibid., 1:19.
35. Ibid., 2:84.
36. Fouquet, "Sensibilité, Sentiment (Médecine)," 15:39.
37. Ibid., 15:49.
38. Shapiro, "Instrumental or Immersed Experience," 265–285. See especially 274.
39. See Wolfe, "Sensibility as Vital Force or Property."

40. Jaucourt, "Sens moral," 15:28.
41. See Irwin, *Development of Ethics*, 354, 362, 419, 679, 682–684; and Norton and Kuehn, "Foundations of Morality."
42. Singy, "Huber's Eyes," 54.
43. Senebier, *L'art d'observer*, 2:161–321.
44. Ibid., 2:279–321.
45. Ibid., 2:201–266. See also Ménuret, "Observateur," 11:311–312.
46. The relationship between moral sense theory and the sentimental novel has been much commentated on. See Keymer, "Sentimental Fiction," 1:578–579; Brewer, "Sentiment and Sensibility," 22; Ellis, *Politics of Sensibility*, 9–14; and Mullan, *Sentiment and Sociability*.
47. For example, see Warman, *Sade*.
48. Rousseau, *Emile, or On Education*, 274–283.
49. Fouquet, "Sensibilité, Sentiment (Médecine)," 15:39–40.
50. Rousseau, *Emile, or On Education*, 266–313.
51. See Sade, "Philosophy in the Bedroom," 304–305; Sade, "La Philosophie dans le boudoir," 119.
52. Sade, "Philosophy in the Bedroom," 257; Sade, "La Philosophie dans le boudoir," 72. Note that Sade elsewhere uses the descriptor *délicieuse tête* in a similar circumstance: in the Grove Press, the standard and widely available English translation of Sade, it is also translated as "mind." For other examples of this usage, see Sade, *Juliette*, 883; Sade, "Histoire de Juliette," 978.
53. Clavier, "Esprit," 659.
54. Descartes, *Passions of the Soul*. See especially articles 32 and 33.
55. Clavier, "Cœur," 16:30–31.
56. Fouquet, "Sensibilité, Sentiment (Médecine)," 15:40. This is also the case for Senebier, *L'art d'observer*, 2:201–266.
57. Jaucourt, "Sens moral," 15:28.
58. Rousseau, *Emile, or On Education*, 266; Rousseau, *Emile, ou de l'éducation*, 320. See also O'Neal, *Seeing and Observing*, 67–68.
59. Rousseau, *Emile, or On Education*, 269–270 (italics added); Rousseau, *Emile, ou de l'éducation*, 324–325.
60. Le Roy, "Homme (Morale)," 8:275. Rousseau argues that it is sensibility which is innate, not ideas: Rousseau, *Emile, or On Education*, 290.
61. Rousseau, *Emile, or On Education*, 273–279. It is worth noting that the division between knowledge of the head and that of the heart is similar to, though it does not match exactly, John C. O'Neal's division in modes of Rousseavian perception between "seeing," understood as the "kind of perception that leads to recognition of one's fellow human beings" and often associated with the heart, and "observing," where perception "stops at the level of the senses […] at most providing intellectual data for reason." *Seeing and Observing*, 6. See also 32. Although O'Neal relies on a close reading of Rousseau's *oeuvre* in the tradition of Starobinski and does not engage with the broader context of sensibility, he is attentive to the epistemological questions I am invoking. For O'Neal:

> From an epistemological standpoint, those who "observe," because of the very limited tendency of their world view, can only have limited knowledge of themselves, their fellow men and women, and their environment. Those who "see," on the other hand, are constrained on both the ethical and epistemological level only by their contact with people who observe. The latter become a stumbling block not only to the attainment of virtue, but also to the attainment of knowledge. (15. See also p. 61.)

62. Condillac, "Treatise on the Sensations"; Condillac, "Traité des sensations." The question of whether it is appropriate for Condiallc to read Locke this way is a topic that is outside the scope of this paper.
63. For example, see Plato, "Phaedrus," 250d.
64. For example: "Here above all is a little tongue-shaped thing – that is the clitoris, and there lies all a woman's power of sensation." Sade, "Philosophy in the Bedroom," 204 ; Sade, "La Philosophie dans le boudoir," 21.
65. And for d'Holbach and Helvétius.
66. Condillac, "Treatise on the Sensations," 177, 242.
67. Ibid., 242.
68. Ibid., 183.
69. Sade, "Philosophy in the Bedroom," 231. See also pp. 292–293. Sade, "La Philosophie dans le boudoir," 48.

70. Krafft-Ebing, *Psychopathia Sexualis*. For a detailed discussion of this issue, see Moore, "Invention of Sadism?"
71. Condillac, "Treatise on the Sensations," 238.
72. It is worth noting that the period does not take heightened sensibility to be without problems: see Vila, *Enlightenment and Pathology*.
73. d'Holbach, *Système de la nature*, 1:14.
74. Ibid., 100; d'Holbach, *System of Nature*, 86.
75. d'Holbach, *Système de la nature*, 12–14; d'Holbach, *System of Nature*, 18.
76. d'Holbach, *Système de la nature*, 40–42.
77. Ibid., 88–89, 94; d'Holbach, *System of Nature*, 78, 81. See also d'Holbach, *Système de la nature*, 91, 92; and d'Holbach, *System of Nature*, 79, 80.
78. d'Holbach, *Système de la nature*, 110.
79. Sade, "Justine," 606.
80. Sade, "Philosophy in the Bedroom," 252; Sade, "La Philosophie dans le boudoir," 67. See also Sade, *Juliette*, 340–341; Sade, "Histoire de Juliette," 482.
81. Sade, "Philosophy in the Bedroom," 208; Sade, "La Philosophie dans le boudoir," 26.
82. See also Rousseau, *Emile, or On Education*, 286.
83. For example, when Mme de Saint-Ange explains that a foetus owes its existence only to a man's sperm, the womb "furthers creation without being its cause" and this is why a child owes filial tenderness to the father alone. Eugénie responds, "it is in my heart I find confirmation of what you tell me, my dear, for I love my father to distraction, and feel a loathing for my mother." Sade, "Philosophy in the Bedroom," 206; Sade, "La Philosophie dans le boudoir," 24. A detailed study of the various operations of the head/intellect and the heart/moral sense in Sade would include a discussion of the relationships Juliette has with Olympe, the Princess Borghese who appeals to Juliette's intellect, and Honorine, the Duchess Grillo who appeals to Juliette's heart. See Sade, *Juliette*, 659; Sade, "Histoire de Juliette," 770.
84. Sade, "Philosophy in the Bedroom," 340; Sade, "La Philosophie dans le boudoir," 154.
85. Sade, "Philosophy in the Bedroom," 341; Sade, "La Philosophie dans le boudoir," 155.
86. Sade, "Philosophy in the Bedroom," 342; Sade, "La Philosophie dans le boudoir," 156.
87. Sade, "Philosophy in the Bedroom," 342; Sade, "La Philosophie dans le boudoir," 156.
88. Sade, "Philosophy in the Bedroom," 215; Sade, "La Philosophie dans le boudoir," 32.
89. Sade, "Philosophy in the Bedroom," 217; Sade, "La Philosophie dans le boudoir," 34. See also Sade, "Justine," 491, 661–662.
90. In particular, see Vila, *Enlightenment and Pathology*.
91. Sade, "Philosophy in the Bedroom," 255; Sade, "La Philosophie dans le boudoir," 70.
92. Sade, "Philosophy in the Bedroom," 255; Sade, "La Philosophie dans le boudoir," 70.
93. See Haakonssen, "History of Eighteenth-Century Philosophy."
94. See Astbury, "Sade and the Sentimental Tale"; and Durante, *Sade ou l'ombre des lumières*.
95. Diderot, "Éloge de Richardson."

Bibliography

Astbury, Katherine. "The Marquis de Sade and the Sentimental Tale: *Les Crimes de l'amour* as a Subversion of Sensibility." *Australian Journal of French Studies* 39, no. 1 (2002): 47–59.

Brewer, John. "Sentiment and Sensibility." In *The Cambridge History of English Romantic Literature*, edited by James Chandler, 21–44. Cambridge: Cambridge University Press, 2009.

Clavier, Paul. "Cœur." In *Dictionnaire Culturel en Langue Française*, edited by Danièle Morvan, 630–631. Paris: Dictionnaires Le Robert, 2005.

Clavier, Paul. "Esprit." In *Dictionnaire Culturel en Langue Française*, edited by Danièle Morvan, 659. Paris: Dictionnaires Le Robert, 2005.

Condillac, Etienne Bonnot de. "Traité des sensations." In *Oeuvres complètes*. Reprint, Genève: Slatkine Reprints, 1970. First published 1754.

Condillac, Etienne Bonnot de. "A Treatise on the Sensations." In *Philosophical Writings of Etienne Bonnot de Condillac*. Hillsdale, NJ: L. Erlbaum Associates, 1982. First published 1754.

d'Holbach, Paul-Henri Thiry. *The System of Nature*. Translated by H.D. Robinson. Manchester: Clinamen, 1999. First published 1770.

d'Holbach, Paul-Henri Thiry. *Système de la nature ou des loix du monde physique & du monde moral*. Vol. 1. N.p., 1781. First published 1770.

Deprun, Jean. "La Mettrie et l'immoralisme sadien." In *De Descartes au romantisme: études historique et thématiques*, 127–132. Paris: Librairie Philosophique J Vrin, 1987.

Descartes, René. *The Passions of the Soul*. Translated by Stephen H. Voss. Indianapolis: Hackett Publishing, 1989. First published 1649.

Diderot, Denis. "Éloge de Richardson, auteur des romans de Paméla, de Clarisse et de Grandisson." In vol. 5 of *Œuvres complètes de Diderot*, edited by J. Assézat, 211–227. 20 vols. Paris: Garnier, 1762.

Diderot, Denis. "Epicuréisme ou Epicurisme." In vol. 5 of *Encyclopédie ou Dictionnaire raisonné des arts et des métiers*, edited by Denis Diderot and Jean Le Rond d'Alembert, 779–785. 35 vols. Paris: Briasson, David, Le Breton & Durand, 2008. First published 1755.

Durante, Danile Castillo. *Sade ou l'ombre des lumières*. Vol. 7 of *Eighteenth-Century French Intellectual History*. Edited by Marc Goldstein and Roland Bonnel. New York: Peter Lang, 1997.

Ellis, Markman. *The Politics of Sensibility: Race, Gender and Commerce in the Sentimental Novel*. Cambridge: Cambridge University Press, 1996.

Fouquet, Henri. "Sensibilité, Sentiment (Médecine)." In vol. 15 of *Encyclopédie ou Dictionnaire raisonné des arts et des métiers*, edited by Denis Diderot and Jean Le Rond d'Alembert, 38–52. 35 vols. Paris: Briasson, David, Le Breton & Durand, 2008. First published 1765.

Gaukroger, Stephen. *The Collapse of Mechanism and the Rise of Sensibility: Science and the Shaping of Modernity, 1680–1760*. Oxford: Oxford University Press, 2010.

Haakonssen, Knud. "The History of Eighteenth-Century Philosophy: History or Philosophy?" In *The Cambridge History of Eighteenth-Century Philosophy*, edited by Knud Haakonssen, 3–25. Cambridge: Cambridge University Press, 2006.

Irwin, Terence. *From Suarez to Rousseau*. Vol. 2 of *The Development of Ethics: A Historical and Critical Study*. Oxford: Oxford University Press, 2008.

Jaucourt, Chevalier Louis de. "Sens moral." In vol. 15 of *Encyclopédie ou Dictionnaire raisonné des arts et des métiers*, edited by Denis Diderot and Jean Le Rond d'Alembert, 28–29. 35 vols. Paris: Briasson, David, Le Breton & Durand, 2008. First published 1765.

Jaucourt, Chevalier Louis de, "Sensibilité, (Morale)." In vol. 15 of *Encyclopédie ou Dictionnaire raisonné des arts et des métiers*, edited by Denis Diderot and Jean Le Rond d'Alembert, 52. 35 vols. Paris: Briasson, David, Le Breton & Durand, 2008. First published 1765.

Kaitaro, Timo. "Can Matter Mark the Hours? Eighteenth-Century Vitalist Materialism and Functional Properties." *Science in Context* 21, no. 4 (2008): 581–592.

Keymer, Thomas. "Sentimental Fiction: Ethics, Social Critique and Philosophy." In vol. 1 of *The Cambridge History of English Literature, 1660–1780*, edited by John Richetti, 572–601. Cambridge: Cambridge University Press, 2005.

Krafft-Ebing, Richard von. *Psychopathia Sexualis: A Medico-Forensic Study*. New York: Pioneer Publications, 1947. First published 1886.

Le Camus, Antoine. *Medecine de l'esprit*. 2 vols. Paris: 1769. First published 1753.

Le Roy, Charles-Georges. "Homme (Morale)." In vol. 8 of *Encyclopédie ou Dictionnaire raisonné des arts et des métiers*, edited by Denis Diderot and Jean Le Rond d'Alembert, 274–278. 35 vols. Paris: Briasson, David, Le Breton & Durand, 2008. First published 1765.

Lever, Maurice, ed. *Catalogue de La Coste*. Vol. 2 of *Papiers de famille: Le marquis de Sade et les siens (1761–1815)*. Paris: Fayard, 1993.

Lloyd, Henry Martyn. "The Discourse of Sensibility: The Knowing Body in the Enlightenment." In *The Discourse of Sensibility: The Knowing Body in the Enlightenment*, edited by Henry Martyn Lloyd. Studies in History and Philosophy of Science. Heidelberg: Springer Dordrecht, 2013.

Lloyd, Henry Martyn. "*Sensibilité*, Embodied Epistemology, and the French Enlightenment." In *The Discourse of Sensibility: The Knowing Body in the Enlightenment*, edited by Henry Martyn Lloyd. Studies in History and Philosophy of Science. Heidelberg: Springer Dordrecht, 2013.

Ménuret de Chambaud, Jean-Joseph. "Observateur." In vol. 11 of *Encyclopédie ou Dictionnaire raisonné des arts et des métiers*, edited by Denis Diderot and Jean Le Rond d'Alembert, 310–313. 35 vols. Paris: Briasson, David, Le Breton & Durand, 2008. First published 1765.

Moore, Alison. "The Invention of Sadism? The Limits of Neologisms in the History of Sexuality." *Sexualities* 12, no. 4 (2009): 486–502.

Mullan, John. *Sentiment and Sociability: The Language of Feeling in the Eighteenth Century*. Oxford: Clarendon Press, 1988.

Norton, David Fate, and Manfred Kuehn. "The Foundations of Morality." In *The Cambridge History of Eighteenth-Century Philosophy*, edited by Knud Haakonssen, 941–986. Cambridge: Cambridge University Press, 2006.

O'Hagan, Timothy. *Rousseau*. The Arguments of the Philosophers. London and New York: Routledge, 1999.

O'Neal, John C. *Seeing and Observing: Rousseau's Rhetoric of Perception*. Stanford French and Italian Studies. Saratoga: Anma Libri, 1985.

Plato. "Phaedrus." In *Plato on Love*, edited by C.D.C. Reeve, 88–153. Indianapolis and Cambridge: Hackett Publishing Company, 2006.

Reill, Peter Hanns. *Vitalizing Nature in the Enlightenment*. Berkeley: University of California Press, 2005.

Rey, Roselyne. *Naissance et Développement du Vitalisme en France de la Deuxième Moitié du 18 Siècle à la fin du Premier Empire*. Edited by Anthony Strugnell. Studies on Voltaire & the Eighteenth Century, vol. 381. Oxford: Voltaire Foundation, 2000.

Rousseau, Jean-Jacques. *Emile, or On Education*. Translated by Allan Bloom. New York: Basic Books, 1979. First published 1762.

Rousseau, Jean-Jacques. *Emile ou de l'éducation*. Paris: Editions Garnier Freres, 1964. First published 1762.

Sade, D.A.F. "Histoire de Juliette, ou les Prospérités du vice." In *Œuvres*, edited by Michel Delon, 179–1262. Paris: Editions Gallimard, Bibliothèque de la Pléiade, 1998. First published 1795.

Sade, D.A.F. *Juliette*. Translated and edited by Richard Seaver and Austryn Wainhouse. New York: Grove Press, 1968. First published 1801.

Sade, D.A.F. "Justine, or Good Conduct Well Chastised." In *Justine, Philosophy in the Bedroom and Other Writings*, edited by Richard Seaver and Austryn Wainhouse, 449–743. New York: Grove Press, 1965. First published 1791.

Sade, D.A.F. "La Philosophie dans le boudoir, ou Les Instituteurs immoraux." In *Œuvres*, edited by Michel Delon, 1–178. Paris: Editions Gallimard, Bibliothèque de la Pléiade, 1998. First published 1795.

Sade, D.A.F. "Philosophy in the Bedroom." In *Justine, Philosophy in the Bedroom and Other Writings*, edited by Richard Seaver and Austryn Wainhouse, 184–367. New York: Grove Press, 1965. First published 1795.

Sade, D.A.F. "Reflections on the Novel." In *The 120 Days of Sodom and Other Writings*, edited by Richard Seaver and Austryn Wainhouse, 97–116. New York: Grove Press, 1966. First published 1800.

Senebier, Jean. *L'art d'observer*. 2 vols. Geneva: 1775.

"Sensations (Métaphysique)." In vol. 15 of *Encyclopédie ou Dictionnaire raisonné des arts et des métiers*, edited by Denis Diderot and Jean Le Rond d'Alembert, 34–38. 35 vols. Paris: Briasson, David, Le Breton & Durand, 2008. First published 1765.

Shapiro, Lisa. "Instrumental or Immersed Experience: Pleasure, Pain and Object Perception in Locke." In *The Body as Object and Instrument of Knowledge: Embodied Empiricism in Early Modern Science*, Studies in History and Philosophy of Science, edited by Charles T. Wolfe and Gal Ofer, 265–285. Vol 25. Heidelberg: Springer, 2010.

Singy, Patrick. "Huber's Eyes: The Art of Scientific Observation Before the Emergence of Positivism." *Representations* 95, no. 1 (2006): 54–75.

Suzuki, Akihito. "Anti-Lockean Enlightenment?: Mind and Body in Early Eighteenth-Century English Medicine." In *Medicine in the Enlightenment*, edited by Roy Porter, 336–359. Amsterdam: Rodopi, 1995.

Vermeir, Koen, and Michael Funk Deckard. "Philosophical Enquiries into the Science of Sensibility: An Introductory Essay." In *The Science of Sensibility: Reading Burke's Philosophical Enquiry*, edited by Koen Vermeir and Michael Funk Deckard, 3–56. Dordrecht: Springer, 2012.

Vila, Anne C. *Enlightenment and Pathology: Sensibility in the Literature and Medicine of Eighteenth-Century France*. London: Johns Hopkins University Press, 1998.

Warman, Caroline. *Sade: From Materialism to Pornography*. Oxford: Voltaire Foundation, 2002.

Williams, Elizabeth A. *A Cultural History of Medical Vitalism in Enlightenment Montpellier*. Burlington: Ashgate, 2003.

Wolfe, Charles T. "Introduction: Vitalism without Metaphysics? Medical Vitalism in the Enlightenment." *Science in Context* 21, no. 4 (2008), 461–463.

Wolfe, Charles T. "Sensibility as Vital Force or as Property of Matter in Mid-Eighteenth-Century Debates." In *The Discourse of Sensibility: The Knowing Body in the Enlightenment*, edited by Henry Martyn Lloyd. Studies in History and Philosophy of Science. Heidelberg: Springer Dordrecht, 2013.

Wolfe, Charles T., and Motoichi Terada, "The Animal Economy as Object and Program in Montpellier Vitalism." *Science in Context* 21, no. 4 (2008): 537–579.

The Artifice of Human Nature: Rousseau and Herder

Anik Waldow

University of Sydney, Sydney, Australia

In the eighteenth century appeals to human nature were often made to refer to universal characteristics found in every human being. Properties and dispositions pertaining to the species as a whole were thus isolated from those through which individuals were classified in terms of their sex, race or social rank. Focusing on the "natural" differences between men and women, Jean-Jacques Rousseau writes in *Emile*: "The only thing we know with certainty is that everything man and women have in common belongs to the species, and that everything that distinguishes them belongs to the sex."[1]

Rousseau invokes the concept of nature not only when trying to explain why we behave the way we do, but also when evaluating specific forms of life. Sketching a life suitable for the purpose of child rearing, he writes that females, in order to "fulfil their functions well," need to acquire "a constitution which corresponds" to their sex (*Emile*, 535). Thus traits and attributes that Rousseau takes to be given to females by nature, namely those that enable them to be pregnant, give birth and nurture their offspring, are used to outline a commendable developmental path.

With this stress on the normative dimension of the concept of nature, knowing one's own nature become paramount: it not only enables us to understand what we are, but also what we ought to be in a situation in which we are – as Rousseau never tires of pointing out – denatured through our lives in society: "The human soul, altered in the bosom of society by a thousand continually renewed causes, [...] has changed its appearance to the point of being nearly unrecognisable."[2] Even though Rousseau is clear that we cannot return to a fictitious state of nature that Rousseau deems inevitably lost,[3] his attempt to present nature as a measure to assess the merits of our "constitution" and social practices suggests that nature circumscribes the direction in which individuals and societies ought to evolve.

In this essay I will argue that although Rousseau often invokes the concept of nature as a fixed point of reference in the evaluation of personal traits, and individual and collective practices, a closer look at the dynamics of the educational programme laid out in his *Emile* shows that for him human nature has to emerge in a process that combines the influence of nature and artifice. This process is essentially enabled by Emile's sensibility that, as I will claim, can be conceived as a natural property geared towards development and change in relation to a specific social environment. By confronting him with artfully orchestrated stimuli, this environment ensures that he "naturally" develops in line with a normatively laden conception of society.

In order to show that the border between artifice and nature becomes increasingly blurred once we start thinking of human beings as forming themselves by affectively responding to their social environment, Part II will relate Rousseau's account of moral education to Herder's account of self-formation. According to Herder, we must actualise our moral capacities by multiplying our sentiments in our engagement with historically shaped representations of human life. By stressing this use of man-made artefacts, Herder renders explicit a point already implicitly contained in Rousseau. That is, that human nature is incomplete and naturally shapes itself by affectively engaging with the artifices around which our existence as humans revolves.

These insights about the entanglement of artifice and nature in the formation of the human being can help us to understand the deficiency of the attempt to introduce the modern distinction between nature and nurture into the analysis of eighteenth-century thinkers.[4] This distinction is typically used to differentiate man-made, cultural influences on our learning from developmental processes determined by nature.[5] As the examination of Rousseau and Herder will reveal, nature often appears to act in the guise of our natural sensibility as the cause that delimits how we learn and what we can learn, while artifice seems to constitute a substantial ingredient in naturally unfolding processes triggered by interactions with surroundings that are genuinely natural to us. The opposition on which the nature-nurture distinction depends (that is, the opposition between natural development and culturally initiated processes of learning) here becomes almost invisible.

What is more, looking at Rousseau and Herder as two examples of thinkers who engaged with the role of nature in moral education can help us to understand how it was possible for many eighteenth-century thinkers to refer to nature when trying to explain genuinely non-natural phenomena.[6] On the account developed here, humans with their moral and social capacities form themselves by interacting with a social environment that is natural to them. In so doing, they act like other animals that develop special aptitudes on the basis of interactions with a specific environmental milieu. Explanatory resources used to explain processes in other parts of nature are thus made available for the explanation of capacities essential to the moral and social life of human beings.

1. Rousseau: natural education

Rousseau begins his *Emile* with a statement about the natural man who, contrary to his domesticated counterpart, is still able to live a solitary life (*Emile*, 164). The ability to be for oneself is here construed as an asset that we have lost with our entry into society, and more specifically when we started to define ourselves in relation to others who then began to dominate our thoughts. Framing our interactions with others in such negative lights, Rousseau moves on to present education as a way to dominate naturally free human beings. Education thus becomes a tool employed to train man like a "school horse" (*Emile*, 161).

These scathing remarks about the value of education at the beginning of *Emile* have the strange effect of rendering pointless the enterprise on which Rousseau is about to embark, namely to show that a carefully designed educational programme is needed to enable human beings to emerge as accomplished moral agents. Of course, the main character of his educational oeuvre undergoes a very specific training, one that has been designed for precisely the purpose of opposing the denaturing effects that society exerts on individuals under normal circumstances. It does so by strengthening and developing dispositions and capacities that Rousseau takes to be naturally given to us.

Emile's education has often been characterised as a "negative education."[7] *Negative* here means that the tutor remains passive in that he merely provides occasion for experiences through which Emile can actively learn and develop himself. On this reading, the tutor's main task consists in shielding Emile from the kind of artifice that is present when others articulate their opinions and try to manipulate and dominate us with their views. Human nature thus emerges as the unspoilt good that must be preserved.

In what follows I will offer an account that challenges the view that Rousseau's ideal of education is negative in the sense that it *protects* a pre-existent, well-defined human nature. Rousseau uses the term "negative education" in a very specific context, namely when he rejects the idea that children can be taught morality before they have reached a certain age (*Emile*, 226). He does not suggest that education as a whole consists in preserving an originally given human nature. On the contrary, a closer look at the role of the tutor reveals that Emile's education must be thought of as a process through which he is actively led beyond that which nature has originally given to him.

The aim of stressing this dimension of the educational programme of Emile is not to say that artifice is what creates the human being in its most accomplished form, nor to stress that education is needed to make visible a human nature hidden under the denatured surface of the victims of civilisation. Rather, my intention is to move beyond the opposition between nature and artifice/society by drawing attention to the fact that artifice and nature converge in the conception of Emile as naturally forming himself in his exchange with an environment that is permeated with artifice. Such artifice is present in the form of opinions he encounters in his social interactions. Given that on this account other persons are part of the environment through which we naturally form ourselves, they cannot be conceptualised as disturbances that block our path to our full actualisation. Rather, other persons must be seen as offering us the opportunity to develop ourselves "naturally" in line with the environment we encounter.

To reveal this interplay between natural and artificial in Emile's education, it is useful to have a closer look at the contrast between nature and habit. Rousseau writes:

> Nature, we are told, is only habit. What does that mean? Are there not habits contracted only by force which never do stifle nature? Such, for example, is the habit of the plants whose vertical direction is interfered with. The plant, set free, keeps the inclination it was forced to take. But the sap has not as a result changed its original direction, and if the plant continues to grow, its new growth resumes the vertical direction. The case is the same for man's inclinations. So long as one remains in the same condition, the inclinations which result from habit and are the least natural to us can be kept, but as soon as the situation changes, habit ceases and the natural returns. Education is certainly only habit. (*Emile*, 163)

Rousseau here opposes the view that habits are natural in the sense that they naturally grow out of prevailing environmental conditions. Contra this view, Rousseau asserts that habits are products of education: they *interfere* with human nature, just as artificial light conditions interfere with a plant's natural growth.

Although this passage is meant to stress that education works against nature, a closer look at the implications of the analogy between humans and plants reveals that for Rousseau humans can develop themselves only in accordance with their environmental conditions.[8] Thus he explains that only if "the situation changes" is it possible to shake off bad habits. The situation for humans is therefore very similar to that of plants: only if an artificial source of light is replaced by natural sunlight, can a plant resume its natural growth.

Just as some light conditions can be considered as more conducive to a plant's natural growth than others, some societal conditions can be seen as enhancing human nature more than others. On this model, teachers like Emile's tutor who put considerable effort into creating learning environments that support their student's development in line with their natural needs are a constitutive part of good environmental conditions: they are like the natural light that enables plants to flourish. Conversely, bad teachers are comparable to those environmental conditions that bend a student's nature similar to the way in which artificial light conditions bend the vertical growth of plant.

By conceiving of Emile's teacher as an integral part of the learning environment through which Emile forms himself, it becomes apparent that his education is as artificial as it is natural. It is artificial because the teacher creates the very environment he deems suitable for Emile's development and even becomes part of this environment when interacting with Emile; and it is natural because Emile spontaneously responds with his sensibility to the challenges his environment poses to him, thus becoming emotionally affected by the events surrounding him.

Interestingly, not only the teacher figures as an element in Emile's learning environment but other persons as well.[9] Emile learns the rudimentary notions of property and justice when being confronted with the gardener, Robert (*Emile*, 232–3). Through this role of other persons in Emile's learning experiences, it becomes clear that the aim of his education is not to protect him from the influence of opinion and other man-made artifices interfering with his nature. Rather, the aim is to arrange artifices in such a way that Emile can respond to them naturally and through this develop himself.

Another insight that can be gained by focusing on Rousseau's analogy between human development and the natural growth of plants is that there is no way around assuming an active role in education. Given that in our natural condition we are exposed to other persons and are susceptible to their influences – similar to plants that are naturally susceptible to the light conditions in their specific situation – it emerges that a passive, hands-off mentality increases the chances that the wrong kind of opinions create the wrong kind of habits. Therefore, the reason why Emile must be educated is not that human nature must be protected from opinion and artifice *tout court*. Rather, education is necessary because it is natural for humans to respond to their environment so that an active control of this environment is required.

We are here far removed from a concept of human nature that stands in opposition to artifice. On the suggested reading, humans naturally form themselves in their interactions with their social environment. So what is taken to be natural about humans is that they become what they are through their embeddedness in a social context, and more specifically through the experiences afforded by this context. In the case of Emile the tutor carefully orchestrates such learning experiences, revealing how artifice and activity in the form of the teacher's knowledge and design permeate the entire process through which Emile develops himself.

We can now see how misleading it is to think of Emile's education as negative and passive in that it simply preserves or drives out features that are naturally given. This reading suggests that human nature is a pre-existing good. However, given that Rousseau clearly sees that in our development it is natural for us to be susceptible to highly contingent environmental conditions, all that nature does is enable highly contingent developments. One might here object that for Rousseau there surely is one developmental path that is preferable to all others in that it actualises our true nature. But on this conception too one operates with an account of human nature that conceives of it as a well-defined set of fixed predispositions, thereby ignoring what even Rousseau accepted, namely that it is natural for us to be essentially malleable.

These considerations reveal how vacuous Rousseau's concept of human nature in fact is.[10] The values determining Emile's education are those of the tutor, that is, a character introduced to teach capacities and skills Rousseau considers essential for individuals forming a society that is to replace the society of his times.[11] Human nature, the actualisation of which is the proclaimed goal of Emile's education, thus becomes an artificial construct that isolates attributes and dispositions that Rousseau believes to be of advantage for properly socialised citizens.

To reinforce this point that human nature is a construct adjusted to a specific vision of society, I will now turn to Rousseau's account of moral education. As pointed out above, Rousseau's man of nature lives for himself and has no regard for others. It is only during puberty, that is, once the passions have been inflamed, that he develops an interest in his fellow companions. Characterizing the developmental stage reached by Emile *before* the onset of adolescence, Rousseau writes at the end of Book III: "He [Emile] considers himself without regard to others and finds it good that others do not think of him. He demands nothing of anyone. He is alone in human society; he counts on himself alone" (*Emile*, 359). Once the passions have created an interest in others,[12] the child's self-love – which by nature is "always good" (*Emile*, 363) – turns into harmful amour-propre. This sentiment derives from the comparison with others and gives way to the irascible passions (*Emile*, 364).

Now, if it holds that in the state of nature there is no place for morality, we cannot conceive of Rousseau's natural man as having original moral dispositions.[13] After all, morality is cultivated *after* we have fallen from the ideal state of nature, that is, after we have developed a *degenerated* form of self-love and have become estranged from our natural self through the company of other persons.[14] If we combine this insight with the fact that the ultimate aim of Emile's education is to teach him how to live as a moral creature,[15] it turns out that for Rousseau the concept of (our original) nature does not normatively determine the direction and goal of self-cultivation. If this were the case, it would become incomprehensible why for Rousseau moral education is of such importance, since it looks like moral capacities are artificially added to our original natural make-up.[16]

A way of dealing with the absolute centrality of morality in *Emile* comes into sight if we think of human nature not as referring to something originally given but as a placeholder concept that acquires meaning against the background of the process that, according to Rousseau, turns humans into citizens. On this reading, the starting point for our development is constituted by a set of original properties that must be transformed such that the asocial natural man becomes capable of a life among others.[17] This transformation can be achieved, as has been suggested above, by interacting with learning environments suitable for this particular purpose.

Approached from this angle, the concept of human nature does not refer to an original set of attributes and capacities that serves as the standard against which certain social practices can be assessed – even though Rousseau often suggests that nature can be seen in this way, as discussed in the introduction of this paper. Rather, a sense of what human nature is and how it can be realised arises out of considerations about the value of certain skills required for a life in society. Since on this account a specific vision of society determines the developmental path through which humans can actualise themselves, Rousseau's concept of human nature emerges as a derivative of his normatively laden concept of society.

It might be objected that his interpretation underplays the fact that in Book V of *Emile* natural differences between the sexes are used to define their respective roles in society.[18] As has been discussed, Rousseau thinks that females should develop a constitution that suits their biological function in relation to childbirth and child rearing. Nature here seems to prescribe what kind of role and educational programme is suitable for females: instead of preparing them for their entry into society, as the education of males does, females are expected to remain confined to the domestic sphere.[19] Although it is hard to deny that Rousseau often brings in the concept of nature to justify a certain developmental path and lifestyle, even in the case of female education it is a specific version of society that informs his normative claims.

Rousseau, as is well known, was a staunch defender of republicanism. Swiss mountain societies as much as the traditional life in Corsica and Poland are idealised in his political writings,[20] while the family is taken to be one of the pillars on which the republic could be erected.[21] If we pay attention to this context, Rousseau's advocacy of the traditional role of females and the demand to confine women to the domestic sphere can be explained by his belief that a society in which family life assumes a central role is best suited to replace the ruling monarchy. Now, if it is the case, as I have argued, that on Rousseau's educational model, individuals are essentially malleable and develop themselves in accordance with their environment, this means that females and males could in principle develop similar skills and attributes if placed in the same kind of learning environment. Rousseau would certainly object to this way of handling female education.[22] If the presented account is correct, however, the reason for his objection is not that he believes that females educated in an Emile-like manner would lead a life that conflicts with their female natures – even though Rousseau sometimes claim this.[23] Rather, what really motivates his objection is his conviction that females must dedicate their attention and care to the family because only a flourishing family can act as a bulwark against moral corruption and political dominion. The urgency of placing females in learning environments so very different from Emile's thus turns out to have a political motivation that is quite independent from considerations related to a specific conception of female nature.

The aim of this section was to reveal that in Rousseau's educational oeuvre artifice and nature merge into one another once we start thinking of Emile as forming himself by interacting with his environment. On the one hand, this is because a normatively laden concept of society embodied in the persona of the teacher determines Emile's development, and through this renders intelligible what kind of nature it is that Rousseau strives to actualise by his educational programme. On the other hand, Rousseau conceives of the education of Emile as experience-based: the cultivation of specific skills and attributes is enabled by his affective openness towards the world and other persons. In this way, the student's natural responses on the basis of his original affective susceptibility enable his learning and make it possible to think of his formation as a *natural* development despite all the artifices that are part of this process.

2. Herder: self-development

In order to further my claim that in many eighteen-century accounts nature and artifice merge rather than oppose one another in their role to actualise human potential, I will now turn to Herder. Herder believes that it is in our imaginative engagement with the cultural diversity of human life as it is represented in poetry, literature, the theatre, history and travel reports that we train our moral sensibility and become truly human. Thus, in *Über die neuere deutsche Literatur* (1768) Herder praises the art of creating sentiment-invoking images as a way of discovering novelty:

> Here we listen to the Greeks, how their poetic imagination, their sensuous thinking was artful enough to dress the truth in images [...] Now that we are surrounded by a new world of discoveries: poets among us, let us taste the mighty honey of the ancients [...] Learn from them the art of creating images for each one of us in our own private and unique sphere. Instead of paling in the face of that appalling image that Homer spit out, firm up your mind to drink from the ocean of images and particularities that surrounds you.[24]

With this stress on the use of man-made artefacts as stimulants of our projective imagination, Herder reveals yet another dimension in which artifice can figure in self-formation: in addition to our *actual* environment, we need artefacts to multiply our sentimental responses, because it is this multiplication that enables us to actualise our natural moral capacities.

Herder, like Rousseau, thinks that an engagement with history assists the cultivation of moral judgement. However, while for Rousseau the study of history is recommended because it enables knowledge of the passions without forcing the student to experience them,[25] Herder values it for the opposite reason. According to him, our engagement with history stimulates the imagination in such a way that we can feel our way into different times and places. He writes, "go into the age, into the climate, the whole history, feel yourself into everything – and now you are on your way towards understanding the world" (503; F 293). The reason why Herder wants the student of morals to immerse herself in imagined feelings, while Rousseau favours an account that places cool-headed observation over affective responses, is that both operate with very different conceptions of the imagination. As a consequence, they come to very different conclusions about the way in which morality can be cultivated, as I will explain now.

For Rousseau, our imaginative responsiveness in principle constitutes the root of all evil. In its capacity to "take[s] us ceaselessly beyond ourselves and often place[s] us where we shall never arrive," (*Emile*, 213) the imagination is seen as a superfluous troublemaker (*Emile*, 212) and the cause of an unbecoming hypersensitivity to matters that should not concern us. As such, the imagination, and the way it holds sway over our passions and desires, is identified as the very reason why humans turn into the degenerated, weak creatures so plentifully populating society.[26]

With this in mind, it becomes clear why for Rousseau the historical judge must remain distanced and avoid the pull of the passions, just as much as why Emile's education would be deemed a failure if he "just once" preferred "to be someone other than himself – were this other Socrates, were it Cato" (*Emile*, 399). Identifying oneself with others, while feeling what we take them to be experiencing, involves an imaginative perspective taking, hence the very faculty that, via its capacity to instigate all sorts of desires, serves to alienate us from a condition in which we are content with what we have.[27]

By studying the passions from a distance, Rousseau argues, these negative consequences can be avoided, since such distance ensures that the contact between judge and the object of study remains rather indirect. Of course, the danger that the imagination will be excited is always present. And it is for this reason that guidance becomes necessary – guidance that in the case of Emile is offered by the tutor who carefully decides which materials, and how much of them, enable the student to acquire a sufficiently distanced perspective to judge the passions appropriately.[28]

Herder does not see the imagination in this negative light. To enter imaginatively into images and sentiments foreign to one's own is not only regarded as a legitimate means in the study of the moral dimension of human life, but stronger than this it is even required if we want to understand morality as such. The reason for this is that it is via our projective imagination that we can acquaint ourselves with the circumstances of peoples and societies so very different from our own.[29] More specifically, the idea is that diversity, and varying moral standards in different societies, can be measured and appreciated for what they are only if considered against the background of a universal feeling of humanity.[30] Thus, Herder stresses that only the noble person would "have the pure eye" and in her "breast *universal natural* and *human sensitivity*,"[31] which would enable her to perceive in the manifold instantiations of human life "the originally good but misused first principles even behind the veil of bad habits."[32] The accomplished moral judge is here conceived in opposition to the base person who "seeks bad company" by trying to find "among a hundred nations [...] one that favors *his* prejudice, that nourishes *his* delusion."[33]

Through this contrast Herder suggests that the search for difference and variety is a crucial step in the cultivation of a unified and inclusive morality that applies to every human being alike.[34] By enabling us to transcend our own moral standards and connect with the feeling of humanity, Herder's imagination prevents premature generalisations exclusively based on the study of our own historical situation. It leads us to a point of view that reveals how much we have in common with all other human beings.[35] In this way, moral practices that we may first find confronting can evoke sympathy, pity and compassion, thereby revealing to us the universal principles of morality. Herder writes: "Travel descriptions [...] expand our horizon and multiply our sensibility for every situation of our brothers. Without losing a word about this they preach, sympathy, tolerance, forgiveness, praise, pity, many-sided culture of the mind, satisfaction, wisdom."[36]

Given that for Herder the imagination performs this positive role, there can be no question about constraining our natural imaginative tendencies in the same way Rousseau's tutor constrains Emile's imagination by controlling the materials used for his moral education.[37] On Herder's account, we can trust our sentimental responses to imagined scenarios, such that spontaneously triggered emotions can function as a guide to moral judgement.[38] Furthermore, since the imagination generates sentiments in response to imagined scenarios – on which we then base our moral judgement –it becomes an extra source of experience in itself, as I will explain now.[39]

Herder's positive assessment of the imagination in principle hinges on his account of "Gefühl" as the base category beyond which we cannot go and to which we must attend in order to organize our life in this world.[40] On this account, sensibility functions as the ultimate basis of cognition. The mind relies on what it finds within itself as a consequence of being immersed in the world as an affective, embodied being.[41] The possibility to think meaningfully about the world thus emerges as a consequence of having sensations and sentiments in relation to a set of specific stimuli, as Herder explains in his *Essay on the Origin of Language*.[42]

In a Lockean, bottom-up approach,[43] he here conceives of sounds as the original names affixed to clusters of sensations and sentiments engendered by a range of sense modalities: "White, soft, woolly – his [the human] soul operating with awareness, seeks a characteristic mark – the sheep bleats!" (Ursprung 723; F 88). By using the bleating of the sheep as the signifier of an object, namely the sheep, nature itself becomes the source of language.[44] It not only presents us with the objects for which we seek names, that is, sheep – thereby determining the content of our concepts – but also offers us the sounds that turn into words when we apply them to the things to which we affectively respond with our sentiments and sensations.[45]

Since for Herder thought and language are intimately related,[46] this model of language acquisition ensures that our thinking is naturally geared towards the world with which we interact: if there are sheep, we can talk and think about sheep by referring to them with words that we gain in our engagement with our environment.[47] However, despite Herder's sympathies with the Lockean model of language acquisition, he firmly rejects the conception that ideas are vehicles of thought.[48] Thus, for him it is not the mind's passing from one idea to another that characterises the way in which our thinking works. Instead, thinking is characterised as being essentially linguistic. Since he dispenses with ideas as a *tertium quid* to which our concepts refer, Herder stresses more than Locke that thinking is a form of feeling. This is because for Herder it is the original mix of sensations and sentiments that gives content to our thoughts, while for Locke concepts refer to general ideas, which have been derived from particular sensory ideas.[49] In this way, for Herder "Gefühl" remains *directly* involved in the performance of thought and cannot be reduced to our ideas' remote and already forgotten origin.

Now, it is due to this understanding of "Gefühl" as a central element in ordinary processes of thought that it is possible to explain why for Herder the imagination ought to be involved in the training of the moral judge. Herder thinks that when we imaginatively enter into different times and places, and participate in cultures fundamentally different from our own, we encounter within ourselves a mix of sensations and sentiments. Since this mix is not dissimilar from the one we encounter in ordinary processes of perception,[50] imaginative processes can be seen as offering us an extra class of experiences. They create the same kind of "Gefühlsurgrund" from which ordinary thought is taken to arise. In this role, imaginative processes can be seen as filling in for experiences we cannot have due to our location in time and space and as enriching our thoughts by offering new material for the creation of linguistic concepts.

Against this background, we can clearly see the reason why Herder and Rousseau assess the merits of the imagination in moral education very differently. While Herder thinks of the imagination as usefully supplementing experiences, thereby acknowledging that it contributes to the goals of experience-focused learning, Rousseau conceives of our imaginings as illegitimate and dangerous substitutes for experiences. It is for this reason, then, that Herder recommends our engagement with fiction, mythology and foreign languages,[51] because such an engagement can produce a species of experience that refines our sentiments and capacity for moral judgement.[52] The case is different for Rousseau: since for him imagining is not a legitimate form of experiencing, but a desire-instigating exercise, it must be supervised and controlled by an experienced moral judge, namely the tutor, in order to prevent it from running wild, and especially so when it is not history but fiction that is used to instruct the student.[53]

With this contrast in mind, it would appear that it is Herder, not Rousseau, who has trust in "human nature." For Herder we need not rely on a teacher who navigates us through the dangerous waters of our seductive sentiments. We are endowed with natural capacities that allow us to progress in our moral development by confronting ourselves with a wide enough range of experiences (real or imagined). This suggests that, rather than depending on other persons, we depend on the availability of man-made artefacts (literature, historical writings, travel reports) that represent to us the diversity of human life in different times and places. Without such artefacts, we would remain trapped within the limited radius of the here and now. As such, we would fail to multiply our experiences, which, as I have argued above, is crucially required if individuals are to develop an understanding of the principles of morality.

Due to this emphasis on multiplication and diversification,[54] Herder's account of moral education stresses that the reason why we must educate ourselves is not that we find ourselves in the wrong kind of social environment, as one could perhaps think with respect to Rousseau. (After all, Rousseau uses his educational programme as a weapon against over-civilization and as a means to promote the right kind of republican virtues.) For Herder moral education is necessary because we are incomplete. We may be endowed with the resources to become accomplished moral judges. However, before we have engaged in the imaginative exercise that connects us with other times and places, we cannot actualise our moral potential appropriately. The reason for this is that this realisation requires encounters with a broad enough variety of examples of human life across different cultures and ages.

Although Herder and Rousseau fundamentally disagree on the details of the process through which humans form themselves, they both stress that experience is central to self-development. Another striking parallel is that both claim that we must acquire those attributes that we deem truly human – most significantly our ability to understand the principles of morality. And we can do so, as has been argued, only if we participate in the world of artifice. Thus, it holds on both accounts that attributes that distinguish us from other animals, and for this reason serve to specify what our *human* nature is, do not exist as a set of fixed pre-dispositions independent of man-made influences. Such attributes emerge once we start interacting with our environment that, in the human case, naturally features other human beings.

3. Artifice in nature

To say that human nature must emerge in a process of social interaction might suggest that human nature is *second* nature, that is, a product of artifice formed, not by nature, but by man-made influences.[55] The relevant contrast is here taken to be that between instincts – conceived as forms of behaviour determined by nature – and acquired behavioural practices that result from our social interactions.

While it is true that one aim of this essay was to show that for Rousseau and Herder artifice is crucially involved in their conception of what human nature is, another aim was to argue that nature figures more prominently in many eighteenth-century approaches to human nature than the artifice of "second nature" would suggest. As we have seen, for Rousseau and Herder human development is essentially enabled by a natural property, that is, our sensibility that renders us susceptible to the way the world affects us. One's learning here takes the form of a natural, affective way of responding to experiences caused by a specific environment. This way of learning is similar to that observable in the adaptability of animals to certain environmental patterns and, as such, parallels processes unfolding in other parts of nature. Furthermore, since for Rousseau and Herder it is clear that in the human case the relevant environment is naturally social, developments that take place as a result of interacting with this environment can be deemed entirely natural. However, to stress that the process of self-formation as it is characterised by Rousseau and Herder is natural is not to deny that artifice forms an integral part of it. Indeed, in this essay much effort has been devoted to arguing that even Rousseau's "natural education" crucially depends on the influence of opinion and revolves around a normatively laden conception of society. The intention of pointing to the various senses in which Rousseau's and Herder's account of self-formation can be seen as describing a natural process therefore merely consists in demonstrating stress that the opposition between nature and artifice collapses at precisely the point where learning is conceived as an affective, stimulus-driven engagement with one's social environment.

Notes

1. Passages from this work are taken from J-J. Rousseau, *Emile or on Education*, 532; henceforth *Emile*.
2. Rousseau, *Discourse on the Origins of Inequality*, 12; hereafter *Second Discourse*.
3. Ibid., 13. Diderot seems to deliberately ignore this aspect of Rousseau's account when claiming that Rousseau preaches "a return to the forest," Diderot, *Réfutation de L'Homme*, 431.
4. E.g. Natasha Gill applies the nature-nurture distinction in her analysis of Locke and Rousseau; see Gill, *Educational Philosophy*, 24–6, 59, 190, 250. Anne Vila also makes use of this distinction when commenting on Diderot in Vila, *Enlightenment and Pathology*, 93. Also see Wirth, "Nature versus Nurture."
5. See, e.g., Prinz, *The Emotional Construction*, 37, 143.
6. Fernando Vidal for instance writes: "Coupled with the appeal to nature as the cognitive and moral authority, the Enlightenment return to nature was supposed to help liberate humanity from passions and false traditions," Vidal, "Onanism," 279.
7. See, e.g., Gill, *Educational Philosophy*, 187–91 and Fuchs, "Nature and *Bildung*," 158.
8. He makes the same point in the *Favre Manuscipt*; see *Emile*, 57.
9. Nicholas Dent notes that for Emile's education it is paramount that his "social environment as well as inanimate surroundings" are structured in a certain way and stresses the active role of the teacher in creating such an environment; see Dent, *Rousseau*, 87, 97.
10. Some have argued that Rousseau operates with the Aristotelian notion of nature, according to which everything that contributes to our well-being and completion in life is deemed natural: see, e.g., Dent, *Rousseau*, 42 and 97 and Roche, *Rousseau*, 3ff, for this claim. Yet, it seems that the tutor decides what is able to bring about the flourishing of Emile. Mark Hulliung remarks, "Nothing can be so unnatural as the education of the natural man," Hulliung, *Autocritique*, 186.
11. Rousseau's *Social Contract* outlines the ways in which this republican society can be realized. The legislator has to alter human nature to make possible a society in which virtue can prevail; see Rousseau, *Social Contract*, 67–70. He writes: "This transition from the state of nature to the civil state produces a most radical change in man, by substituting justice for instinct in his behavior, and endowing his actions with the morality they previously lacked," ibid. 53.
12. It has been noted that the original cause of amour-propre is the child's desire to command the rage felt when confronted with opposing wills; see Dent, *Rousseau*, 89–91, and *Emile*, 197. But of course, the wish to command requires the child to take notice of others and presupposes an interest in them, namely the interest to make them do what one wants them to do. So apparently amour-propre presupposes for its emergence the child's interest in others.
13. See Cooper, *Nature*, 107, for the claim that virtue is not natural.
14. See Dent, "Species," for the refutation of this "standard" interpretation. According to him, Rousseau allows for one's opening up towards others "without thereby acquiring a deformed and distorted character and a miserable and perverted mode of life," ibid., 27.

15. Morals that then enable Emile to live harmoniously in society which constitutes his natural environment. See Timothy O'Hagan for the claim that on Rousseau's naturalist vision individuals "strive to realize an ideal of integrity, which can be attained only when an equilibrium is established or re-established between the individual and its environment," O'Hagan, *Rousseau*, 271.

16. This is not to deny that amour-propre can in itself be deemed natural in that it is a natural response to an individual's confrontation with others. Such confrontations are unavoidable given that children are raised by others and live among them. For the distinction between healthy and corrupted amour-propre see Dent and O'Hagan, "Rousseau on 'Amour-Propre.'"

17. Rousseau distinguishes between "man as a natural being and man as social being," a distinction that, as Fuchs puts it, creates the paradox that "without sociality, rationality, and history" the man of nature "cannot be human yet, while the human being is no longer natural," Fuchs, "Nature and Bildung," 158–9.

18. The opening passage of Book IV reads: "Sophie *ought* to be a woman as Emile is a man – that is to say, she *ought* to have everything which suits the constitution of her species and her sex in order to fill her place in the physical and moral order," *Emile*, 531 (emphasis added).

19. See Gatens, "Rousseau and Wollstonecraft," for an analysis of Rousseau's attempt to deny women access to the public sphere of society, which according to Gatens is tantamount to denying them the right to transform their natures. The question that needs to be asked here is how the concept of nature can *both* justify the kind of society to which Rousseau aspires *and* provide the starting point from which we must depart in order to acquire sociability.

20. Rousseau, *Lettres écrites de la montagne*, and *Considération sur le Gouvernement de Pologne*. Also see Rousseau, *Letter to d'Alembert*, and Rousseau, *Social Contract,* 162.

21. See Hulliung, *Autocritique*, 137–45, for the claim that not only Rousseau, but even the philosophes, Diderot and d'Holbach, at the height of their dissatisfaction with the monarchy, sought to revitalize the traditional family model as a bulwark against the corruption of the world. The interesting point about this is that they did so, although they attacked Rousseau for his reactionary views on the role of women in society.

22. Rousseau openly attacked the *salonnières* of his time for their participation in *le monde*; see i.e. Rousseau, *Letter to d'Alembert*, 324–9. In *La Novelle Héloïse* Rousseau presents Julie who has been formed by her life in the countryside as an alternative female ideal. See Vila, *Enlightenment and Pathology*, 198–224, for an analysis of Julie's female virtues; see Garrard, *Rousseau's Counter-Enlightenment*, ch. 4, for a characterisation of Rousseau's republic as manly.

23. See for instance Rousseau, *Letter to d'Alembert*, 311–15, where he refers to nature in order to justify female chastity.

24. Herder, *Fragmente 1768*, 449 (my own translation).

25. Rousseau writes, "It is by means of history that, without the means of philosophy, he [the student] will read the hearts of men; it is by means of history that he will see them, as a simple spectator, disinterested without passion, as their judge and not as their accomplice or as their accuser," *Emile*, 392.

26. At the end of Book III, Rousseau notes that it is through his received training that Emile's imagination is somewhat atypical in that it is "in no way inflamed and never enlarges danger," *Emile*, 359. This means that an untrained imagination typically affects the mind negatively, revealing once again the crucial importance of actively forming human nature into something it cannot be by itself.

27. Rousseau describes the negative consequences of the imagination in the example of a man who receives a letter with supposedly bad news. This man would ignore "the place that nature assigns to [him]," *Emile*, 214, and unnecessarily trouble himself with things he could safely ignore. The same logic applies to insatiable desires: we only need to stop imagining unattainable things to restore us to a peaceful state of mind; see *Emile*, 363–4.

28. The tutor not only offers guidance, but forces his influence upon Emile at a critical point in his development when Emile wants to break away from him. Interestingly, the method here consists in manipulating Emile's imagination; see *Emile*, 494–7.

29. There are limits to our ability to understand another person's situation. Herder concedes that it is difficult for us to understand someone who has been socialized entirely differently; see Herder, *Ideen*, 331.

30. See Frazer, *Enlightenment of Sympathy*, ch. 6, for this interpretation.

31. Herder, *Letters*, 397.

32. Ibid.

33. Ibid.

34. Herder suggests that an understanding of human nature depends on one's ability to feel one's way into the sensibility of human kind; see *Ideen*, 294. This shows that not only with respect to moral issues, but

also in relation to the broader question of what we are, the acknowledgement of variety and difference is crucial.

35. Again, the rationale behind this is that for Herder understanding is relative to the way we have learnt to conceptualize the world on the basis of our interactions with a given social environment. In order to develop a *general* understanding of human nature (as opposed to a culturally conditioned understanding), it is therefore necessary to imagine and feel our way into a variety of different manners of thinking. See Herder, *Abhandlung*, 782–3, for the claim that it is by "Einfühlung" that we come to know other people's thoughts. I will say more about this shortly.

36. Herder, *Letters*, 397. In *Auch eine Philosophie der Geschichte zur Bildung der Menschheit* (1774) Herder applies the method of imaginative projection in order to produce an understanding of morality in history. As such, it covers both a synchronic and diachronic dimension.

37. Yet Herder recognizes that an excessive stimulation of the imagination tends to overwhelm the rather limited capacity of the human mind and for this reason must be avoided; see *Ideen*, 332.

38. Herder claims that even in science there is a place for the imagination (in the sense of using metaphors and analogies); see Herder, *Vom Erkennen und Empfinden*, 330.

39. For a more detailed account of the suggested parallel between imagining and experiencing see Waldow, "Back to the Facts."

40. Stressing the fundamental character of sensibility and our connectedness with the world in the processes of knowledge acquisition, Marion Heinz writes: "Since man can acquire an understanding of the world only when his sensibility is affected, the disposition of his organs and the concrete location of his body in the world become most basic determinants of knowledge beyond which he cannot go," Heinz, *Sensualistischer Idealismus*, 24.

41. Heinz calls this relation of the individual to her world "Kreaturgepräge," a term that stresses the importance of the subject's needs in her specific situation that impact on the way concepts are formed; see Heinz, *Sensualistischer Idealismus*, 163.

42. For passages from this work I have used Michael Forster's translation in Herder, *Philosophical Writings*; I will refer to these passages by *Ursprung*, page number in the German original, F and the page number in English translation. References without citations will be given to the German original only.

43. See Sikka, "Herder's Critique," for an account that recognizes the Lockean legacy in Herder's philosophy of language. See Taylor, "The importance of Herder," especially 50–1, for an account that stresses dissimilarities between Locke and Condillac on the one hand and Herder on the other.

44. To claim that nature functions as the starting point for the development of language is not to deny that for Herder the emergence of language is necessary, given that humans are put in the state of "Besonnenheit" (*Ursprung* 722). See Nigel DeSouza, "Language, Reason and Sociability," for a discussion of Herder's critique of Condillac who, according to Herder, ignores the difference in kind between human and animal language.

45. This is not to say that Herder suggests that nature entirely fixes the way we think and use language. He is clear that "Besonnenheit" sets us free from instinct, and through this enables us to develop language, precisely because we can freely overlook ("freistehend") and freely organise ("frei wirkend") our sensory inputs; see *Ursprung*, 716–19.

46. *Ursprung*, 770.

47. DeSouza makes this point in relation to the faculty of reason. For Herder, he claims, the "flooding of the senses" is a necessary prerequisite for the actualization of human reason: see DeSouza, "Language, Reason and Sociability," 227.

48. See Heinz, *Sensualistischer Idealismus*, 159, for the contrast between Locke's and Herder's theory of representation.

49. See Locke, *Essay*, 158–9.

50. For Herder it is the fact that we feel something when being affected by the world that matters to his theory of language and thought; it is not the fact that we can trace a sensation to its original physical cause that makes for our ability to think meaningfully and develop reason. Feelings stimulated by our imagination and those caused by perceptual stimuli therefore both stand on the same footing: they offer us the raw materials for developing a more diverse conceptual scheme and through this offer us novel ways of understanding the world. See Waldow, "Back to the Fact," for a longer version of this argument.

51. Herder describes translation and the study of the grammar and syntax of another language as ways to "discover" new ways of thinking; see his *Fragmenten* 1767, 199–207. The use of mythology is described in *Fragmente* 1768, 449.

52. So imagining is not only important to develop cross-cultural tolerance, as Frazer claims – see Frazer, *The Enlightenment of Sympathy*, 158 – more fundamentally, imagining also helps us to complete our naturally scant experiences of human life and morality. It thereby helps us to develop an understanding of what morality consists in, not just with respect to our narrow circle but in general.

53. For a critical assessment of the use of literature and theatre in Emile's moral instruction see *Emile*, 516. For Rousseau's claim that the theatre leads to moral corruption see Rousseau, *Letter to d'Alembert*. See Vila, *Enlightenment and Pathology*, 182–224, for an account of how Rousseau uses fiction, namely his own novels, to portray a superior state of morality.

54. If we follow Heinz's claim that for Herder assimilation is the principle that rules our engagement with the world, the multiplication of one's own sentiments by imagining oneself into culturally diverse situations can be construed as a process through which we assimilate bits and pieces of human life as it exists in its diverse manifold instantiations; see Heinz, *Sensualistischer Idealismus*, 106–8, 135, 155.

55. See, e.g., Gill, *Educational Philosophy*, especially 250. Second nature in this sense just is what others today call nurture; see note 5 above.

Bibliography

Cooper, L. *Nature: The Problem of the Good Life*. University Park: Penn State University Press, 1999.

Dent, N. "'An integral part of the species … '?" In *Jean-Jacques Rousseau and the Sources of the Self*, edited by Timothy O'Hagan, 25–37. Aldershot: Avebury, 1997.

Dent, N. *Rousseau*. Abingdon: Routledge 2005.

Dent N., and T. O'Hagan. "Rousseau on 'Amour-Propre.'" *Proceedings of the Aristotelian Society* 99 (1999): 91–107.

DeSouza, N. "Language, Reason and Sociability: Herder's Critique of Rousseau." *Intellectual History Review* 22 (2012): 221–240.

Diderot, D. *Réfutation de L'Homme*. 2 Vols. Edited by J. Assézat Garnier. Paris, 1875–77.

Frazer, M. *The Enlightenment of Sympathy, Justice and Moral Sentiments in the Enlightenment and Today*. Oxford: Oxford University Press, 2010.

Fuchs, E. "Nature and *Bildung*, Pedagogical Naturalism in Nineteenth-Century Germany." In *The Moral Authority of Nature*, edited by L. Daston and F. Vidal, 155–181. Chicago: University of Chicago Press.

Garrard, G. *Rousseau's Counter-Enlightenment*. Albany: State University of New York Press, 2003.

Gatens, M. "Rousseau and Wollstonecraft: Nature vs. Reason." *Australasian Journal of Philosophy* 64, Supp. (1986): 1–15.

Gill, N. *Educational Philosophy in the French Enlightenment: From Nature to Second Nature*. Burlington, VT: Ashgate, 2010.

Heinz, M. *Sensualistischer Idealismus: Untersuchungen zur Erkenntnistheorie und Metaphysik des jungen Herder (1763–1778)*. Hamburg: Meiner, 1994.

Herder, J. G. *Abhandlung über den Ursprung der Sprache*. Vol. 1 of *Werke in zehn Bänden*. 1772. Frankfurt: Deutscher Klassiker Verlag, 1985–.

Herder, J. G. *Auch eine Philosophie der Geschichte zur Bildung der Menschheit*. Vol. 4 of *Werke in zehn Bänden*. 1774. Frankfurt: Deutscher Klassiker Verlag, 1985–.

Herder, J. G. *Ideen zur Geschichte der Menschheit*. Vol. 6 of *Werke in zehn Bänden*. 1784. Frankfurt: Deutscher Klassiker Verlag, 1985–.

Herder, J. G. *Letters for the Advancement of Humanity*. 1793–7. In *Philosophical Writings*, translated and edited Michael Forster. Cambridge: Cambridge University Press, 2002.

Herder, J. G. *Philosophical Writings*, translated and edited Michael Forster. Cambridge: Cambridge University Press, 2002.

Herder, J. G. *Über die neuere deutsche Literatur. Zwote Sammlung von Fragmenten*. Vol. 1 of *Werke in zehn Bänden*. 1767. Frankfurt: Deutscher Klassiker Verlag, 1985–.

Herder, J. G. *Über die neuere deutsche Literatur. Fragmente, erste Sammlung, zweite überarbeitete Ausgabe*. Vol. 1 of *Werke in zehn Bänden*. 1768. Frankfurt: Deutscher Klassiker Verlag, 1985–.

Herder, J. G. *Vom Erkennen und Empfinden*. Vol. 4 of *Werke in zehn Bänden*. 1778. Frankfurt: Deutscher Klassiker Verlag, 1985–.

Hulliung, M. *The Autocritique of the Enlightenment: Rousseau and the Philosophes*. Cambridge, MA: Harvard University Press, 1998.

Locke, J. *An Essay Concerning Human Understanding*. Edited by P. Nidditch. Oxford: Clarendon Press, 1975.

O'Hagan, T. *Rousseau*. London: Routledge, 1999.

Prinz, J. *The Emotional Construction of Morals*. Oxford: Oxford University Press, 2007.

Roche, K. F. *Rousseau: Stoic and Romantic*. London: Methuen, 1974.

Rousseau, J.-J. *Considération sur le Gouvernement de Pologne*. Vol. 3 of *Oeuvre Complète*. Edited by Ch. Lahure. Paris: Hachette, 1856.

Rousseau, J.-J. *Discourse on the Origins of Inequality*. Vol. 3 of *The Collected Writings of Rousseau*. Edited by Roger D. Masters and Christopher Kelly. Hanover, NH: University Press of New England, 2009.

Rousseau, J.-J. *Emile or on Education*. Vol. 13 of *The Collected Writings of Rousseau*. Translated and edited by C. Kelly and A. Bloom. Hanover, NH: University Press of New England, 1992.

Rousseau, J.-J. *Letter to d'Alembert about the Theatre*. Vol. 10 of *Complete Works of Rousseau*. Edited by A. Bloom and C. Kelly. Hamburg: University Press New England, 2004.

Rousseau, J.-J. *Lettres écrites de la montagne*. Vol 3. of *Oeuvre Complète*. Edited by A. Belin. Paris: Imprimeur-Libraire, 1817.

Rousseau, J.-J. *The Social Contract and Other Later Political Writings*. 2 Vols. Edited by Victor Gourevitch. Cambridge: Cambridge University Press, 1997.

Sikka, S. "Herder's Critique of Pure Reason." *Review of Metaphysics* 61 (2007): 31–50.

Taylor, C. "The Importance of Herder." In *Isaiah Berlin: A Celebration*, edited by Edna Margalit and Avishai Margalit, 40–63. Chicago: University of Chicago Press, 1991.

Vidal, F. "Onanism, Enlightenment Medicine, and the Immanent Justice of Nature." In *The Moral Authority of Nature*, edited by L. Daston and F. Vidal, 254–281. Chicago: University of Chicago Press.

Vila, A. *Enlightenment and Pathology*. Baltimore: John Hopkins University Press, 1998.

Waldow, A. "Back to the Facts – Herder on the Normative Role of Sensibility and Imagination." In *Contemporary Perspectives on Early Modern Philosophy*, edited by M. Lenz and A. Waldow, 115–133. New York: Springer, 2013.

Wirth, Marvick E. "Nature versus Nurture: Patterns and Trends in Seventeenth-Century French Child Rearing." In *The History of Childhood*, edited by L. deMause. Northvale, NJ: Jason Aronson, 1995.

Seduced by System: Edmund Burke's Aesthetic Embrace of Adam Smith's Philosophy

Michael L. Frazer

Harvard University, Cambridge, MA, USA

There is little scholarly agreement about how to understand the relationship between Adam Smith and Edmund Burke. Philosophical commentators often see the two in fundamental opposition, reading Smith's *Wealth of Nations* as precisely the sort of unflinching, systematic critique of existing society which Burke is held to have so abhorred.[1] There is much truth to this; Smith himself described his magnum opus as "a very violent attack […] upon the whole commercial system of Great Britain."[2] Yet historians point out that Smith and Burke were personal friends who not only shared a sentimental attachment, but also considered themselves to be in fundamental agreement on most philosophical and political issues. Burke repeatedly praised Smith's writings as both beautiful and true, not only in his conversation and in his correspondence, but also in at least one published review. For his part, Smith is alleged to have commented that Burke "was the only man, who, without communication" thought on topics of political economy "exactly as he did."[3] Scholars must confront the fact of this mutually recognized similarity in viewpoints before describing Smith as fundamentally anti-Burkean or Burke as fundamentally anti-Smithian.[4]

We must be careful, however, not to replace one unduly reductive thesis on this subject with its equally reductive opposite.[5] The record of their interaction does no more to support the thesis that Burke and Smith were in full agreement than it does to support the view that they were in full disagreement.[6] If nothing else, it forces us to recognize that Smith and Burke lived very different lives, and as a result engaged in very different modes of thinking and writing.[7] This difference between both the biographies and the philosophies of Smith and Burke is best captured by noting that the former was primarily an academic, and the latter primarily a politician, albeit one with philosophical predilections. This essay will argue that Burke's and Smith's respective understandings of their different social roles are central both to the complex relationship between their respective worldviews and to their deep mutual admiration. For Burke, Smith was always the model of a wise philosopher. For Smith, Burke grew into the model of a prudent statesman.

The contrast between the philosopher and the statesman was a constant theme for Burke and Smith alike. They shared an opposition to the "man of system," the hybrid philosopher/statesman who attempts to shape actual societies according to some preconceived theoretical model. The man of system, both argue, is enchanted by the aesthetic appeal of his imagined ideal society, and is made blind to the suffering which occurs in the futile attempt to actualize this ideal. Yet while Smith joins Burke in warning against the dangers of sublime and beautiful systems, Smith does not refrain from constructing systems of his own. Indeed, both *The Theory of Moral Sentiments* and *The Wealth of Nations* contain intricate intellectual systems. In the reviews of both these works in Burke's *Annual Register*, Smith's systems are lauded for their remarkable degree of beauty and sublimity.[8] As a result, it is entirely possible to be caught up in the aesthetic enchantments of Smith's systems, and to become a man of system blind to the suffering that the actualization of Smith's theories may bring.

With his evident enthusiasm for the aesthetic aspect of Smith's philosophy, Burke is particularly vulnerable to becoming such a dangerous utopian. And in his posthumously published *Thoughts and Details on Scarcity*, the great opponent of philosophical systems reveals that, for at least a moment, he has indeed fallen prey to their aesthetic allure. Burke here calls for the implementation of free market policies with dogmatic zeal, regardless of the consequences, equating the laws of the market with the commands of God. The power of his Smith's ideas were such that they could, with terrible irony, turn a man of refined aesthetic sensibility like Burke into precisely the sort of man of system Burke himself is so famous for opposing.

1. Burke on Smith's two systems

1.1. *The Theory of Moral Sentiments*

On April 12, 1759, David Hume wrote to Smith from London, informing Smith that he and Alexander Wedderburn had distributed copies of Smith's newly published *Theory of Moral Sentiments* to "such of our acquaintances as we thought good judges and proper to spread the reputation of the book." Among these is Burke, described as "an Irish gentleman, who wrote lately a very pretty treatise on the sublime."[9] Smith's response to Hume's letter has not survived, but it seems that he expressed some interest in the "Irish Gentleman." Hume describes him further in his next extant letter to Smith, from the following July 28. "I am very well acquainted with Burke," he writes, "who was very much taken with your book. He got your direction [i.e., postal address] from me with a view of writing to you, and thanking you for your present, for I made it pass in your name. I wonder he has not done it."[10]

Burke was not to write Smith until September 10, after he had returned to London. He explains his lateness in giving thanks to Smith for the copy of his "very agreeable and instructive work" as stemming from a desire to "defer [...] [his] acknowledgements until I had read your book with proper care and attention."[11] Burke then goes on to describe at some length the merits of the *Theory*. The following year, parallel arguments for the greatness of the work were made in an unsigned review for the second volume of Burke's *Annual Register*, that for 1759.[12] Considering that Burke was not only editing the successful almanac at this time, but also writing almost all of its nearly 500 pages of content, it is a safe assumption that the review is Burke's own; it has been universally identified as such in the literature.

In his initial letter to Smith on the *Theory*, Burke writes that he is "not only pleased with the ingenuity of your theory," but also "convinced of its solidity and truth."[13] Rather than discuss the validity of any of Smith's arguments in particular, however, Burke praises the soundness of its construction as a systematic whole. He writes:

> I have ever thought that the systems of morality were too contracted and that this science could never stand well upon any narrower basis than the whole of human nature. All the writers who have treated this subject before you were like those gothic architects who were fond of turning great vaults upon a single slender pillar; there is art in this, and there is a degree of ingenuity without doubt; but it is not

sensible, and it cannot long be pleasing. A theory like yours, founded on the nature of man, which is always the same, will last, when those that are founded on his opinions, which are always changing, are gone and forgotten.[14]

Note that Burke believes Smith's method to not only ground his moral system on a stronger foundation than all other such systems, but also to render it more "pleasing." Burke devotes the rest of his letter to Smith to the praise, not of Smith's philosophical acuity, but of his literary skill. Smith makes expert use of "easy and happy illustrations from common life"; he provides an "elegant painting of the manners and passions"; his prose style is "lively" and "well varied."[15] Burke even makes use of the categories of his own aesthetic theory to analyze the appeal of Smith's work – in which beauty is understood as a source of love and joy arising from ordered harmony, and sublimity as a source of delight and awe arising from glorious power. Not only does the *Theory* show countless "beauties," Burke writes, but it also "is often sublime too, particularly in that fine picture of the Stoic philosophy [...] which is dressed out in all the grandeur and pomp that becomes that magnificent delusion."[16] If Smith's literary achievement bears any flaws, it is "rather a little too diffuse," though this is "a fault of the generous kind."[17]

In his review of the *Theory* for the *Annual Register*, Burke continues his effusive praise of the book along these same aesthetic lines. He begins by questioning a reviewer's ability to "give the reader a proper idea of this excellent work."[18] Burke rhapsodizes:

> A dry abstract of the system would convey no juster idea of it, than the skeleton of a departed beauty would of her form when she was alive; at the same time the work is so well methodized, the parts grow so naturally and gracefully out of each other, that it would be doing it equal injustice to show it by broken and detached pieces.[19]

After insisting that the only possible solution is for the reader of his review to purchase a copy of Smith's book, Burke then goes on to praise, not only the work's beauty (though he continues to insist it presents "one of the most beautiful fabrics of moral theory, that has perhaps ever appeared"[20]) but also the book's "ingenious novelty."[21] Such praise may strike the contemporary ear as strange coming from the author who was to become Britain's most famous defender of the old against the new, and Burke indeed maintains that "with regard to morals, nothing could be more dangerous" than sheer novelty.[22] Smith avoids this danger, however, because his philosophical system "is in all its essential parts just, and founded on truth and nature."[23] The review, as was customary in the eighteenth century, then provides an extended quotation from the work being discussed. Burke selects "the first section, as it concerns sympathy, the basis of his [Smith's] theory; and as it exhibits equally with any of the rest, and idea of his style and manner."[24]

1.2. *The Wealth of Nations*

While Burke and Smith by now had certainly established an intellectual camaraderie based on their published work and personal correspondence, there is no indication that the two men met in person at any time for nearly two decades. This is reason alone to doubt the traditional tale that Smith consulted Burke and paid great deference to his opinions during the composition of the *Wealth of Nations*. Jacob Viner traces this tradition to the editor's preface to the posthumous *Thoughts and Details*.[25] Viner, however, argues that this story is improbable considering that on the basis of what is known about Smith's and Burke's respective activities, the earliest they could have met in person would have been in London late in 1775, only a few months before the *Wealth* was published.[26] It was at this time that Smith was elected to the London literary institution known as "The Club," of which Burke was an original member. Smith attended his first meeting on December 1, 1775, and probably attended semi-regularly through the publication of the *Wealth* in April of the following year.[27] It is almost certain that Smith and Burke met in the capital sometime before Smith left London shortly after the publication of the *Wealth* in April of 1776, though some have suggested that the meeting took place only upon Smith's return to London early in 1777.[28]

The review of *The Wealth of Nations* in that year's *Annual Register* closely parallels Burke's earlier review of Smith's *Theory* in terms of both style and content. The latter review begins with the observation that while "the growth and decay of nations" has "sometimes exercised the speculations of the politician" the subject has "seldom been considered [...] by the philosopher."[29] It then goes on to compare Smith's work favorably with the writings of the physiocratic school of "French economical writers," lauding the *Wealth* for its unparalleled "sagacity and penetration of mind, extent of views, accurate distinction, just and natural connection and dependence of parts" and its completeness as a systematic "analysis of society."[30] The review even makes the same criticism of the *Wealth* that Burke earlier made of the *Theory*, that it "may be sometimes thought diffuse," though it excuses this literary fault by noting that "the work is didactic, [and] that the author means to teach, and teach things that are not obvious."[31] Like the review of the *Theory*, the piece then concludes with an extended quotation, in this instance, Smith's entire introduction to the *Wealth*.[32]

It is uncertain what role, if any, Burke himself played in the composition of this review. While some scholars have attributed it to Burke, others have questioned this attribution.[33] Burke had certainly relinquished control of the *Annual Register* by this time, though he continued to write book reviews and to provide editorial guidance. The *Register*'s review of the *Wealth* in 1776 is so similar to that of the *Theory* in 1759, however, that we can have some confidence that it is an accurate reflection of Burke's position on the work, even if it was not composed by him directly.

In the years between the publication of *The Wealth of Nations* in 1776 and Smith's death in 1790, Burke and Smith maintained an active correspondence. Smith repeatedly expressed support for Burke's practical political work, and Burke repeatedly expressed his admiration for Smith as a sagacious philosopher.[34] After Smith's death, in his 1796 *Letter to a Noble Lord*, Burke claimed to "have made political economy an object of my humble studies from my very early youth to near the end of my service in Parliament."[35] Burke takes considerable pride in the fact that "great and learned" political economists "thought my studies were not wholly thrown away, and deigned to communicate with me now and then on some particulars of their immortal works."[36] Smith was certainly foremost among those political economists to whom Burke could have been referring.

2. Smith on system

2.1. *The aesthetic appeal of system*

Before he abandoned the life of the philosopher for that of the statesman, the young Burke was widely hailed as a savant in the field of philosophical aesthetics. Yet even those well aware of Burke's aesthetic predilections must be surprised to find Burke praising Smith's work primarily through the categories of the sublime and beautiful rather than those of the true and the good. Burke was only speaking metaphorically when he described Smith's prose as "rather painting than writing" and yet he consistently describes moral philosophy and political economy of what now seems a dry and technical nature as if they were works of art.[37] Nor can this striking feature of Burke's reviews be merely attributed to the conventions of his time, in contrast to those of ours. Although aesthetic criteria were more often used when assessing philosophical works in the eighteenth century than they are today, the almost exclusively aesthetic emphasis in this review is unusual, both among eighteenth-century book reviews in general and among the reviews in Burke's *Annual Register* in particular. To cite just one obvious example, Burke's review of Rousseau's *Letter to D'Alembert* – which immediately precedes his review of Smith's *Theory* – does not take this aesthetic approach, instead engaging in a substantive critique of Rousseau's arguments against the theater.[38]

Smith himself was well aware that aesthetic considerations can play an important role in science and philosophy, terms which he uses interchangeably for the construction of explanatory systems. Smith makes note of this fact in his posthumously published essay on "The Principles Which Lead and Direct Philosophical Enquiries as Illustrated by the History of Astronomy." "A [philosophical] system," Smith writes, "is an imaginary machine invented to connect together in the fancy those different movements and effects which are already in reality performed."[39] Some explanatory systems, though, are created with "a more simple and intelligible as well as more beautiful machinery" than others.[40] Typically, scientific systems are created to dispel the unpleasant sensation of ignorant awe one feels upon contemplating the unexplained. Yet an especially well-crafted scientific theory, with its "novelty and unexpectedness" may itself become a sublime object of wonder, if not outright awe. Such was the case with Copernican astronomy, which "excited more wonder and surprise than the strangest of those appearances, which it had been invented to render natural and familiar, and these sentiments still more endeared it [to humanity]."[41]

Smith's two great systems – the system of sympathy as the foundation of ethical life and the system of natural liberty that would, if realized, maximize the wealth of nations – are both designed to so endear themselves to our aesthetic sensibilities. The author's system of political economy in particular makes use of complex mechanics of ingeniousness perhaps even surpassing those of Copernican or Newtonian astronomy.[42] The paradoxical power of the invisible hand to guide the pursuit of private interests so as to maximize the wealth of all is perhaps the single most striking element of Smith's system, and hence the one most closely embraced by the mass of his readers. Smith dismissively attributes the popularity of physiocratic economics precisely to the fact that "men are fond of paradoxes, and of appearing to understand what surpasses the comprehension of ordinary people."[43] Smith was surely aware, however, that the same cause would lead to the popularity of his own economic theory.

2.2. *The danger of system*

Over the course of his intellectual development, Smith came to see the beauty and sublimity of imaginary, philosophical systems, not only as a source of aesthetic delight, but also as a source of considerable danger. He outlined this position in a small section of Part VI of the *Theory*, the entirety of which was added to the work for the sixth and final edition of 1790, the year of Smith's death. Smith's analysis of the dangers of systemic thinking is part of a larger discussion of political loyalties, for it is only with regard to systems describing the interactions among human beings that this frightening phenomenon arises. The excessive love of system in natural philosophy is basically harmless; perhaps its worst effect is the rather absurd cult of the scientist that formed at the altar of the deceased Newton. Yet the intellectual systems of a moral philosopher, unlike those of a natural scientist, describe imaginary social systems, and a moral philosopher can never remain wholly satisfied as long as the utopia in his imagination has not been actualized as a social reality. In this way, "a certain spirit of system" can inflame "even to the madness of fanaticism" the reformist drive of an opposition party, as its members become "intoxicated with the imaginary beauty of [...] [some] ideal system, of which they have no experience, but which has been presented to them in all the most dazzling colors in which the eloquence of their leaders could paint it."[44]

The man of system, the unholy union of the philosopher and the politician, is to be contrasted with the prudent statesman. The statesman, "prompted altogether by humanity and benevolence," will, in reforming the ills of society, "content himself with moderating, what he cannot annihilate without great violence […] When he cannot establish the right, he will not disdain to ameliorate the wrong; but like Solon, when he cannot establish the best system of laws, he will endeavor to establish the best that the people can bear."[45] The man of system, however, is "often so enamored with the supposed beauty of his own ideal plan of government, that he cannot suffer the smallest deviation from any part of it." The result is that a society governed by men of system will function "miserably" and "at all times in the highest degree of disorder."[46] Blind to the defects in his idealized plan, the man of system cannot see the suffering its enactment will cause.[47]

3. The statesman and the philosopher

3.1. *Burke as a prudent statesman*

There is reason to believe that Smith was thinking of Burke as he contrasted the prudent statesman with the man of system. While constantly working to enact practical improvements in the body politic, Burke always insisted that radical political change according to philosophical schemes of perfection was to be entirely avoided. There is more direct evidence that Smith thought of Burke as a model statesman when the passages in the *Theory* on the subject are considered in conjunction with a certain relevant section of the *Wealth*. At the end of a chapter on the corn trade in that latter work, Smith discusses a law Burke had marshaled through the House of Commons in 1773, reforming but hardly eliminating bounties for the export of grain.[48] Smith argues that Burke's bill "seems to have established a system with regard to the Corn Laws, in many respects better than the ancient one, but in one or two respects perhaps not quite so good."[49] In the first edition of the *Wealth*, this chapter then concluded with a critique of Burke's reform. For the second edition of 1778, however, Smith added an additional paragraph at the very end of the chapter:

> So far, therefore, this law seems to be inferior to the ancient system. With all its imperfections, however, we may perhaps say of it what was said of the laws of Solon, that, though not the best in itself, it is the best which the interests, prejudices, and temper of the times would admit of. It may perhaps in due time prepare the way for a better.[50]

Smith, then was thinking specifically of a reform championed by Burke when he referred to Solon's laws in the 1778 edition of the *Wealth*, good evidence that he was also thinking of Burke when he made an identical reference 12 years later in the 1790 edition of the *Theory*. It is probably not a coincidence that Smith seems to have first made Burke's personal acquaintance sometime between the composition of the *Wealth* and its revisions for the second edition, which suggests that the statesman himself may have objected to Smith's critique of his 1773 reforms. Such, at least, is the tradition preserved in an 1804 article by Francis Horner. After discussing Smith's statements on the laws of Solon, Horner observes that the philosopher "probably bore in mind when he used these expressions, the answer which Mr. Burke had made to him, on being reproached for not effecting a thorough repeal."[51] Burke, with his usual gift for metaphor, is reported to have argued, "that it was the privilege of philosophers to conceive their diagrams in geometrical accuracy; but the engineer must often impair the symmetry, as well as the simplicity of his machine, in order to overcome the irregularities of friction and resistance."[52]

There is another account of Burke addressing Smith on the differing natures of philosophy and statesmanship quoted in the papers of Thomas Jefferson. "You, Dr. Smith, from your professor's chair, may send forth theories upon freedom of commerce as if you were lecturing on pure mathematics," Burke is reported as saying. "But legislators must proceed by slow degrees, impeded as they are in their course by the friction of interest and the fiction of preference."[53] Regardless of whether Burke expressed such a position to Smith sometime between 1776 and 1778, however, he certainly adhered to this view concerning the respective social positions of the pair. "A statesman differs from a professor in a university," the MP wrote. "The latter has only the general view of society; the former, the statesman, has a number of circumstances to combine with those general ideas, and to take into consideration."[54]

3.2. *Smith as a systematic philosopher*

If Burke is the model of a prudent statesman, then Smith must consider himself as (at least attempting to be) the model of a true philosopher, and certainly not a man of system. Such philosophers are in a difficult position. It is not enough that they themselves resist the spirit of system; they must also help their followers avoid this danger. Nonetheless, it is still the philosopher's responsibility to provide the ideals toward which societies must strive. As much as he feared the man of system, Smith also saw that "the same principle, the same love of system, the same regard to the beauty of order, of art, and contrivance" that so intoxicates such an individual also "frequently serves to recommend those institutions which tend to promote the public welfare."[55] After all, the vast majority of the projects of humanity began as imaginary systems in the mind of some philosophical designer, and these plans were made into reality through the work of others acting out of a commitment to this imagined machine. The realization of Smith's system of natural liberty, however, requires less the action than the inaction of humanity, or at least of humanity's governmental institutions.[56] In systematically presenting the mechanisms of the natural economic order, Smith thus turns the love of system against itself.

This system of natural liberty, moreover, while remaining a source of ideals for the orientation of political action, is itself riddled with numerous flaws.[57] It is beyond the scope of this essay to detail these many imperfections – from the dehumanizing alienation of the working class, to an ultimate end to economic growth. Nonetheless, his foregrounding of the many flaws in this system is evidence that Smith was capable of designing a model social order while immunizing both himself and his readers from the intoxicating effects of imagined perfection.

Indeed, Smith repeatedly cautions his reader that the total realization of even this imperfect utopia may be practically impossible. Smith's discussion of Burke's reform of the Corn Laws can certainly be read as an admission that it may be infeasible to legislate the immediate adoption of perfectly free trade. Elsewhere, Smith is even more explicit on the matter. "To expect, indeed, that the freedom of trade should ever be entirely restored in Great Britain," the philosopher writes, "is as absurd as to expect that an Oceana or Utopia should ever be established in it. Not only the prejudices of the public, but what is much more unconquerable, the private interests of many individuals, irresistibly oppose it."[58] Even if it were politically feasible to actualize Smith's still imperfect utopian vision instantly and immediately, it would nonetheless not be economically feasible to do so. One of "the unfortunate effects of all the regulations of the mercantile system," Smith writes, is to "not only introduce very dangerous disorders into the state of the body politic, but disorders which it is often difficult to remedy, without occasioning, for a time at least, still greater disorders."[59]

In short, the refusal to directly apply philosophical systems to political decision-making is a central element of Smith's nonetheless highly systematic thought. James Boswell reportedly marveled at the strangeness of this seemingly anti-philosophical philosophy. "Mr. Smith," Boswell recounts, "wrote to me some time ago, 'Your great fault is acting upon system.' What a curious reproof to a young man from a grave philosopher! It is, however, a just one, and but too well founded with respect to me."[60] It is certainly possible that Burke sometimes acted for Smith as Smith himself acted for Boswell, serving to help warn the philosopher against the dangers of system.

4. Men of system

4.1. *Richard Price and the French revolutionaries as men of system*

Smith's discussion of the man of system in the *Theory* is immediately preceded by arguments concerning the alteration of a nation's constitution and the loyalty one owes to one's fatherland and its existing regime. Here, Smith argues that "the love of our own country seems not to be derived from the love of mankind," adopting a thesis directly contrary to Richard Price's in the radical Dissenter's November 4, 1789 sermon, "A Discourse on the Love of Our Country."[61] It was in response to this sermon that Burke composed his 1790 masterpiece *Reflections on the Revolution in France*. While Burke makes it clear that he is directly addressing Price's sermon, however, Smith does not. There is, moreover, some reason to believe that Smith was unaware of Price's sermon when composing these passages. While the sixth edition of the *Theory* was not printed until January 1790, the papers of Smith's friend Thomas Cadell record that Smith finished "the very last sentence" of his revisions to the work on November 18, 1789.[62] It is unlikely that Price's text of November 4 would have reached Smith in Edinburgh in time for him to have composed a refutation of the speech a mere two weeks later.

Smith, however, was certainly aware of Price's earlier work, and displayed an antipathy toward the radical Dissenter almost as great as Burke's own. "Price's speculations cannot fail to sink into the neglect that they always deserved," Smith wrote in a 1785 letter to George Chalmers. "I have always considered him as a factious citizen, a most superficial philosopher and by no means an able calculator."[63] Regardless of whether Smith was directly addressing either the French Revolution or Price's sermon in the sixth edition of the *Theory*, it is undeniable he was adding his views to the debate of the day on the constitutions of nations, and that his position was at least sympathetic to that later adopted by Burke in the *Reflections*.[64]

Certainly, the *Reflections* paints the French revolutionaries and their British sympathizers as men of system of the type we have seen denounced by Smith. "They conceive, very systematically," the statesman writes, "that all things which give perpetuity are mischievous, and therefore they are at inexpiable war with all establishments. They think that government may vary like modes of dress, and with as little ill effect."[65] It is therefore that the revolutionaries feel free to rebuild society to conform with their rationalistic conception of the rights of man. The resulting behavior of the "abettors of this philosophic system" inevitably devolves into "frauds, impostures, violences, rapines, burnings, murders, confiscations, compulsory paper currencies, and every description of tyranny and cruelty to bring about and to uphold this Revolution."[66]

In his rhetorically overheated attack, Burke never makes a general, philosophical case against the man of system, and freely mixes general denunciations of philosophically systematic politics with specific arguments against the particular utopian system advanced by the revolutionaries of his day. "In the system itself," Burke writes of the constitution put forward by the French National Assembly, "I confess myself unable to find out anything which displays in a single instance the work of a comprehensive and disposing mind or even the provisions of a vulgar prudence."[67] Later, the statesman rails against the "imbecility [...] of the puerile and pedantic system, which they [i.e., the National Assembly] call a constitution."[68] So flawed is the new regime in its design, that Burke questions whether it even "deserves such a name" as "system" at all.[69]

While this attack on the French constitution may function quite well rhetorically, it serves to undermine any more general attack on the man of system. As Smith recognized, it is not the flaws, but the very perfection of utopian political systems that renders them so dangerous. Burke, too, recognizes that "in a new and merely theoretic system, it is expected that every contrivance shall appear, on the face of it, to answer its ends, especially where the projectors are no way embarrassed with an endeavor to accommodate the new building to an old one, either in the walls or on the foundations."[70] Burke argues, of course, that the new French constitution fails in this regard, but in doing so he weakens his argument that even a perfect philosophical system ought not to be actualized through sudden, revolutionary change. Burke, however, wishes to portray the revolutionaries of his day as villains or fools, and hence could not admit the truth if they were in fact merely misguided lovers of beauty, blinded by the philosophical genius of their utopian dreams. Smith, who has no such ideological axe to grind, is free to present a more sympathetic, and hence also more realistic, portrait of the revolutionary man of system, a character who the philosopher nonetheless denounces as surely as does Burke.

Indeed, throughout his discussion of patriotism, the constitutions of nations, and (perhaps) Price, Smith adopts a far more moderate position than does Burke. After establishing that the love of country has a different source from the love of humanity, Smith sees that the former sentiment "seems, in ordinary cases, to involve in it two different principles; first, a certain respect and reverence for that constitution or form of government which is actually established; and secondly, an earnest desire to render the condition of our fellow-citizens as safe, respectable and happy as we can." Fortunately, "in peaceable and quiet times, those two principles generally coincide," for the maintenance of the established regime will be the best means of promoting the welfare of the citizenry. "But in times of public discontent, faction and disorder, those two different principles may draw different ways." The decision as to whether to dismantle a nation's system of government completely, of course, requires "the highest effort of political wisdom." The statesman who chooses correctly has the opportunity to "assume the greatest and noblest of all characters, that of the reformer and legislator of a great state."[71] It is only after his praise of the great legislator that Smith launches his analysis of the man of system, thus robbing this analysis of any rhetorical force it might have in condemning the revolutionaries of the day.

Smith's dispassionate analysis and Burke's partisan speechifying are characteristic rhetorical modes of the philosopher and the politician, respectively. Smith is engaged in the rational construction of model social systems, while Burke is rallying his fellow citizens to action, and this divergence in purpose serves to alter the very nature of the thought conveyed. Smith, concerned with the consistency and completeness of his philosophical investigations, offers a highly systematic refutation of acting upon system. Burke, striving to corral all possible arguments in support of his position into a single, rhetorically effective package, constructs a powerful, if haphazard and often contradictory case, a case which is anything but systematic.

Thomas Paine, in his 1791 response to Burke, argued that the statesman not only refused to engage in systematic thinking, but was also incapable of doing so. Paine argues that Burke, as a brilliant orator but a second-rate philosopher, was unable to see the wise order provided by the constitution put forth by the French National Assembly. Interestingly, Paine contrasts Burke with a philosopher of the day famed for observing the hidden order underlying political and social phenomena. Paine writes:

> Had Mr. Burke possessed talents similar to the author of *On the Wealth of Nations*, he would have comprehended all the parts which enter into, and, by assemblage, form a constitution [...] It is not from his prejudices only, but from the disorderly cast of his genius, that he is unfitted for the

subject he writes upon. Even his genius is without a constitution. It is a genius at random, and not a genius constituted.[72]

The works of Burke and Smith, according to Paine, both display aesthetic brilliance in their critiques of acting upon system, but aesthetic brilliance of very different sorts, corresponding to the primary categories of Burke's own aesthetic theory. The beauty of the *Theory* and the *Wealth* is akin to that found in the ordered harmony of classical architecture, and is greeted with joy and love for the systems constructed therein. The sublimity of the *Reflections* is akin to that of a bombastic tragedy, and is greeted with weeping and the gnashing of teeth. Both such forms of aesthetic achievement have their dangers. Smith's philosophy could potentially give rise to men of system who pursue natural economic liberty in a radical manner never intended by the author, and the staid professor took great steps to inoculate his readers against this utopian madness throughout his books. Burke's oratory, for its part, might beget counter-revolutionary fanatics with an unreasonable and unreasoning fear of change. It is not evident that Burke was aware of the threat to human welfare posed by his own work, as Smith was undoubtedly aware of the threat posed by his.[73]

4.2. *Burke as a man of system*

Adam Smith died the same year that Burke published the *Reflections*, so it is impossible to say whether the philosopher would have been moved by his friend's rhetoric. Burke, however, was clearly moved by Smith's philosophy, both in the field of ethics and that of political economy. The historical evidence also indicates that the statesman continued to embrace Smith's economic doctrines with considerable enthusiasm throughout his career.

The fullest statement of Burke's economic views was not composed until late 1795, less than two years before his death; it was published posthumously in 1800 as *Thoughts and Details on Scarcity*. Here, Burke argues against any interference in the market to counteract rising food prices – be they regulations of the trade in grain, the establishment of public granaries, minimum wage laws, or even direct payments to supplement the wages of laborers of the sort first enacted in Speenhamland at this time. While Smith himself did not address the possibility of a policy akin to that in Speenhamland, he did argue against regulation of the trade in food staples, even during times of scarcity. "The unlimited, unrestrained freedom of the corn trade," Smith maintained, "is the only effectual preventative of the miseries of a famine," as well as "the best palliative of the inconveniences of a dearth; for the inconveniences of a real scarcity cannot be remedied; they can only be palliated."[74] Burke certainly provides arguments against Speenhamland-type programs along these Smithian lines, maintaining that redistribution of wealth would impede the efficient operations of self-interest, and that interfering in the operations of the market is generally an ineffective choice of policy. "Such is the event of all compulsory equalizations," Burke writes. "They pull down what is above; they never raise what is below; and they depress high and low together beneath the level of what was originally the lowest."[75] It is not necessary here to evaluate the validity of Burke's argument that even a temporary redistribution of wealth from the rich to the poor would prove deleterious to the material welfare of all, though this argument does demonstrate that Burke possessed more than a moderate facility for political economy in the Smithian mold.

It is critical to note, however, that Burke also includes a second line of argument against Speenhamland-type policies independent of their ineffectiveness, a deontological moral argument grounded in natural theology. "We, the people," Burke piously proclaims, "ought to be made sensible that it is not in breaking the laws of commerce, which are the laws of Nature, and consequently the laws of God, that we are to place our hope of softening the Divine displeasure to remove any calamity under which we suffer or which hangs over us."[76] With a single rhetorical flourish, Burke has transformed scientific, positive laws with no more moral weight than the laws of physics into divine commands whose violation is a grave sin. Christian charity, Burke acknowledges, is also God's law, but with such admittedly obligatory acts of mercy "the magistrate has nothing at all to do; his interference is a violation of the property which it is his office to protect." While feeding the poor is the duty of all, "the manner, mode, time, choice of objects, and proportion [of charitable donation] are left to private discretion; and perhaps for that very reason it is performed with the greater satisfaction, because the discharge has more the appearance of freedom."[77] That is, even if a magistrate were able to design some scheme of payments to the poor during times of famine which would prevent their starvation effectively and efficiently, he would be morally wrong to do so, as he would be acting contrary to the will of God.

Such theological arguments could not be further from Smith's own views.[78] Never in the *Wealth* does Smith describe the laws of commerce given free reign under the system of natural liberty as possessing any moral authority independent of their uncanny ability to maximize the wealth of nations to the benefit of all. Indeed, talk of God and divine law, while still present in the *Theory*, has been entirely excluded from Smith's later work, and nowhere in any of his writings does the philosopher ever indicate that the laws of commerce carry some supernatural sanction.

To the contrary, Smith gives several examples of circumstances in which it will advance the common good for a magistrate to interfere with the free operation of the market. A government official "may prescribe rules, therefore, which, not only prohibit mutual injuries among fellow-citizens, but command mutual good offices to a certain degree," though "it requires the greatest delicacy and reserve" to lay down such laws "with propriety and judgment."[79] For example, although Smith called for a reform of existing "poor laws," which had required localities to provide aid to the indigent since Elizabethan times, he nowhere called for their wholesale abolition.[80] The criterion according to which such policies are to be judged is not their conformity with divinely ordained laws of the market, but rather their ability to improve the welfare of the populace. "No society can surely be flourishing and happy," Smith memorably insisted, "of which the far greater part of the members are poor and miserable."[81]

In pursuing the welfare of the people, moreover, the prudent statesman must be willing to defer to popular opinion as necessary. And nowhere is this more necessary, Smith argued, than with regard to the people's very sustenance and survival. "The people feel themselves so much interested in what relates either to their subsistence in this life, or to their happiness in a life to come, that government must yield to their prejudices, and, in order to preserve the public tranquility, establish that system that they approve of."[82] There is thus reason to believe that, had he lived to see the sharp rise in food prices in the second half of the 1790's, Smith might have advocated accommodating popular demands for a governmental response.[83] Yet Burke seems to reject, not only any new response to sudden scarcity, but even the existing scheme of poor laws. He rejects them, independent of their consequences, as a kind of blasphemy, a wanton flouting of the divine laws of the free market.

Burke's description of the laws of commerce as normatively binding laws of God, a description never intended by Smith, cannot be explained as simply the tendency of a religious man to see the hand of God at play in fields addressed in a secular manner by irreligious scientists. After all, a religion must select which natural phenomena are to be given moral authority as the work of its deity, and which are to be rejected as the work of chance, chaos, or even Satan himself. From a Christian perspective, as C.B. Macpherson observes, "That the capitalist order is part of the divine and natural order is not self-evident; indeed, at least until the end of the sixteenth century, most writers and preachers would have treated it as nonsense."[84] J. R. Poynter sees such a view as highly uncommon even at the end of the eighteenth century, and argues that

"Burke's tract resembles the lesser writings of the generation after Malthus rather than its contemporaries."[85]

It seems, then, that Burke could not imagine that the machinery of commerce described by Smith was anything other than the handiwork of God. Only an artist of divine sublimity could be responsible for a system of such overpowering aesthetic power. Burke thus insisted that this imaginary system be actualized, regardless of the human suffering that such a project might cause. Here, the proper roles of the philosopher and the statesman are reversed, with the philosopher advocating political caution, the statesman becoming enamored with the perfection of an imagined ideal.[86] This is a classic example of the madness of system that Smith so accurately described in the last edition of the *Theory*. Although it may come a surprise to many that Edmund Burke, of all people, would fall prey to this particular folly, it is one to which those who judge works of social science and moral philosophy according to aesthetic rather than ethical criteria are all too prone.[87] Had Smith lived to see Burke's overheated economic essay, the prudent Scottish philosopher might have repeated the warning he gave Boswell against acting upon system. Considering the brilliant and impassioned attack on such behavior in his own writings, Burke might have heeded his friend's warning well.

Acknowledgements

A very early version of this article was written for Daniel J. Cohen's undergraduate seminar on British Conservatism at Yale University. Revised versions were then presented at meetings of the American Political Science Association, the New York Political Science Association, and the Brown University Political Philosophy Workshop. In addition to all those who offered feedback at these meetings, I would also like to thanks Jennifer Page for her research assistance, Anik Waldow for her editorial guidance, and the anonymous reviewers at *Intellectual History Review* for their helpful suggestions.

Notes

1. W.C. Dunn writes that it is "in these lights – Smith as an economic liberal, and Burke as a political conservative – [that] these men have been traditionally considered" (Dunn, "Adam Smith and Edmund Burke," 330–346). And the view has long outlived Dunn; see, for example, Pack, *Capitalism as a Moral System*, 121.
2. Smith, *Correspondence*, no. 208, 251. As with all quotations from eighteenth-century texts in this essay, the spelling and punctuation have been modernized for purposes of clarity.
3. Bisset, *The Life of Edmund Burke*, vol. 2, 429; as cited in Winch, *Riches and Poverty*, 125. Winch laments how this undocumented anecdote has found its way into virtually all biographies of both Smith and Burke (*Riches and Poverty*, 128) – see, for example, Rae, *Life of Adam Smith*, 387.
4. Some have attempted, rather unconvincingly, to deny the importance of this fact. Peter Minowitz, for example, writes, "Although Burke proclaimed himself Smith's disciple, Smith contributed to the Enlightenment enterprise that Burke decried: tearing away life's "decent drapery" and "pleasing illusions"" (Minowitz *Profits, Priests and Princes*, 44; quoting Burke, *Reflections*, 67).
5. On this point, see Willis, "The Role in Parliament."
6. The best non-reductive overview of the relationship between Smith's ideas and Burke's is Winch, *Riches and Poverty*, esp. 125–220. Winch compares and contrasts Smith's and Burke's respective positions on such issues as the independence of the American colonies (ibid., 137–165), the social utility of aristocracies and established churches (ibid., 166–197), and support for the laboring poor (ibid., 198–220). Yet Winch's nuanced study never focuses on the respective social roles of the philosopher and the statesman, or the aesthetic appeal of system, which are the subject of the present essay.
7. As Palyi, "The Introduction of Adam Smith," 181, has observed, "their ideas, their methods, even their problems were decidedly different, as different as the men themselves and their personal careers."
8. Burke, "*The Theory of Moral Sentiments*, by Adam Smith," and Burke, "*An Enquiry into the Nature and Causes of the Wealth of Nations* by Adam Smith." (Authorship disputed for the latter.)
9. Smith, *Correspondence*, no. 31, 33. For the treatise to which Hume is referring, see Burke, *A Philosophical Enquiry*, 49–200.

10. Smith, *Correspondence*, no. 36, 42–43.
11. Ibid., no. 38, 46.
12. Burke, "*An Enquiry into the Nature and Causes of the Wealth of Nations* by Adam Smith." (Authorship disputed.)
13. Smith, *Correspondence*, no. 38, 46.
14. Ibid., 46–47.
15. Ibid.
16. Ibid., 47.
17. Ibid.
18. Burke, "*The Theory of Moral Sentiments*, by Adam Smith," 484.
19. Ibid., 484–485.
20. Ibid., 485.
21. Ibid.
22. Ibid.
23. Ibid.
24. Ibid., 485–489; citing Smith, *The Theory of Moral Sentiments*, 9–13
25. Viner, "Guide," 24.
26. Ibid.
27. During this time, Samuel Johnson is alleged to have remarked "Smith too is now of our club. It has lost its select merit." See Rae, *Life of Adam Smith*, 268. The other details on Smith's admission to The Club are drawn from Bell, "Adam Smith, Clubman'; as well as Ross, *The Life of Adam Smith*, 251–252.
28. See Mossner and Ross's notes to Smith, *Correspondence*, 47.
29. Burke, "*An Enquiry into the Nature and Causes of the Wealth of Nations* by Adam Smith," 241.
30. Ibid.
31. Ibid.
32. Ibid., 241–243; citing Smith, *Wealth of Nations*, 10–12.
33. Eindaudi, "The British Background," 589, is one of such works in which the attribution is given to Burke, whereas it is questioned, e.g., in Cone, *Burke and the Nature of Politics*, vol. 2, 490.
34. For Smith's political support of Burke, see letters 216 and 217 in Smith, *Correspondence*, 258–259. For Burke's praise of Smith as a wise philosopher, see Letter 230. *Ibid.*, 268.
35. Burke, *A Letter to a Noble Lord*, 192.
36. *Ibid.*
37. Burke, "*The Theory of Moral Sentiments*, by Adam Smith," 485.
38. Burke, "A Letter by M. Rousseau," 479–484. The essentially aesthetic character of Burke's reviews of the *Theory of Moral Sentiments* and the *Wealth of Nations* has yet to receive adequate attention in the secondary literature. Winch, for example, attributes Burke's enthusiastic reception to the *Theory* to his substantive philosophical agreement with Smith on the issue of moral anti-rationalism, to their common belief that morality is a product of our moral sentiments, and not of our reason alone (Winch, *Riches and Poverty*, 170).
39. Smith, "The Principles," 66.
40. Ibid., 74.
41. Ibid., 115.
42. Winch, for one, cannot help but marvel at the intricate "connections between the overlapping sub-systems that compose Smith's highly ambitious and systematic enterprise – the most ambitious enterprise to be carried through to near-completion in an age and place that was notable for the compendious quality of its intellectual projects" (Winch, *Riches and Poverty*, 253).
43. Smith, *Wealth of Nations*, 678.
44. Smith, *The Theory of Moral Sentiments*, 232.
45. Ibid., 233.
46. Ibid., 234.
47. Smith's man of system thus represents one example of a larger phenomenon described by Kateb, "Aestheticism and Morality," 5–37, in which aesthetic considerations lead individuals to act immorally.
48. *Burke's Act 1773*, 13 Geo. III, c. 43.
49. Smith, *Wealth of Nations*, 541.
50. Ibid., 542–543.
51. Horner, *The Economic Writings*, 98.
52. Ibid.

53. Jefferson, *Papers*, vol. 8, 59; see also Viner, "Guide," 26–28.
54. Burke, "Speech on a Petition of the Unitarians," as cited in Dunn, "Adam Smith and Edmund Burke," 66.
55. Smith, *Wealth of Nations*, 185.
56. On this topic, see Griswold, *Adam Smith*, 308; as well as Winch, *Riches and Poverty*, 94–96.
57. See Griswold, *Adam Smith*, 302.
58. Smith, *Wealth of Nations*, 471.
59. Ibid., 606.
60. Cited in Viner, "Guide," 32–33; see also Dankert, "Adam Smith and James Boswell," 331.
61. The quote appears in Smith, *The Theory of Moral Sentiments*, 229. See also Price, "A Discourse."
62. See Ross, *The Life of Adam Smith*, 391–394.
63. Smith, *Correspondence*, no. 251, 290.
64. For a plausible account of the specific historical circumstances which may have inspired Smith's account of the "man of system," see Rothschild, "Adam Smith and Conservative Economics," 54–55.
65. Burke, *Reflections*, 77.
66. Ibid., 108.
67. Ibid., 146.
68. Ibid., 190.
69. Ibid., 116.
70. Ibid., 152.
71. Smith, *The Theory of Moral Sentiments*, 231–232.
72. Paine, *Rights of Man*, 472.
73. For more on the moral dangers of the aesthetic elements of Burke's political writings, see Kateb, "Aestheticism and Morality," 24–27.
74. Smith, *Wealth of Nations*, 527.
75. Burke, *Thoughts and Details on Scarcity*, 142–143.
76. Ibid., 156–157.
77. Ibid., 146.
78. Indeed, the differences between Smith's actual views and the views advanced by Burke are so great that Emma Rothschild has argued that the *Thoughts and Details* "is close, at several points, to being an open attack on Smith" (Rothschild, "Adam Smith and Conservative Economics," 87). If this is taken to mean that a close reader of both Burke's work and Smith's will notice that the two are often in important disagreement, then it is certainly true. Yet if Rothschild is suggesting that Burke intended the *Thoughts and Details* as an attack on Smith, then the claim is a false one. Such a view is incompatible with the considerable evidence, outlined earlier in this essay, that Burke believed himself to be in full agreement with Smith on matters of political economy, however much he may have been blind to the real differences between them. Indeed, Rothschild acknowledges that almost all of Burke's contemporaries were also blind to these real differences. Rothschild writes that Burke's work "was received as little more than an exposition of Smith's 'principles,'" with these "principles" understood to be nothing more than "the simple prescription for economic freedom" (ibid., 87). This oversimplification of Smith's position survives to our own day, as does the interpretation of the *Thoughts and Details* as a correct application of Smith's views (ibid., 88, fn. 83). There is no reason to believe that Burke himself was immune from this widespread error. To the contrary, there is considerable evidence he was one of the first to fall prey to it. In this respect, my own interpretation of the relationship between Burke and Smith is close to that of Gertrude Himmelfarb; see Himmelfarb, *The Idea of Poverty*, 68–79.
79. Smith, *The Theory of Moral Sentiments*, 81.
80. Smith's main suggestion for reform of the poor laws is not to abolish, or even lessen, governmental aid, but to remove local residency requirements to allow for the free movement of labor; see Smith, *Wealth of Nations*, 152–157. For more on Smith's position on the poor laws, see Himmelfarb, *The Idea of Poverty*, 61.
81. Smith, *Wealth of Nations*, 96.
82. Ibid., 539.
83. For further discussion of this issue, see Winch, *Riches and Poverty*, 208–212.
84. Macpherson, *Burke*, 62.
85. Poynter, *Society and Pauperism*, 55.
86. For a similar observation, see Winch, *Riches and Poverty*, 204.

87. Many previous commentators have noted the disjoint between Burke's arch-libertarian economic views in the *Thoughts and Details* and the social conservatism of the *Reflections*, especially given that local forms of poor relief were well-established traditional practices in Britain at this time. For an overview of many competing attempts to resolve this inconsistency, all ultimately unsuccessful, see Himmelfarb, *The Idea of Poverty*, 71–73. To mention only the most prominent such argument, Macpherson argues that Burke was able to be both a laissez-faire capitalist and a defender of traditional social institutions because "the capitalist order *had in fact been* the traditional order in England for a whole century" (Macpherson, *Burke*, 51). Yet this argument ignores *both* the all-important differences between a highly regulated mercantilist system and a system of genuine free trade which would be obvious to any reader of Smith *and* the entire history of the poor laws dating back to the reign of Elizabeth I; see Himmelfarb, *The Idea of Poverty*, 73. Judith Shklar offers a more promising solution when she finds a deeper consistency behind Burke's seeming inconsistency only insofar as insistence on strict logical coherence is one of the qualities that "conservatives have resented most in their opponents" (Shklar, *After Utopia*, 225).

Bibliography

Barrington, Donald. "Edmund Burke as an Economist." *Economica, New Series* 22, no. 83 (1954): 252–258. doi:10.2307/2551325.

Bell, J.F. "Adam Smith, Clubman." *Scottish Journal of Political Economy* 7, no. 1 (1960): 108–116. doi:10. 1111/j.1467-9485.1960.tb00120.x.

Bisset, Robert. *The Life of Edmund Burke*. London: G. Cawthorn, 1798.

Burke, Edmund. "*An Enquiry into the Nature and Causes of the Wealth of Nations* by Adam Smith, LL.D., F.R.S.*" In *The Annual Register, or a View of the History, Politics and Literature of the Year 1776*, 241–243. London: J. Dodsley, 1777. (Authorship Disputed.)

Burke, Edmund. "A Letter by M. Rousseau of Geneva to M. d'Alembert of Paris Concerning the Effects of Theatrical Entertainments on the Manners of Mankind." In *The Annual Register, or a View of the History, Politics and Literature of the Year 1759*, 479–484. London: R. and J. Dodsley, 1760.

Burke, Edmund. *A Letter to a Noble Lord on the Attacks Made Upon Mr. Burke and his Pension in the House of Lords[...]*, Vol. 5 of The *Works of the Right Honourable Edmund Burke*, 171–232. London: John C. Nimmo, 1887. Facsimile published New York: Georg Olms Verlag, 1975.

Burke, Edmund. *A Philosophical Enquiry into the Sublime and the Beautiful and Other Pre-Revolutionary Writings*. Edited by David Womersley. New York: Penguin Books, 1998.

Burke, Edmund. *Pre-Revolutionary Writings*. Edited by Ian Harris. New York: Cambridge University Press, 1993.

Burke, Edmund. *Reflections on the Revolution in France*. Edited by J.G.A. Pocock. Indianapolis, IN: Hackett Publishing Company, 1987.

Burke, Edmund. "*The Theory of Moral Sentiments*, by Adam Smith, Professor of Moral Philosophy, in the University of Glasgow." In *The Annual Register, or a View of the History, Politics and Literature of the Year* 1759, 484–489. London: R. and J. Dodsley, 1760.

Burke, Edmund. *Thoughts and Details on Scarcity*. Vol. 5 of *The Works of the Right Honourable Edmund Burke*, 131–170. London: John C. Nimmo, 1887. Facsimile published New York: Georg Olms Verlag, 1975.

Cone, Carl B. *Burke and the Nature of Politics*. 2 vols. Lexington: University of Kentucky Press, 1964.

Dankert, Clyde E. "Adam Smith and James Boswell." *Queen's Quarterly* 68, no. 2 (1961): 323–332.

Dunn, W.C. "Adam Smith and Edmund Burke: Complementary Contemporaries." *Southern Economic Journal* 7, no. 3 (1941): 330–346. doi:10.2307/1053043.

Einaudi, Mario. "The British Background of Burke's Political Philosophy." *Political Science Quarterly* 49, no. 4 (1934): 576–598. doi:10.2307/2143466.

Griswold, Charles L. Jr. *Adam Smith and the Virtues of Enlightenment*. New York: Cambridge University Press, 1999.

Himmelfarb, Gertrude. *The Idea of Poverty: England in the Early Industrial Age*. New York: Vintage Books, 1985.

Horner, Francis. *The Economic Writings of Francis Horner in the Edinburgh Review*. Edited by Frank W. Fetter. London: London School of Economics and Political Science Press, 1957.

Jefferson, Thomas. *The Papers of Thomas Jefferson*. Edited by Julian P. Boyd. 39 vols. Princeton, NJ: Princeton University Press, 1950.

Kateb, George. "Aestheticism and Morality: Their Cooperation and Hostility." *Political Theory* 28, no. 1 (2000): 5–37. doi:10.1177/0090591700028001002.

Macpherson, C.B. *Burke.* New York: Oxford University Press, 1980.

Minowitz, Peter. *Profits, Priests and Princes: Adam Smith's Emancipation of Economics from Politics and Religion.* Stanford, CA: Stanford University Press, 1993.

Muller, Jerry Z. *Adam Smith in His Time and Ours: Designing the Decent Society.* New York: Free Press, 1993.

Pack, Spencer J. *Capitalism as a Moral System: Adam Smith's Critique of the Free Market Economy.* Brookfield, VT: Edward Elgar, 1991.

Paine, Thomas. *Rights of Man.* In *Collected Writings*, edited by E. Foner, 431–662. New York: Library of America, 1995.

Palyi, Melchior. "The Introduction of Adam Smith on the Continent." In *Adam Smith, 1776–1926*, edited by John Maurice Clark. Chicago: University of Chicago Press, 1928.

Poynter, J.R. *Society and Pauperism: English Ideas on Poor Relief, 1795–1834.* London: Routledge and Kegan Paul, 1969.

Price, Richard. "A Discourse on the Love of our Country." Delivered on November 4, 1789, at the Meeting-House in the Old Jewry, to the Society for Commemorating the Revolution in Great Britain. http://www.constitution.org/price/price_8.htm.

Rae, John. *Life of Adam Smith.* Introduction by Jacob Viner. New York: August M. Kelley, 1965.

Ross, Ian Simpson. *The Life of Adam Smith.* New York: Oxford University Press, 1995.

Rothschild, Emma. "Adam Smith and Conservative Economics." *Economic History Review, New Series* 45, no. 1 (1992): 74–96. http://www.jstor.org/stable/2598329.

Rothschild, Emma. *Economic Sentiments: Adam Smith, Condorcet and the Enlightenment.* Cambridge, MA: Harvard University Press, 2001.

Shklar, Judith N. *After Utopia: The Decline of Political Faith.* Princeton, NJ: Princeton University Press, 1957.

Smith, Adam. *Correspondence of Adam Smith.* Edited by Ernest Campbell Mossner and Ian Simpson Ross. Indianapolis, IN: Liberty Fund, 1987.

Smith, Adam. *An Inquiry into the Nature and Causes of the Wealth of Nations.* General Editing by R.H. Campbell and A.S. Skinner. Textual Editing by W.B. Todd. Indianapolis, IN: Liberty Fund, 1981.

Smith, Adam. "The Principles Which Lead and Direct Philosophical Enquiries as Illustrated by the History of Astronomy." In *Essays on Philosophical Subjects*, edited by W.P.D. Wrightman and J.C. Bryce, 33–105. Indianapolis, IN: Liberty Fund, 1982.

Smith, Adam. *The Theory of Moral Sentiments.* Edited by A. L. Macfie and D. D Raphael. Indianapolis, IN: Liberty Fund, 1984.

Viner, Jacob. "Guide to John Rae's *Life of Adam Smith*." Introduction to John Rae, *Life of Adam Smith*. New York: August M. Kelley, 1965.

Willis, K. "The Role in Parliament of the Economic Ideas of Adam Smith: 1776–1800." *History of Political Economy* 11, no. 4 (1979): 505–544. doi:10.1215/00182702-11-4-505.

Winch, Donald. "Adam Smith's "Enduring Particular Result': A Political and Cosmopolitan Perspective." In *Wealth and Virtue: The Shaping of Political Economy in the Scottish Enlightenment*, edited by Istvan Hont and Michael Ignatieff, 253–270. New York: Cambridge University Press, 1983.

Winch, Donald. *Riches and Poverty: An Intellectual History of Political Economy in Britain, 1750–1834.* New York: Cambridge University Press, 1996.

Index

www.ingramcontent.com/pod-product-compliance
Ingram Content Group UK Ltd.
Pitfield, Milton Keynes, MK11 3LW, UK
UKHW010021280225
455677UK00023B/722